The Dance Catalog

The DANCE CATALOG

Edited by Nancy Reynolds
Designed by Joan Peckolick

H

Harmony Books/New York

Editor: Marcy Posner
Art Director: Ken Sansone
Art Assistant: Sally Cooney
Production: Celie Fitzgerald, Murray Schwartz
Editorial Consultant: Manuela Soares

Cover photograph of Lael Evans by Marjory Dressler.
Chapter title illustrations by Heather Taylor.

Published simultaneously in Canada by General Publishing Co., Ltd.
Printed in the United States of America.

Library of Congress Cataloging in Publication Data

Reynolds, Nancy, ed.
The dance catalog.
1. Dancing.   I. Title.
GV1594.R49   1979   793.3   78-25553
ISBN 0-517-53642-0
ISBN 0-517-53643-9 pbk.

For ETP, who will have a wonderful life

CONTENTS

ACKNOWLEDGMENTS

A book of this kind, covering such a range of specialized material and attempting countrywide representation, could not have been compiled without the help of many people. It is amazing to me that so many friends, acquaintances, and strangers took time to answer numerous questions, some of them lengthy and some requiring tricky value judgments; often the replies came by return mail. The dance world is still a generous place, and it is a pleasure to be part of it.

The arrival of my baby son in the midst of the preparations made expert assistance an even greater necessity than would ordinarily have been the case; for, in addition to needing supplements to my knowledge, I was dependent on vast supplements to my time. For their sympathy and understanding of the situation, and for their attention to detail as well as to deadline, I would like to express my appreciation to those who contributed chapters to the book. The speedy cooperation of photographers was also an inestimable aid.

In addition, for advice cheerfully and abundantly given, I would like to thank: Mindy Aloff, Jack Anderson, Chrystelle Bond, Patricia Boyer, Edith d'Addario, *Dance in America,* Dixie Durr, Carol Elsner, Martha Hill, Billie Kirpich, Louise Kloepper, Don McDonagh, Constance Nadel Miller, Elvi Moore, National Association for Regional Ballet (N.A.R.B.), Janis Pforsich, Peter Ramsey, Janice Ross, Nancy Ruyter, Suzanne Shelton, Barbara Thuesen, Muriel Topaz, Marian van Tuyl, Norman Walker, and Theodora Wiesner. For the early American material I am indebted to the lectures of Selma Jeanne Cohen and Julian Mates.

Robert Cornfield (as he has on other occasions) helped in refining the concept of the book. Assistance in manuscript preparation was provided by Barbara Newman. With speed and unflagging energy Ken Sansone orchestrated the devoted efforts of my editor Marcy Posner, my designer (and fellow recent mother) Joan Peckolick, and me to produce the pages that follow. To all of these collaborators, my gratitude.

N.R.

CONTRIBUTORS

NANCY REYNOLDS, a former dancer with the New York City Ballet, is author of a prize-winning history of that company, *Repertory in Review: 40 Years of the New York City Ballet*. A Phi Beta Kappa graduate of Columbia University, she has worked as a book editor and has contributed articles on dance and art to magazines and encyclopedias. She has done graduate work and has lectured in dance history, and she is copublisher of Pictura Dance, producers of audiovisual materials in dance education. Her future projects include a history of theatrical dance in the twentieth century.

JOAN PECKOLICK has been art director of *Working Woman* magazine and promotion art director for *Penthouse* and *Viva* magazines. She now has her own design studio, Joan of Art. Her work in graphic design has won over a dozen awards from the American Institute of Graphic Arts, New York Printing Industries, The Type Director's Club, and a silver medal from the New York Art Director's Club.

Her most recent creative accomplishment is the birth of her daughter, Thea, a constant source of inspiration.

LINDA GRANDEY received an M.A. from Smith College and studied dance notation with Ann Hutchinson, Helen Priest Rogers, and Lucy Venable. She has taught notation at various colleges and universities, including Smith, Mount Holyoke, SUNY at Binghamton, Hunter, and the University of Otago at Dunedin, New Zealand, as well as at Jacob's Pillow, Connecticut College School of Dance, and the American Dance Festival.

HENLEY HASLAM, educated at Goucher and the Sorbonne, has been extensively trained in ballet, including four summers in Copenhagen studying the Bournonville School, for which she received a Marshall Fondet grant. She is on the faculty of The New Ballet School (school of the Eliot Feld Ballet) and is guest teacher and rehearsal coach for the Ballet Repertory Company. She has contributed articles to *Ballet Review* and *Dance Magazine*.

DAWN LILLE HORWITZ has worked in modern dance as a performer, teacher, and coach. A graduate of Barnard College, she holds M.A.s from Columbia and Adelphi. She has taught dance history while on the faculties of Barnard, Brooklyn College, and Adelphi; she is currently Director of Education at the Dance Notation Bureau. Her articles have appeared in *Dance News* and *Ballet Review*.

ELLEN JACOBS is a publicist and dance writer whose articles have been published in the *Soho Weekly News*, the *New York Times Sunday Magazine, Arts in Society,* and *Playbill,* among others. She has also worked for government and government-related agencies, including the New York State Council on the Arts (NYSCA) and the Creative Artists Public Service Program (CAPS).

BILLIE MAHONEY has headed the dance notation faculty of the Dance Division at the Juilliard School, New York, since 1970. As a solo variety performer, with an act based on tap and jazz dance, she was featured with Lionel Hampton and his band and in personal appearances with Bob Hope. She has appeared in films, musical theater, and on television. After working as assistant to John Gregory and then to Eugene "Luigi" Louis, she taught jazz classes in New York City for ten

years. In 1972–73, as rehearsal director, she accompanied the Jose Limon Dance Company to the Soviet Union.

MATTEO has been acclaimed by the *New York Times* as "the most versatile artist in the field of ethnic dance" and has concertized throughout the world. He is founder and director of the EthnoAmerican Dance Theater, now completing its ninth tour under the aegis of the National Endowment for the Arts. As a lecturer and teacher, he has been engaged by major centers of learning throughout the United States, including New York University, SUNY Purchase, Connecticut College, and twelve years at Jacob's Pillow. His monograph "Woods that Dance" is the definitive history of the castanets, and his articles on many subjects appear in the comprehensive *Enciclopedia dello Spettacolo*. He is also founder and director of the Foundation for Ethnic Dance, Inc., in New York City, an organization devoted to dance research.

BARBARA NEWMAN, a graduate of Vassar College, is Associate Critic for *Dance Magazine* and has written for such varied publications as *The Encyclopedia of Dance and Ballet, Library Journal*, the Covent Garden quarterly *About the House*, the London biweekly *Classical Music*, John Curry's *Ice Dancing* souvenir program, *Show Magazine*, and a new 8-million-word general encyclopedia to be published by the Dutch company Arete. She is currently working on a book about dance and dancers.

ROBERT J. PIERCE is dance critic for the *Soho Weekly News* and has written extensively for *Dance Magazine* and the *Village Voice*. A graduate of Rutgers, he now teaches dance history and aesthetics at Brooklyn College. He contributed chapters on modern dance to the Pictura Dance 300-slide survey of dance in the twentieth century.

MARY PAT ROBERTSON came to New York with her husband, dance writer Michael Robertson, in 1975. She has studied with Martha Graham, Twyla Tharp, and Merce Cunningham, and has taught ballet at New York University and Dancer School. A native of Tulsa, she received her B.A. from Stanford University.

JILL SILVERMAN, a graduate of Trinity College, Hartford, has done graduate work in theater history at Tufts University and CUNY Graduate Center. Her writing has appeared in *Dance Magazine, Ballet Review, Performing Arts Journal*, the Pictura Dance twentieth-century dance text-catalogue, and *Skylines*; she is currently covering performance art for *Art in America*. She has taught dance history and criticism at C. W. Post and Dowling College and is now writing the introduction to a forthcoming translation of Andre Levinson's *The Old and The New Ballet*.

KAYLA KAZAHN ZALK, a certified Laban movement analyst, received her B.A. from the University of Michigan. She has been guest lecturer at the Laban Art of Movement Centre, London, and has been on the faculties of the Effort/Shape Certification Program (Dance Notation Bureau), the American Dance Festival, N.Y.U. School of the Arts, and the American Academy of Dramatic Arts. She is currently teaching and choreographing at SUNY Purchase, and she is president of the American Dance Guild.

PHOTO CREDITS

FOREWORD

t seems no exaggeration to say that dance fever is sweeping the nation. There are more than 850 companies now performing (amateur and professional), and countless other groups give occasional recitals. In ten years, audience attendance has increased an incredible 1500 percent; in 1978 it was expected to reach 25 million. On campus the most popular entertainments are not rock concerts but dance concerts. Government support on the federal level alone runs in the neighborhood of $7 million annually; corporations and foundations have been lavish in their giving as well. During 1978 the United States Post Office issued four dance stamps, and National Dance week was proclaimed.

And "everybody" is dancing: thanks to the current concern with health and environment, exercise of all kinds has become a craze. Dancing, jogging, and tennis head the list, practiced not only to tone the body but to elevate the mind. Running has been invested with almost mystical properties; serious runners speak of the runner's "high." Being physically exhausted from strenuous exercise is considered more "real" and certainly more satisfying than being worn out from nervous tension, insomnia, and too many cigarettes. Even those who don't exercise spend some time thinking that they should. Dance studios now sometimes assume the function of social centers, and dance clothes—tights, legwarmers,

leotards (as bathing suits) have been adapted for streetwear. The look of dance is all around us.

How has this happened?

For almost four centuries ballet was considered a hothouse entertainment for the rich, the aesthetes, the snobs, and the bohemians. Modern dance, by contrast, was the province of a handful of poverty-stricken fanatics during its first forty-five years. And dancing, although acceptable in small doses as an aid in developing poise, was not considered a "nice" profession. Furthermore, one could hardly make a living at it.

During the 1960s Americans started becoming "culture conscious." Whether this attitude was prompted by the government's new financial commitment to the arts, or whether increased cultural activity generated pressure in Washington for arts support is hard to say. Businessmen began to see the economic potential of the arts in revitalizing neighborhoods and attracting tourists; corporations decided there was prestige attached to underwriting cultural ventures.

All the arts benefited, but the most explosive growth has been in dance (which started the furthest behind in popularity). Perhaps this is because, of the performing arts, dance has engendered considerably more creative experimentation in our time than music or drama, and it has remained less tied to traditional concepts of form and content (although these, too, continue to be relevant) while for the most part retaining its essential identity as dance. (Compare the activity of contemporary choreographers with that of modern opera composers, for example.) For another thing, it is only within the past few years that the male half of the population has embraced dance in any widespread way. The example of such superior dancers as Edward Villella and Jacques d'Amboise, who laid the groundwork for American men in ballet, and today's superstars, including the two dynamic Russians Rudolf Nureyev and Mikhail Baryshnikov, has made a tremendous difference. Finally, not until staged works were televised was there a way of disseminating them widely, analogous to tapes and records for music, books and prints for art. (As an interesting footnote, it has been remarked that when Americans at large finally "discovered" dance, they were well equipped to respond to it, from years of watching sports events, which had accustomed them to following movement patterns.)

For generations dance suffered from being considered unintellectual and decadent, not worth analytical attention in print, a no-credit or "gut" course in college if given at all. But these attitudes are also going out the window. Harvard has just begun to give credit for the study of dance history; *The New Yorker* has employed a dance critic since 1973. (The value of music and art was recognized by these institutions many years ago.)

All of this activity has given rise to a multitude of new careers or has expanded horizons in careers already existing for those who are not dancers themselves. There are opportunities in administration, therapy, notation, filmmaking, clothing manufacture, entertainment law, college teaching, photography, journalism, recording, grant writing, consultation, television, book editing, studio or company management, research, scholarship, archiving, and much more—all with a dance orientation for which there was no demand just a few years ago. Today there is more to read, more to study, more to write about, more to do, and more to see in dance than ever before.

The Dance Catalog is designed to help both laymen and specialists alike to find their way around this wonderful new world of dance. Resources are now so numerous and varied that no one can keep up with all of them. A professional in one area may know nothing about another. And the neophyte might like an inkling of the vast amount of activity in the field. Thus, this introductory "Yellow Pages" to Dance U.S.A., 1979.

The book can be used as a "tool kit," manual, reference, and career guide: It is intended for the spectator, the participant, the student, the trainee; it covers dance as an avocation and as a profession; dance for work and dance for fun; dance all over the country.

Background as well as practical information is provided. Each topic is explained and described; this is followed by a listing of names and addresses that will answer your questions as to where, when, and how. For example, in the chapter on jazz dance you will find: a description of jazz dance; history of jazz dance; some influential jazz teachers; what to wear in class; where to study; what to look for in a jazz class; what to read; and where to see jazz currently. The section on dance criticism deals with the history and problems of critical writing on dance; courses to take; important critics to read; where to publish your own criticism; a listing of anthologies of critical writing; a note on the Dance Critics Association. Organizations serving each area of activity are listed under "For more information"; books are mainly restricted to current English-language titles, and, wherever possible, paperbacks are given. Sometimes material is repeated from chapter to chapter, but generally cross-references are made to relevant information elsewhere in the book. Some sources are so important they appear again and again; foremost among these is the *Dance Magazine Annual*, a publication of more than 300 pages listing dance and dance-related services.

For those who need less extensive information, *The Dance Catalog* provides quick answers to a variety of questions. How to get reduced-price tickets? See page 251. Where to buy toe shoes? Page 124. How and where to borrow dance films at no charge? Page 202. A look at the index should get you going.

A compilation of this nature is, at best, a thorny undertaking. Whenever selections must be made, as travel and restaurant writers know all too well, many worthy names will be omitted. There is too much going on in dance to be able to cover it all. The most difficult decisions involved the sections on ballet and modern dance schools. Anyone can open a studio; no accreditation is required. And so there are thousands. Except in rare cases, there are no guidebooks or even comprehensive mailing lists of studios. The schools listed here are based on recommendations from specialists all over the country, with full awareness of the limitations of the result. For children's studios, no attempt was made to list names; there are simply too many, and it is not logistically possible to give a reasoned opinion on even a fraction of them. Your own participation in the classes and the advice of your friends and respected professionals are still the best guides to picking a teacher for your child. For ballet *Balanchine's Complete Stories of the Great Ballets* (Garden City, N.Y.: Doubleday, 1977) has a lengthy section on what parents might look for in a teacher as well as what a career in ballet entails.

So, inevitably, some good studios, companies, college dance departments, and sources will not be found here. Future editions of the book may help correct this; other books will surely improve on this initial effort. At the least, however, if what you want to know about dance isn't in *The Dance Catalog*, the book ought to give you some ideas about where to go looking.

N.R.
January 1979

I.
For the
Audience:
Dance in
Performance

HISTORY OF
THEATRICAL DANCING
IN THE WEST
By Nancy Reynolds

Commedia dell'arte: Pantalone. Engraving.

Early Court Dances

 ance has existed since the beginning of time—as ritual, as recreation, as spectacle. But the roots of theatrical dance in the West, which developed into what we call "the ballet," are believed to lie in the court entertainments of sixteenth-century France, which were themselves based on the triumphal processions of Renaissance Italy.

The elaborate presentations at the court of Louis XIV, in which the Sun King himself participated, took place on the ballroom floor, where the audience (the court nobles) joined the performers for the final dance (the use of the proscenium stage was just beginning). The Sun King amplified the grandeur of his prowess in government and warfare by appearing in these spectacles, lavishly clothed, usually in the role of a god. The subject matter of the early ballets was almost always allegorical, and the godlike figure, of course, could easily be equated with the King. Most of these works were given once only and were enormously expensive; the *Ballet-Comique de la Royne Louise* of 1581, for instance, produced at a cost of 3,600,000 francs, was seen by ten thousand people at its single performance, which lasted from 10:00 P.M. until 3:00 in the morning. Sometimes the productions celebrated royal weddings or other state occasions; sometimes, it seems, they provided diversion for the overprivileged and underactive nobles whom Louis purposely kept too busy with occupations that flattered their vanity for them to have time to intrigue against him. The fantastically costumed dancing consisted primarily of ballroom forms (courante, sarabande, branle, and so forth) along with walking, posturing, and gesturing. (Louis's entire life, of course, was a staged theatrical presentation, beginning with each morning's ritualistic *levée*—bathing and dressing in full view of an audience.)

The First Ballet School

In 1661, Louis founded the first ballet school, L'Académie Royal de la Danse; and ballet steps have been known by their French names ever since (the word "ballet," however, actually comes from the Italian for "to dance"). In the Academy, steps and sequences began to be codified for the first time, and from this a syllabus for uniform teaching would be shaped.

Early technique was not precisely on the Baryshnikov level. A new language was being formulated—a language of the body—and its refinement and elaboration took time. The concept of turn-out and the famous five positions of the feet were present almost from the beginning, but there were no professional dancers and no training at a virtuoso level. Also, the enormous costumes and high-heeled shoes prohibited complex movements.

The First Ballets

Louis XIV was not the first king to dance; Louis XIII also appeared in pageants (he reportedly loved light

Ballet-Comique de la Royne Louise, *1581. Entry of the Tritons. Engraving.*

Opposite: **The Ballet of the Provinces of France, *1573. Engraving.***

comedies and women's roles), and England's Queen Elizabeth is known to have enjoyed social dancing, especially the galliard. England was also home of the masque, made famous by Inigo Jones and Ben Jonson, which was a more literary, less movement-oriented relative of the French ballet.

The early ballets would not be recognized as such, for they consisted of songs and recitations as well as dancing. Italian influence predominated, coming from two sources: the triumphal entries (a series of floats in giant parades) and the commedia dell'arte tradition, with its robust gallery of stock characters whose impersonation required dexterity in vocal production and body control. Harlequin and Pulcinella (from whom "Punch" derives) were the most famous of the commedia dell'arte figures. Lively, comic, oversized, and sympathetic, they have been immortalized in the engravings of Callot.

Among the noted names associated with the early balletic entertainments are those of Jean-Baptiste Lully, a musician, Pierre Beauchamps and Baldassare Beaujoyeulx, dancing masters, and Molière, who obviously took the new form seriously: he and Lully developed the *comédie-ballet*. This did not glorify allegorial figures but examined the human foibles of contemporary men, whom Molière loved to make appear ridiculous.

In 1670, Louis XIV retired (too stout to dance, although still in his thirties). This, plus the rise of the Paris Opera, with its own dance troupe, ushered in a new era of professional dancing and the decline of court ballet.

In the Baroque age, due to the increased use of the proscenium stage (with its wings and flies and its distance from the audience), special effects had almost no limitation. Sets as well as costumes were unbelievably ornate. Waterfalls, erupting volcanoes, and deities descending from the heavens were all well within the capability of current stage technology, and ballets on horseback were not uncommon.

In 1713, the Paris Opera Ballet school opened its doors, and training in dance as a profession was assured. An early star pupil, Louis Dupré, was the teacher of Gaetan Vestris, sire of a famous ballet family and nicknamed "god of the dance." His son Auguste developed an advanced technical ability emphasizing turns and jumps, and one of today's superstars, Mikhail Baryshnikov, commemorates Auguste Vestris in a virtuoso vehicle, *Vestris*, created for him by Leonid Jacobson in 1969. With its gallery of roles, ranging from an old man to a drunk, a coquette, and a preacher, the solo provides Baryshnikov with a chance to display the versatility of his acting as well as his superior dance technique.

Early Women Dancers

Female dancers were also beginning to attract attention.

Opposite: Mikhail Baryshnikov in Vestris.

Marie Sallé was a choreographer (certainly one of the first women to be one) as well as a dramatic actress and dancer of taste and propriety. To attain greater range and freedom of movement, she danced in heelless shoes and discarded the hooped petticoat and wig that had weighed dancers down for years. A more flamboyant performer of the time, Marie Camargo, had greater technical proficiency than her peers and, to show off her unusual jump, which she embellished with beats (feet clicking together in the air), she daringly shortened her skirt to reveal her ankles. A more complex version of her jump was made famous by Nijinsky and is today performed regularly by any male virtuoso worth his salt.

Sometime later, La Barberina gained the affections both of the Paris public and of Frederick the Great. She was probably not the first and certainly not the last favorite of monarchs (the prima ballerina assoluta of Imperial Russia, Mathilde Kchessinska, was mistress to Tsar Nicholas II and eventually married his cousin, the Grand

Seventeenth-century stage setting by Lodovico Burnacini. Engraving.

Duke André, before ending her days in poverty in postwar Paris, riding the Métro to her ballet studio). La Barberina was noted for her technical virtuosity. It is perhaps equally remarkable that she was the only female in Frederick the Great's intimate retinue and that she ended her days in a nunnery. Dancers, of course, were still not "respectable," and in general, especially in the United States, would not truly be so considered until the 1960s.

The Eighteenth Century

An important new dance form was developing. The ballet of Louis's time—the *ballet à entrées*—had been a series of more or less unconnected divertissements, interspersed with scenes presenting a story, often told in words and music. Later, in Rameau's day (the Baroque period), danced divertissements appeared here and there in operas, still in isolated segments. Now, in the eighteenth century, the *ballet d'action*, or ballet with the story continuously told in dance without speaking or "entertainment interludes," began to gain favor. Its

Ballet d'action: Les Scythes. *Engraving.*

foremost apologist, or spokesman, and, incidentally, a ballet master employed all over Europe, foreshadowing a trend among today's jetsetting dance practitioners and choreographers, was Jean-Jacques Noverre, who was also one of the first eloquent writers on dance. (He remains among the best in a field which is still plagued by the lack of a critical vocabulary.) Noverre proposed extensive costume reform—the abolition of heeled shoes, corsets, and "boning"; he also argued for the unity of the dance work, for making all actions relevant to the main theme or story and against empty technical display. Ballet, now stripped of song and recitation, was becoming an autonomous art, complete in itself and expressive on its own terms. Noverre's treatise, *Letters on Dancing and Ballet* (1760), lives on.

The *ballet d'action* was actually pioneered in the work of John Weaver (although Noverre was far more famous). In 1717, he produced *The Loves of Mars and Venus*, starring the first English ballerina of note, Hester Santlow. Weaver, called the father of English pantomime, advocated the portrayal of drama exclusively through movement, mime, and music, without words or

Scene from eighteenth-century ballet, Amsterdam. Engraving.

interludes of declamation. Weaver also wrote extensively on dance.

Noverre's actual dances have disappeared, as have all that preceded his. The earliest ballet that is still performed is *The Whims of Cupid and the Ballet Master*, choreographed in 1786 by Vincenzo Galeotti, now seen in occasional performances by the Royal Danish Ballet and still mildly amusing. Present-day American audiences might be surprised to see the tiny child Cupid dancing on pointe (teachers here would not approve!). Another ballet of the period, of much greater impact, *La Fille Mal Gardée* (1789), is also still performed, but with varying choreography, little of it original. Created on the eve of the French Revolution, this ballet was the first to take peasant life as its subject (earlier works had dealt with mythological figures, ancient heroes, allegory, and, very occasionally, with royal personages). In so doing, the ballet introduced rustic dances to the stage. Called character dances—that is, folk or national dances theatricalized for greater effect—these would be an important component of the evening-long ballets of the nineteenth century such as *Swan Lake*. The mazurka, the czardas, the polonaise, and Spanish dancing were all, until recently, in the curriculum of serious ballet studios, but since the nineteenth-century classics are now but a small percentage of today's repertoires, dancers are tending to put their energies into other types of classes.

Character dancing is still important in the Soviet Union, however, and there are some dancers who do little else. Their classification as *demi-caractère* dancers indicates that they specialize in character dancing, and, just as important, that they lack the classical purity of movement required for the hero or heroine. In fact, the term character dancer is analogous to "character actor"—the one who never gets the girl. *La Fille Mal Gardée*, a comic story of a young girl, a young man, and the wealthy simpleton the girl's mother wants her to marry, has been performed for nearly two centuries. Sir Frederick Ashton's version, which he choreographed for the Royal Ballet in 1960, is acclaimed as one of his finest works.

In the eighteenth and nineteenth centuries, ballets of heroic dimensions pleased the public. These revolved around larger-than-life figures, Shakespearean heroes, or ancient kings whose valor had increased with time. Foremost producer of these works, which he called *choreodrammi*, was Salvatore Viganò (for whom Beethoven wrote *The Creatures of Prometheus*). Viganò combined dancing and mime (instead of alternating them as had been done previously), and arranged a large chorus in classical poses and tableaux.

Viganò's contemporary, Charles Didelot, staged ballets throughout Europe and spent many years in Russia, where his influence was profound; the later greatness of ballet

Opposite: Marie Camargo. Engraving.

there owes much to him. Perhaps his most important contribution was inventing a system of wires that lifted the dancers into the air, so they looked as though they were flying, and set them down again on the tips of their toes. This was not the same as dancing on pointe, which would evolve in another thirty years or so, but, visually speaking, it was a step in that direction (*Zephyr and Flora*, 1796).

The Nineteenth Century

Romanticism, which swept Europe (and America) in the early nineteenth century, transforming art and literature,

La Sylphide. *Engraving (1845).*

was tellingly realized in ballet as well. The ethereal, the otherworldly, and the exotic all found expression on the ballet stage, as did overt emotionalism, a revolt against the Age of Reason, against Neoclassicism, against science, and against authority. Death, particularly in the form of suicide or tuberculosis, was the most fashionable end for the love-sick hero. In dance, several important technical innovations helped project the Romantic sensibility. The new gas lighting made possible many more eerie and supernatural stage effects than candles could provide. Even more important, the development of the toe shoe

"Heroic" Ballet. Salvatore Vigano with his wife, Maria Medina. Engraving by Gottfried Schadow.

aided the dancers portraying ethereal creatures in creating a greater sense of lightness and spirituality, of elusiveness and weightlessness. A new gauzy skirt was introduced, adding to the illusion. As so often happens in history, the perfect embodiment of the desired qualities appeared at just the right time. Marie Taglioni, a long, slender dancer, possessed the ideal Romantic body, and a work created for her, *La Sylphide* (1831), became the standard Romantic ballet of that era and this, although it is not possible today to say how much of the original choreography remains. (Much is new, in any case.) The story of a mortal who deserts his betrothed for a woodland sylph, whom he then unwittingly kills (through the

Hermine Blangy in Giselle. *Lithograph by Charles Currier.*

intervention of a witch) when he tries to claim her as his own, has all the Romantic ingredients—earthy characters, otherworldly sprites, a hero torn between the real and the ideal, tragic death, and the search for the unattainable. A few years after the premiere of *La Sylphide*, another even more famous ballet with some of the same themes was created. This was *Giselle*, which, next to *Swan Lake* and *The Nutcracker*, is the most popular and durable ballet ever produced. *Giselle* also dramatized the dual currents of the age—real vs. ideal, flesh-and-blood vs. spiritual—in its Rhenish tale of a peasant girl who is turned into a Wili (sister to a sylph) because she was betrayed before marriage, and then saves her former fiancé from being danced to death by her fellow Wilis. *Giselle* has been called the "Hamlet of ballet" for the acting and dancing range required to portray the leading role.

The Age of the Ballerina

When Marie Taglioni established a new feminine ideal, the glorification of the ballerina began. Love letters and poems were written to these exalted creatures while the male dancer became less and less important until, later in the century, he disappeared almost completely, and male roles were danced by women *en travesti*. Under the circumstances, there could not be any intricate partnering or lifts; nor could there be much in the way of a "male variation." The leaps, turns, and beats at which men excelled were seldom seen. The ballerina was the object of veneration; the esteemed Gautier was among the many who were completely captivated, and when Taglioni's rival, Fanny Elssler, danced in America, champagne was drunk from her slipper. Like the movie stars of another age, there was mad jealousy among the dancers (and perhaps even more among their admirers). Somehow, however, four of the leading Romantic ballerinas were persuaded to appear together, amid much bickering, in a display piece given only four times, *Le Pas de Quatre* (1845). Queen Victoria and Prince Albert attended the third performance, an indication of the prestige the art of ballet then enjoyed, which has not always been the case in the United States. Robert Joffrey has choreographed a clever parody of this rivalry among beauties, *Pas de Déesses* ("Dance of the Goddesses," 1954), and the Paris Opera sometimes performs an approximation of the original version.

Romanticism was not all fragility and suffering. Its more robust, fiery, and erotic side was represented in ballet by Elssler, the most traveled ballerina of her time. She went as far east as Russia, as far west as America and Cuba. A smoldering presence, Elssler captivated audiences, particularly in her Cachucha and in *La Esmeralda* (based on Hugo's *The Hunchback of Notre Dame*), the first ballet, incidentally, in which the crowd was given truly individual movements.

During the Romantic era, Copenhagen was the scene of

Fanny Elssler in La Cracovienne. *Engraving by Johann Wenzel Zinke.*

lively activity in dance, thanks to the work of Auguste Bournonville (see page 120). Through the efforts of Harald Lander in the 1930s, the legacy of Bournonville has been preserved. The style he developed, characterized by lightness, springiness, gaiety, and charm, with virtuoso footwork for the men, lives on today at the Royal Danish Ballet and in the dancing of Erik Bruhn, Peter Martins, and Peter Schaufuss, all of whom trained in Denmark.

Generally speaking, however, since the age of Louis XIV, French ballet had reigned supreme in Europe, although from time to time there had been important contributions from London, Stuttgart, Copenhagen, and Italy. The situation was to change. True, the most delightful comic ballet of all time, *Coppélia*, was produced in Paris (1870), but just after this "last gasp," preeminence in ballet moved from France to an unexpected new location, the still half-feudal Russia.

Acalista, 1857. Engraving.

Russia and Petipa

St. Petersburg, Peter the Great's "Window on the West," was by far the most cosmopolitan city in the land, and for many years, foreign artists in all fields—architecture, painting, music, and dance—had been imported to satisfy the demand for culture. Russian artists were little esteemed, but Noverre, Didelot, and Saint-Léon (choreographer of *Coppélia*) had all worked in Russia, and many foreign teachers of note had also been employed there. Italian ballerinas were all the rage. In 1847, another Frenchman was brought to St. Petersburg. His reign would be long, and during his tenure Russian dance and dancers would be established as the greatest in the world, a notion that is still popularly believed, although it is no longer exclusively the case. In the late nineteenth century, Russia was the cradle of the classical ballet as we know it today. And it was Marseilles-born Marius Petipa who made all the difference.

Petipa dominated Russian ballet for sixty years, and under his regime the great age of Classicism reached full flower. The excellent state-supported ballet academies and the challenging influence of foreign ballerinas produced dancers of greater and greater virtuosity. Petipa took full advantage of them; his ballets demanded diamond-sharp quickness and large movements of grandeur and sweep rather than the filigreed lightness of the Romantic age. In addition to his role in the creation of *Sleeping Beauty, Swan Lake,* and *The Nutcracker,* which remain the backbone of the traditional repertory, Petipa choreographed at least sixty other ballets, two of which, *Raymond* and *La Bayadère,* now enjoy new popularity.

With Petipa, the construction of a ballet settled into something of a formula, but one that allowed a great deal of variety. Petipa's ballets were full-evening stories that developed at a leisurely pace, liberally punctuated with divertissments that had nothing to do with the plot but were inserted purely for pleasure and diversion. These were dances of all kinds—peasant, ethnic, classical. He also used a complete mime vocabulary (see page 177).

A setpiece of the Petipa ballet was the grand pas de deux, which had a standard form designed to display the dancers' majesty and virtuosity: it opened with a stately supported adagio; then came a variation for the man, a variation for the woman, and a lively and exciting coda, or closing, for them both, which built to a smashing climax. Some of these pas de deux are such excellent showpieces that they have often been performed as independent concert numbers, divorced from narrative reference.

Petipa was surely one of the most inventive choreographers who ever lived. George Balanchine, the most prolific choreographer of our day, whose training began in Imperial Russia, has often spoken of his debt to him.

Opposite, top: **Le Pas de Quatre, 1845. Bottom: 1940s.**

Russian Ballet in the West

Early in the twentieth century, the Russian choreographer Michel Fokine began to criticize Petipa's formulas, arguing against divertissements and mime passages that stopped the action and proposing that every movement of a dancer be expressive of his character. He called for authenticity of locale (in Petipa's ballets, Egyptians, Spaniards, and slaves alike frequently wore classical tutus) and for full integration of the corps de ballet in the dance design. He also advocated the equal collaboration of composer, designer, choreographer, and librettist in the creation of a ballet.

This last idea, in particular, put him on a common wave length with another extraordinary figure in the history of dance, Serge Diaghilev. While he was not a creator in any given sphere, Diaghilev was a catalyst who brought talents

Apollon Musagete *(Balanchine), 1928.*

together and drew from them creations they might not have been able to produce without his influence.

Diaghilev organized a season of Russian ballet (and opera) in Paris in 1909, which launched a new era in dance. Fokine, Stravinsky, Bakst, Benois, and later, the electric Nijinsky, Picasso, Nijinska, Massine, Prokofiev, Cocteau, Ravel, Matisse, and Balanchine were among those associated with Diaghilev's Ballets Russes during its twenty-year history. *Les Sylphides, The Firebird, Schéhérazade, Petrouchka, Prince Igor, Le Spectre de la Rose, Le Sacre de Printemps* (with new choreography), *Les Noces, Les Biches, La Boutique Fantasque, Apollo,* and *Prodigal Son* are some of the ballets created under his aegis that are still performed.

Although not strictly "Russian" in style (that is, not emulative of the ballet it left behind in Russia), Diaghilev's company introduced a living classical tradition to the West. His legacy remains to this day; his creative artists scattered literally throughout the world after his death in 1929, spreading the classical technique and the art of ballet to five continents.

Anna Pavlova, the "immortal swan," was the other pivotal force in the dissemination of the Russian ballet tradition. Trained to the highest standards at the Imperial School, a ballerina at the Maryinsky Theater in St. Petersburg and later with Diaghilev, Pavlova began to tour independently in 1907 and never stopped till her death in 1930. She traveled extensively in Europe and the United States as well as to remote outposts in Asia, Central and South America, Australia, New Zealand, Java, India—dancing in vaudeville theaters as well as opera houses—creating a legend.

Early American Dance

Before the twentieth century, America was not, as is popularly believed, a vast wasteland for the performing arts. George Washington was a great theater lover and was entertained at Valley Forge, although during the American Revolution theater was officially banned. Dance and theater were considered immoral in early America but music was not, and by the 1790s there were concerts all over the Colonies, during which theatrical scenes were also presented. The concerts were followed by balls.

The earliest entertainers (who often sang, danced, pantomimed, and did circus acts) were imported, and since no city in America was then large enough to support a resident troupe, performers were forced to tour extensively, so shows reached even small towns. By 1800, however, there were resident performing companies in New York and Philadelphia.

Most of the earliest professional dancers were French, arriving here in the wake of the Revolution at home. Alexandre Placide presented New York's first dance season in 1792 and toured with his company to other parts of the country. In the cast of *La Forêt Noire,* called the "first serious ballet performed in the United States," which opened in Philadelphia in 1794, were the lovely Mme. Gardie, a refugee from the race riots in Santo Domingo and the first ballerina of fame here, and John Durang, the first noted American dancer, whose hornpipe, famous in his own day, has come down to us in his description. (He learned it from a Frenchman.) It has been called the forerunner of tap dancing. In 1795, the French choreographer M. Francisquy formed a small touring troupe consisting of M. and Mme. Val, M. Dubois, Mme. Gardie, and John Durang. Among their spectacular productions was *The Independence of America, or the Ever Memorable 4th of July, 1776,* starring Mme. Gardie as America. When the troupe broke up, Durang found employment with the circus, and all of his children were

Left top: **L'Apres-midi d'un Faune (Nijinsky), 1912. Diaghilev's Ballets Russes. Bottom: Le Spectre de la Rose (Fokine), 1911. Tamara Karsavina and Vaslav Nijinsky. Diaghilev's Ballets Russes. Opposite: The Firebird (Fokine), 1910. Diaghilev's Ballets Russes.**

trained as dancers. In the late 1820s, a ballet troupe at the Bowery Theater, New York, offered the New World an introduction to "the French style of dancing," which probably meant pointe work and supported partnering, unknown here before then. Stars of the group were M. and Mme. Achille and Mme. Hutin, and the dancers included the adolescent Mlle. Celeste, who would later have a brilliant fifty-year career as a dancer and melodramatic actress, traveling all over the United States (including the frontier) and Europe, where she eventually played Shakespeare. In her heyday, she rivaled Fanny Elssler in both earning and drawing power.

Clearly, the French influence was still dominant, but in the later 1830s, three American dancers of importance made their débuts—Mary Anne Lee, Augusta Maywood, and George Washington Smith (who was originally a stonecutter). Lee, America's first Giselle, trained here and also studied in France; she thus learned authentic versions of *Giselle* and other classics as well as a large part of the Elssler repertory, taught to her by Elssler's American partner, James Sylvain (né Sullivan). Lee's Albrecht in *Giselle* was George Washington Smith, America's first premiere danseur, active as a dancer, actor, and ballet producer for forty-five years. At one point he joined the Ronzani Ballet, whose members included the seven-year-old Enrico Cecchetti, later a master teacher in the Imperial Russian academy and still later a teacher, coach, and dancer for Diaghilev (see page 118). Smith's technical prowess may have included the ability to do triple turns in the air; his son, at any rate, could do them, and it is not impossible that he learned them from his father. Augusta Maywood danced in America for only a year; she then went on to Europe and was the first American-trained dancer to become internationally famous.

More typical of entertainers in America was the Ravel family (also from France), composed of dancers, acrobats, tumblers, highwire artists, contortionists, rope dancers—the works. In keeping with the tastes of the time, their repertory included a piece that featured Harlequin landing in China in a burning balloon. In the name of high art, they also performed *Giselle, La Sylphide,* and *Esmeralda.* The Ravels traveled as far as California during the 1850s; dancing had spread across the continent.

In 1840, Fanny Elssler visited America and caused a sensation; Congress adjourned early so that members could attend her performances. Elssler had such a good time that she stayed two years, instead of the planned three months, breaking her contract with the Paris Opera, the most prestigious house in Europe, to do so. Taglioni's

Opposite: Autumn Leaves (Pavlova), 1918. Anna Pav-lova and Aubrey Hitchins. *Top:* Mary Anne Lee in The Maid of Cashmere, 1836. *Bottom:* Mlle. Paladino and Arnold Kiralfy in unidentified work. America, late nineteenth century.

brother Paul and his wife Amélie also toured the States. But in the 1850s, possibly as a result of the Civil War, the Romantic ideals began to die. Sylphides skimming the air were no longer acceptable; empty pointe technique was all that was left. Spectacular effects serving no artistic function seemed bombastic instead of supernatural, and the age of serious ballet was at an end. "Showgirls" were in; their prancing on pointe in brief costumes was what Loie Fuller, Isadora Duncan, and Ruth St. Denis would later rebel against, not the finest in classical ballet, which was not in evidence at the turn of the century when these three women came along.

The Minstrel Show

In addition to the "all around" entertainment provided by the Ravels and the Placides, another popular—and indigenous—form of theater developed. The minstrel show spread all over the country in the 1840s (including the frontier), as well as to Europe and Africa. At first, John Durang and others performed in blackface; later, Juba, a black dancer who was also a singer and tambourine virtuoso, won fame. In the 1830s, "Jumping Jim Crow," a southern plantation Negro but not a caricature, was created by a white man, "Daddy" Rice, who performed regional dances, and delivered monologues spiced with local anecdotes and political commentary. The soft shoe was born in the minstrel show. The early Negro imitators stressed the authenticity of their material; it was only later that the stock black character, singing and dancing for happiness in the fields, became an apology for slavery. By the 1860s, the minstrel show was bloated and slick, burlesquing everything. It had lost its heart. Its stuffed size and the coming of vauderville caused its decline in the 1880s.

The most spectacular extravaganza of the nineteenth century, which enjoyed a run of *forty years* and was a seminal influence on American music hall and vaudeville, was *The Black Crook*, which opened in 1866. Its complicated plot was bolstered by the "Great Parisienne Ballet Troupe" and the dancing talents of Marie Bonfanti and Rita Sangalli, as well as by elaborate scenery depicting a fairy grotto and a "wild pass in the Hartz Mountains," among other things. An opening night critic wrote: "It was played by easy stages from 7 ¾ o'clock until 1 ¼. . . . The scenery is magnificent; the ballet is beautiful; the drama is—rubbish."

A Revolution in Dance

In 1892, an American with no dance training, Loie Fuller, conquered Paris by performing in costumes made of yards of fabric illuminated by colored lights. The costumes had a life of their own; they virtually danced themselves. Around the turn of the century, the American Isadora Duncan danced barefoot in flowing robes, preaching the beauty of natural movement and citing the inspiration of Classical Greece. About the same time for-

mer "toe dancer" and vaudeville performer, Ruth St. Denis, was creating dances based on mystical Eastern themes.

None of these Americans felt the need for toe shoes, corsets, or even a touch of classical ballet technique. They dispensed with elaborate fairy-tale plots and danced to the music of great composers, rather than to traditional "ballet music" (generally characterized by a sturdy beat and melodic invention of a secondary order). These three women were the forerunners of modern dance, a dramatic artistic movement that was almost wholly American. Ruth St. Denis and her husband Ted Shawn (who later organized a troupe of male dancers) formed the Denishawn company, from which three members—Martha Graham, Doris Humphrey, and Charles Weidman—broke away to evolve personal dance techniques and to begin the modern dance revolution.

Most modern dancers through the years have gone their separate ways but all have basically worked toward the same end—to develop techniques that could be used to express the human condition, which they felt the "artificial" language of ballet was unable to do. Graham, in particular, sought to chart "interior landscapes," especially of mythic heroines, with a technique, based on the contraction and release of the torso, which incorporated the floor as a positive element in the dance design. Now in her eighties, Graham still directs her company.

During the 1930s and 1940s, other modern dancers began to create, often using social issues as points of departure. It was a time of Depression, then war, and these subjects found expression in the works of such modern dance exponents as Anna Sokolow (who is still active), José Limón, Lester Horton, and Hanya Holm (who also choreographed *My Fair Lady* and *Kiss Me, Kate*). American themes were at last considered worthy of dance treatment (*Appalachian Spring*, by Graham), as, eventually, were black themes, many of which were danced to spirituals (*Revelations*, by Alvin Ailey). Two influential foreigners in the development of modern dance were Mary Wigman and Kurt Jooss, both from Germany (Jooss fled to England before World War II).

The Avant-Garde

Three Graham dancers, Erick Hawkins, Paul Taylor, and Merce Cunningham, went on to found companies which have proved more durable than most in the modern dance field. With Cunningham, in particular, we reach the age of the avant-garde. Never neglecting substantive dance technique, Cunningham composed by chance, sometimes rolling dice to decide on a movement sequence. Rather than collaborating, designer, composer,

Opposite: Isadora Duncan with her students. Page 32: Isadora Duncan, 1904. Page 33: Loie Fuller, 1901. Page 34: Martha Graham. Drawings by Charlotte Trowbridge. Page 35: Top: Clytemnestra (Graham), 1958. Bottom: New Dance (Humphrey), 1935.

Loie Fuller

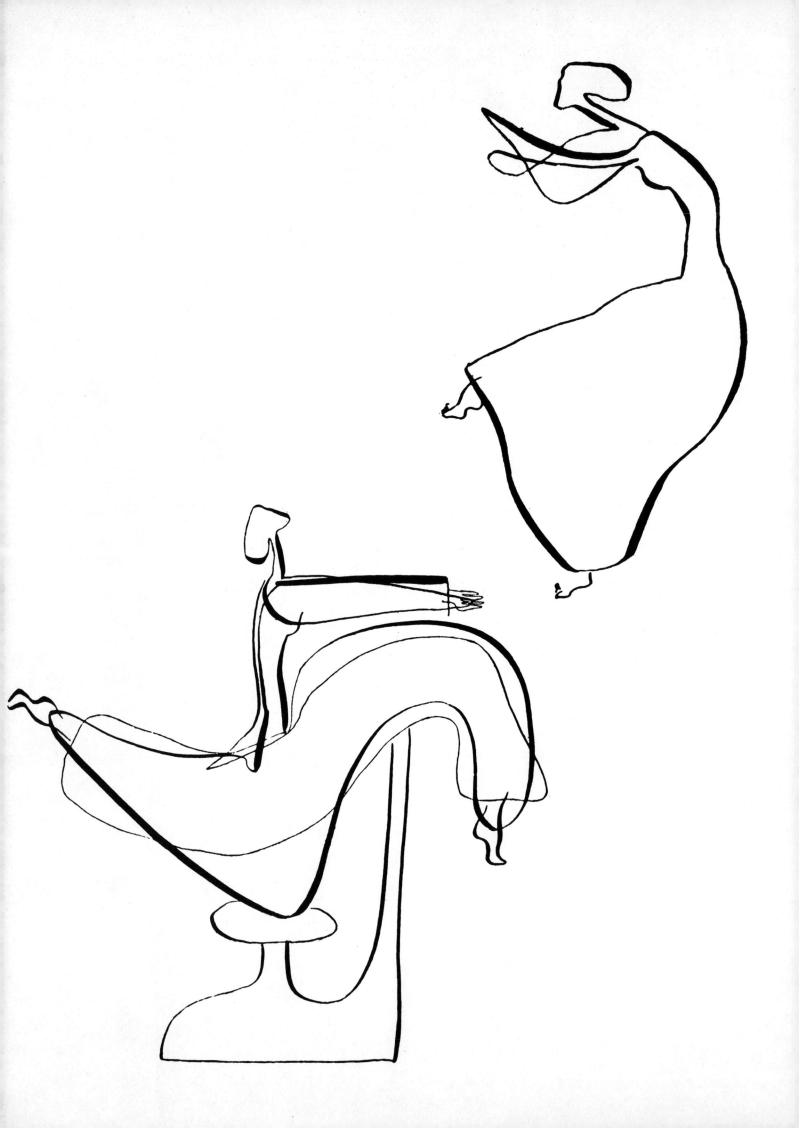

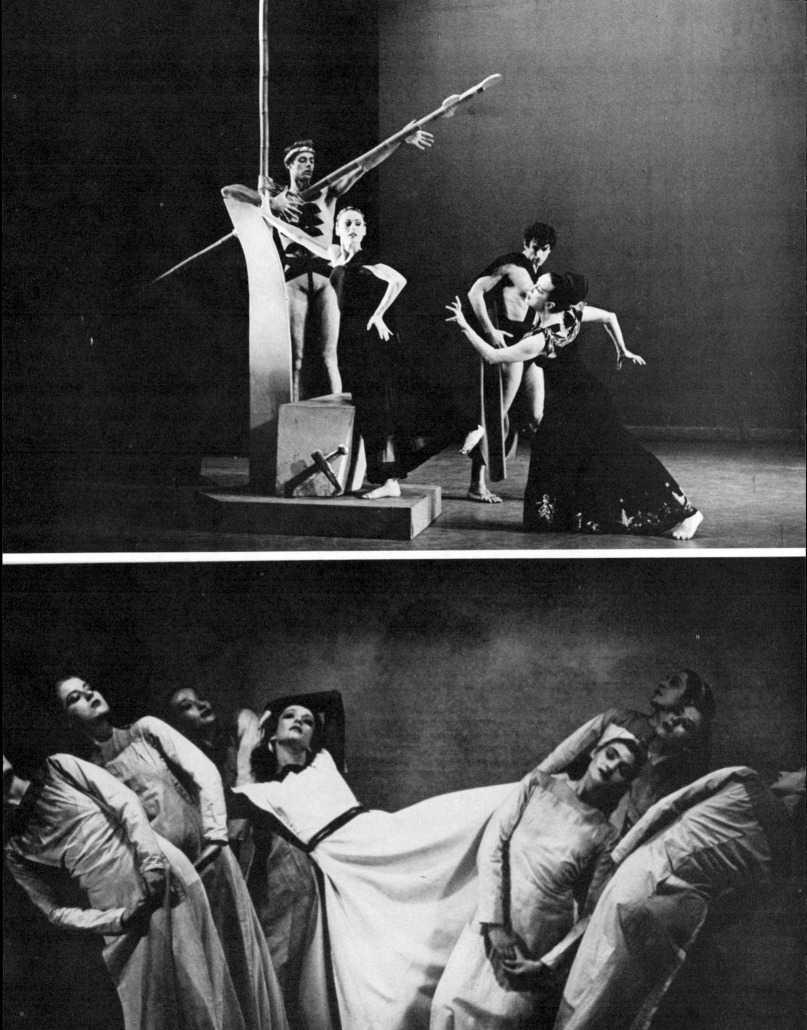

and choreographer each created independently, only assembling their creations at the final rehearsals or in performance. Incredibly, Cunningham has been in the forefront of the avant-garde for thirty years. Other notable avant-gardists are Alwin Nikolais, with his psychedelic light shows, Lucinda Childs, Kei Takei, Yvonne Rainer, Meredith Monk, Pilobolus, and Trisha Brown. Twyla Tharp is a most unusual case: her slinky, slithery movements, often set to popular music, fit into no category.

A fuller discussion of some modern dance techniques begins on page 136; profiles of modern dance, contemporary dance, and avant-garde companies now before the public will be found starting on page 72.

Ballet After Diaghilev

In 1933, George Balanchine, Diaghilev's last choreographer, came to America at the invitation of Lincoln Kirstein, and stayed to found a ballet company and to evolve a technique and an American style that revolutionized the classical ballet. Balanchine's contribution is the more unusual in that he did not throw out the past, as many revolutionaries tend to do. He used the Russian classical technique as a basis for his streamlined new movement, which represents a heightening and quickening of the basic vocabulary that originated in the days of Louis XIV. Although Balanchine is best known for his rigorous plotless ballets to modern music—most notably to Stravinsky (*Apollo, Agon, Movements*)—he has also created lush works to Brahms, Tchaikovsky, Mozart, and numerous other composers, both popular and "serious." He has been Artistic Director of the New York City Ballet since its founding in 1948.

Balanchine is probably the most towering creative figure in twentieth-century dance (equalled only by Martha Graham), but there are other great talents in the ballet field. In England, Sir Frederick Ashton has had a long career, mostly with the Royal Ballet, and is noted for his affecting and decorous story ballets. Antony Tudor's psychological ballets—*Pillar of Fire, Lilac Garden*—now performed by American Ballet Theatre, reveal his characters' inner torments and longings. He and Graham have translated the preoccupations of Freud into dance.

Jerome Robbins has been phenomenally successful as a choreographer and director of Broadway shows (*West Side Story*) and as a most original ballet creator. No two Robbins works look alike. Although he burst on the scene with the breezy and topical *Fancy Free* (premiered in 1944 and still performed), in recent years he has concentrated on plotless dance works such as *Dances at a Gathering* and *The Goldberg Variations*, created for the New York City Ballet.

Robbins, Tudor, and the younger Eliot Feld (who now has his own troupe) have all been associated with America's second major ballet company, American Ballet Theatre, founded in 1939 by Lucia Chase and Richard Pleasant. Its expressed intent was to perform the classics as well as new American works, with native dancers and internationally famous stars. Still going strong after almost forty years, American Ballet Theatre, with its long years of touring throughout the country, has probably been highly influential in the development of regional ballet, which is now firmly established all over America. (The Ballet Russe de Monte Carlo, another large-scale touring troupe, active in the 1930s, 1940s, and 1950s, also played a role in this.)

America's third major ballet company, the Joffrey Ballet, is more modest in size and does not perform any nineteenth-century classics at all. Like American Ballet Theatre, however, the company has two distinct concerns: capturing the spirit of the times in the "hip" ballets of Gerald Arpino and presenting revivals of distinguished works of this century. Thus, Ashton, Kurt Jooss, and Léonide Massine are represented in the repertory.

A more extensive view of the ballet troupes performing today, including the foreign companies most often seen here, begins on page 60.

The Musical Comedy

Ballet was a European invention; modern dance, until recently, evolved almost wholly in America. So too, in the popular sphere—musical comedy and movie dancing—America led the way.

Musical comedy is an original American creation. Its jaunty combination of song, dance, and story owes little to the musical theater of other countries. In the 1920s, with the coming of sound movies and the consequent slow death of vaudeville, musical comedy began to develop. At first, it was mostly a string of production numbers, given class by such performers as Fred Astaire. Later, Balanchine joined the act; his "Slaughter on Tenth Avenue" for *On Your Toes* (1936) was the first ballet in a musical to have its own plot. In 1943, Agnes de Mille's dream ballet for *Oklahoma!* added dimension to both story and character; and after that, a number of "serious" choreographers worked on Broadway, including Anna Sokolow, Hanya Holm, Jerome Robbins, and Helen Tamiris. In more recent times, particularly in the work of Bob Fosse, dance has been exploited more for its virtuoso potential than as a means for creating character or amplifying the story; his *Dancin'* has no plot at all. And with interest in dance and dancers now at an all-time high, it is perhaps not

---

Opposite: **Witch Dance I (Wigman), 1926. Page 38: Orpheus (Balanchine), 1948. Maria Tallchief and Nicholas Magallanes. Page 39: Ballet Russe de Monte Carlo. Gâité Parisienne (Massine), 1938. Alexandra Danilova and Léonide Massine. Page 40: Dances at a Gathering (Robbins), 1969. Patricia McBride, Edward Villella, Sara Leland. Page 41: Lilac Garden (Tudor), 1936. Hugh Laing, Nora Kaye, Tanaquil LeClercq.**

surprising that in the super-hit, *A Chorus Line*, dancers themselves are the characters and the focus of the action, rather than decoration for (and distraction from) a headlining group of principals.

Hollywood

In Hollywood, dance first received major attention in Busby Berkeley's *42nd Street* (1933), where the production numbers actually had more to do with camera angles than with dance as dance. During the 1930s and 1940s, Fred Astaire, with his debonair bearing and unusual ease, grace, and technical skill, made the greatest contribution by far to dance in the movies. According to Rudolf Nureyev, his films are well known even in Russia.

On the Town (1949) was the first great Hollywood musical to integrate plot, character, song, and dance. This starred Gene Kelly, next to Astaire the most important male dancing star in movies. It was followed by *An American in Paris, Singin' in the Rain, The Band Wagon, Funny Face,* and *Silk Stockings.* A period of decline in movie musicals in the 1960s was perhaps triggered by the onslaught of rock music and staggering production costs. In the 1970s, the magnetic John Travolta, in *Saturday Night Fever* and *Grease,* seems the most likely successor to Astaire and Kelly.

In a different vein, two romantic movies about the lives of dancers, *The Red Shoes* (1948) and *The Turning Point* (1977), have inspired thousands of girls and, one hopes, boys to get into practice clothes and find a ballet studio.

Television

On television, dance has been more extensively treated than is popularly supposed (see page 202). Still more or less in the experimental stages is videodance—dance created specifically for television, transformed by such video devices as changing colors and elongation and fractioning of the body.

Jazz and tap techniques, most often used as the basis for dances on the musical stage, film, and television, are discussed on pages 154 and 164.

The biggest story in dance today—aside from its sheer proliferation—is the coexistence and sometimes the mingling of so many styles. The boundaries have been broken; what dance is can no longer be easily defined. Almost "anything" goes—from the most traditional *Nutcracker* performances to contemporary minimalist choreography, which often unfolds in slow motion. About all that can be said is that dance still concerns movement. As such, it remains one of the basic impulses of man.

WHAT TO READ

Anderson, Jack. *Dance.* New York: Newsweek, 1974.
Balanchine, George. *Complete Stories of the Great Ballets.*
  Edited by Francis Mason. New York: Doubleday, 1977.
Beaumont, Cyril. *Complete Book of Ballets.* Rev. ed., New

York: Putnam, 1949. *Supplement* 1952.

———.*Ballets of Today*. New York: Putnam, 1954.

———.*Ballets Past and Present*. New York: Putnam, 1955.

———.*Bookseller at the Ballet*, incorporating *The Diaghilev Ballet in London*. Rev. ed., London: Beaumont, 1975.

Chujoy, Anatole, and Manchester, P. W. *The Dance Encyclopedia*. Rev. ed., New York: Simon and Schuster, 1967.

Clarke, Mary, and Crisp, Clement. *Ballet: An Illustrated History*. 1973. Paperback, New York: Universe, 1977.

Clarke, Mary, and Vaughan, David (eds.). *The Encyclopedia of Dance and Ballet*. New York: Putnam, 1977.

Guest, Ivor. *The Dancer's Heritage: A Short History of Ballet*. 1960. Paperback, London: Dancing Times, 1977.

Jackson, Arthur. *The Best Musicals*. New York: Crown, 1977.

Kirstein, Lincoln. *Dance: A Short History of Classic Theatrical Dancing*. 1935. Paperback, New York: Dance Horizons, 1962.

———.*Movement and Metaphor*. New York: Praeger, 1970.

Koegler, Horst. *The Concise Oxford Dictionary of Ballet*. New York: Oxford, 1977.

Lloyd, Margaret. *The Borzoi Book of Modern Dance*. 1949. Paperback, New York: Dance Horizons. 1970.

McDonagh, Don. *The Complete Guide to Modern Dance*. 1976. New York: Popular Library, 1977.

McGriel, Paul (ed.). *Chronicles of the American Dance*. 1948. Paperback, New York: Da Capo, 1978.

Martin, John. *America Dancing*. 1936. Paperback, New York: Dance Horizons, 1967.

———.*Introduction to the Dance*. 1939. Paperback, New York: Dance Horizons, 1965.

———.*Modern Dance*. 1933. Paperback, New York: Dance Horizons, 1965.

Mazo, Joseph. *Prime Movers: The Makers of Modern Dance in America*. New York: Morrow, 1977.

Palmer, Winthrop. *Theatrical Dancing in America*. Rev. ed., South Brunswick and New York: A. S. Barnes, 1978.

Reimer, Susan, and Reynolds, Nancy (eds.). *Dance of the Twentieth Century*. New York: Pictura Dance, 1978.

Opposite and right: **The Band Wagon, *1953*. Cyd Charisse and Fred Astaire. Page 44: Top:** **The Red Shoes, *1948*. Moira Shearer (center). Bottom:** **On the Town, *1949*. Page 45: Singin' in the Rain, *1952*. Gene Kelly. Pages 46-47: A Chorus Line** *(Bennett)***, *1975*.**

PERFORMING TODAY

This section describes and lists the companies most frequently appearing before the American public at the present time. Included are the most prominent ballet troupes across the country, foreign ballet companies who make appearances in the United States, and smaller regional American companies who perform in areas which are rarely reached by the larger ones. This section by no means exhausts the number of companies actively performing. There are many others!

Ballet Troupes
By Barbara Newman

AMERICAN BALLET THEATRE
888 Seventh Avenue
New York, N.Y. 10019
(212) 757-7053

Lucia Chase and Oliver Smith, Directors
Joyce A. Moffatt, General Manager

This company was established in 1939 by Lucia Chase and Richard Pleasant as a museum for the classics and an open forum for the development of new American works. Agnes de Mille was one of its original eleven choreographers, and Jerome Robbins joined the list shortly. Having created *Lilac Garden* and *Dark Elegies* for the Ballet Rambert in England, Antony Tudor contributed them to the repertory at the company's inception. His unbroken affiliation has continued to this day; he now serves as Associate Director. His great psychological studies of behavior, like *Pillar of Fire* and *Undertow*, created expressly for the company in the forties, further enhanced its reputation. Today's repertory is still an assortment of nineteenth-century classics and newer American works by de Mille, Robbins, Tudor, and the contemporary choreographers Twyla Tharp and Alvin Ailey. The company has made over fifteen international tours, and was the first American ballet company to appear in the Soviet Union. It has also been featured on television's "Live from Lincoln Center." Leading the dancers are company stars Fernando Bujones, Cynthia Gregory, Gelsey Kirkland, and Natalia Makarova, and guest artists Anthony Dowell and Rudolf Nureyev, who demonstrate the company's continuing star-orientation.

Eighty dancers.

Barnes, Clive. *Inside American Ballet Theatre.* New York: Hawthorn, 1977.
Payne, Charles. *American Ballet Theatre.* New York: Knopf, 1978.

ATLANTA BALLET
1404 Spring Street
Atlanta, Ga. 30309
(404) 873-5811

Robert Barnett, Artistic Director
Charles Fischl, General Manager

Dorothy Alexander founded a small company in 1929 to stimulate career-minded dancers, encourage a greater local appreciation of dance as an art form, and improve the level of grass-roots performances. This group evolved slowly into the present Atlanta Ballet which, in 1973, was named the State Ballet Company of Georgia by the Georgia State Legislature. The repertory has featured an annual *Nutcracker*, a full-length *Sleeping Beauty*, works by Balanchine, Fokine, Pauline Koner, and the company's own Carl Ratcliff and Robert Barnett, as well as more than eighty ballets by Alexander. The company has appeared regularly with the Atlanta Symphony Orchestra. In 1968, it joined the Atlanta Opera Company and the Atlanta Repertory Theatre to perform Purcell's *King Arthur* at the opening of the short-lived Memorial Arts Center. Either the full company, or its special touring group of fourteen, the Atlanta Ballet Touring Ensemble, has danced in thirty states, abroad, and at the Delacorte Festival in New York.

BALLET REPERTORY COMPANY
322 West 78 Street
New York, N.Y. 10024
(212) 799-1861

Richard Englund, Director

Since its establishment under the sponsorship of American Ballet Theatre in 1972, this company has graduated twenty-eight dancers into that parent organization, eighteen of whom still remain with it. Formed primarily to tour to those communities in which the larger company could not perform, this company offers young dancers vital touring experience and training in a variety of dance styles and techniques. Its repertory includes a *Nutcracker* pas de deux, selections form Bournonville, Tudor, Lucas Hoving, and works by Richard Englund and the Israeli choreographer Domy Reiter-Soffer.

Twenty dancers; lecture-demonstrations, residencies, seminars, master classes.

LES BALLETS TROCKADERO DE MONTE CARLO
c/o Sheldon Soffer Management
130 West 56 Street
New York, N.Y. 10019
(212) 757-8060

Natch Taylor and Peter Anastos, Directors
Eugene McDougle, General Manager

This all-male ballet company affectionately mocks

choreographic styles and stage managers with productions of *Le Pas de Quatre, Swan Lake* Act II, *Don Quixote* Pas de Deux, and original satires such as *Go for Barocco,* a takeoff on Balanchine. Using names like Olga Tchikaboumskaya, Veronika-Malaise du Mer and Eugenia Repelskii, the men perform *en travestie,* often on pointe and wearing Romantic tutus. Their serious approach and commitment to classical standards yield hilarious results.

Ten dancers.

BALLET WEST
P.O. Box 11336
Salt Lake City, Utah 84147
(801) 364-4343

Bruce Marks, Artistic Director
Robert Bradford, General Manager

William Christensen left the San Francisco Ballet in 1951 for the University of Utah, where he started a conservatory program in ballet out of which this company emerged, in 1963, as the Utah Civic Ballet. It became Ballet West in 1968 when the Federation of the Rocky Mountain States named it the official company of the Federation. Based in Salt Lake City but a frequent visitor to both farm communities and major cities in the surrounding states, it performs many of Christensen's own stagings of the classics, among them *La Fille Mal Gardée, Cinderella, Coppelia,* and an annual *Nutcracker.* Shorter pieces in the repertory are by Lew Christensen, Balanchine, Jacques d'Amboise, Michael Smuin, Tom Ruud, and company director Bruce Marks, who recently staged a full-length *Don Quixote.* The company has appeared in all the major cities of the Midwest and Pacific coast, and in Europe. Its summer residency for the last nine years has been in Aspen/Snowmass, Colorado, where it offers two three-week sessions of classes and seminars.

Thirty-nine dancers; 150 performances per year; lecture-demonstrations, master classes.

BOSTON BALLET
19 Claredon Street
Boston, Mass. 02116
(617) 542-3945

E. Virginia Williams, Artistic Director
Jan Chester, Business Manager

Organized into a fully professional company in 1963 by its present director, this troupe's versatile repertory has ranged from *Giselle* and *Sleeping Beauty* to Merce Cunningham's *Summerspace* and *Winterbranch,* with the work of Balanchine (the company's original artistic

Top: **Napoli** *(August Bournonville),* **Ballet Repertory Company. Center: Sanctus** *(Bruce Marks),* **Ballet West. Bottom: Pillar of Fire** *(Antony Tudor),* **American Ballet Theatre.**

advisor), Robbins, Cullberg, Lichine, and Norman Walker between those two stylistic extremes. One of this country's most respected teachers, Williams has concentrated on educating both her dancers and her public in the broadest possible spectrum of dance experience. As a result, the company had presented thirty-eight world premieres by 1976. It currently sponsors a yearly "Choreographers' Series" and presents free performances on Boston's Esplanade and during its tours throughout the New England area.

Thirty-two dancers; principals Anamarie Sarazin, Tony Cantanzaro, Elaine Bauer; lecture-demonstrations, workshops.

CINCINNATI BALLET COMPANY

1216 Central Parkway
Cincinnati, Ohio 45210
(513) 621-5219

David McLain, Artistic Director

Chartered in 1958 as the Cincinnati Civic Ballet, this company originally gave only occasional performances to taped accompaniment. It now has twenty-four dancers, its own orchestra, and a repertory of twenty-five classical and contemporary ballets highlighted by a group of Lester Horton's modern works which have been staged by James Truitte. Affiliated from the start with the Cincinnati Conservatory of Music, where it still performs regularly in the 800-seat Corbett Auditorium, it has recently transferred its subscription season of repertory to Cincinnati's even larger Music Hall. The company offers an annual full-length *Nutcracker*, staged by Resident Choreographer Frederic Franklin, and a series of lecture-demonstrations for students. It is the only professional ballet company of its size in the immediate tri-state area comprising Ohio, Kentucky, and Indiana.

Twenty-four dancers.

CLEVELAND BALLET

1375 Euclid Avenue
Cleveland, Ohio 44115
(216) 621-3634

Ian Horvath, Artistic Director
Gerald Ketelaar, General Manager

Founded in 1976 by two soloists from American Ballet Theatre, Dennis Nahat and Ian Horvath, this is Cleveland's first professional ballet company. Resident Choreographer and Associate Director Nahat has supplied most of the repertory, primarily contemporary works rooted in classical technique, to music by Mendelssohn, Tchaikovsky, and Brahms. His *Things Our Fathers Loved* is a

Top: **Spring Waters,** *Eglevsky Ballet.* **Bottom:** **Swan Lake,** *Les Ballets Trockadero de Monte Carlo.*

theatrical slice of Americana, while *US*, co-choreographed with Horvath, depicts popular American dance styles from square dances to the jitterbug. Agnes de Mille's comic *Three Virgins and a Devil* and Horvath's rock ballet *Ozone Hour* complete the small but varied repertory. Despite its youth, the company now boasts a live orchestra for its eight-week season and has arranged short tours to Chicago and Columbus.

Thirty dancers.

DANCERS
450 Avenue of the Americas
New York, N.Y. 10011
(212) 260-0453

Dennis Wayne, Artistic Director
Martin Kagan, General Manager

Dancer Dennis Wayne left American Ballet Theatre in 1976 to establish this "chamber ensemble ballet company." Its repertory of modern works by Norbert Vesak, Todd Bolender, Maurice Béjart, Paul Sanasardo, and Norman Walker (Wayne's first teacher) was designed to challenge and satisfy both a modern audience and the company's young, ambitious dancers. In 1977, this company was the United States representative to the Festival of Two Worlds in Spoleto, Italy.

Fourteen dancers.

DANCE THEATER OF HARLEM
466 West 152 Street
New York, N.Y. 10031
(212) 690-2800

Arthur Mitchell and Karel Shook, Directors
Richard A. Gonsalves, Company Manager

When Arthur Mitchell founded the Dance Theater of Harlem in 1969, he was the only black man who had ever established an international reputation as a ballet dancer. Abandoning his position as the first and only black principal at the New York City Ballet, he decided to create a company in which black dancers could perform the classical works which had never been available to them. Rigorously trained in the classical vocabulary by Mitchell and his co-director, Karel Shook, former ballet master of the Netherlands National Ballet, the company performs four Balanchine ballets and assorted excerpts and pas de deux from the standard classical repertory. Such works as *Dougla* by Geoffrey Holder, *Forces of Rhythm* by Louis Johnson, and *Every Now and Then* by William Scott celebrate the African origins and native traditions of all American blacks. The company also dances contemporary pieces by Robert North, Choo San Goh, and Carlos Carvajal. It has toured major cities in the United States, and in Europe, and gave a command performance for Queen Elizabeth II in London.

Fourteen dancers; fifteen performing apprentices; lecture-demonstrations.

Hodgson, Moira. *Quintet: Five American Dance Companies.* New York: Morrow, 1976.

DAYTON BALLET COMPANY
140 North Main Street
Dayton, Ohio 45402
(513) 222-3661

Josephine Schwarz, Artistic Director
Diane Dean, General Manager

Thanks to Josephine Schwarz, Dayton has had a small resident ballet company since 1937 when she formed the Experimental Group for Young Dancers. Known today as the Dayton Ballet Company, the active group performs in public schools, for senior citizens, and at city recreation centers, giving both lecture-demonstrations and lecture-recitals called "Dancers and Dialogues." Dancer Bess Saylor and Resident Choreographer Jon Rodriguez are frequent contributors to the repertory, and Fernand Nault, Violette Verdy, Yuriko, E. Virginia Williams, and Robert Barnett have all served as guest choreographers. The company has performed at Jacob's Pillow, at the Delacorte Festival, and in the Dayton Opera Association's production of Saint-Saens's *Samson and Delilah*.

EGLEVSKY BALLET
P.O. Box 43
Massapequa Park, N.Y. 11762
(516) 798-8296

Leda Anchutina Eglevsky, Artistic Director
Mark W. Jones, Administrator

The great dancer André Eglevsky organized this company in 1961 to present the classics and the ballets of Balanchine to the local community and the residents of New York State, many of whom had never seen them before. The company now dances five Balanchine works and full-length versions of *Sleeping Beauty, Cinderella,* and *Nutcracker,* as well as William Dollar's *Combat* and James Waring's *Au Café Fleurette.* It has toured widely in the Northeast, and offers a total of twenty-five performing weeks annually. Fernando Bujones and Marina Eglevsky were once company members; the latter has returned several times as a guest artist.

Twenty-six dancers; guest artists Galina and Valery Panov.

ELIOT FELD BALLET
890 Broadway
New York, N.Y. 10003
(212) 777-7100

Overleaf: **Forces of Rhythm *(Louis Johnson)*, Dance Theater of Harlem.**

Eliot Feld, Artistic Director
Cora Cahan, Administrator

Eliot Feld danced for six years with American Ballet Theatre, founded his first company, the American Ballet Company, in 1969, and his second, the present company, in 1974. With a few exceptions, its repertory is drawn from the twenty-nine ballets he has choreographed since 1967. *Harbinger* and *At Midnight* are lyrical abstract works, *A Soldier's Tale* is strident and theatrical, *The Real McCoy* is satiric. The company has appeared at the first Spoleto Festival in Charleston, N.C., on television "Live from Wolf Trap," and in Mexico and South America as the United States cultural representative to Latin America for the Bicentennial. It is the resident dance company of the New York Shakespeare Festival. Its alphabetically listed dancers are indisputably led by Christine Sarry, who is occasionally partnered by guest star Mikhail Baryshnikov.

Twenty-three dancers.

Hodgson, Moira. *Quintet: Five American Dance Companies.* New York: Morrow, 1976.

FIRST CHAMBER DANCE COMPANY

P.O. Box 66252
Seattle, Wash. 98166
(206) 246-4313

Charles Bennett, Artistic Director
Merilyn D. Hatheway, Administrator

Originally a quartet based in New York, this company added several members before making three world tours under United States State Department auspices. After a series of residencies in the Pacific Northwest, it moved west for good in 1974, establishing Seattle as a home base, and continued its extensive touring. It has given more than 100 performances in the last few years before more than 75,000 schoolchildren, under the sponsoring banner of the Washington State Cultural Enrichment Program. While part of its repertory consists of original modern ballets, many of them by company founder Charles Bennett, the company also performs the work of Tudor, Sokolow, Limón, Goslar, and Sanasardo, all of whom it has introduced to the Northwest public.

Seven dancers; twenty-five performances per year; intensive educational program at Summer Dance Laboratory, Fort Worden Park.

HARTFORD BALLET

308 Farmington Avenue
Hartford, Conn. 06105
(203) 525-9396

Michael Uthoff, Artistic Director
Ellsworth Davis, Managing Director

With Michael Uthoff at the helm since 1972, this company concentrates on a contemporary repertory, predominantly choreographed by Uthoff to music ranging from bluegrass to Brahms, Mahler, and Foss. The repertory also features modern ballets by Limón, Sokolow, and Jennifer Muller; Balanchine's *Allegro Brilliante*, Uthoff's own *Nutcracker*, and a comic work, *Leggieros*, by Lotte Goslar. The company's first full-length production, Ernst Uthoff's *Carmina Burana*, is scheduled to premiere shortly. Lengthy tours, often a succession of one-night stands, have taken the company throughout Connecticut and New England (including Jacob's Pillow), and as far afield as Arkansas, Michigan, North Dakota, and South Carolina.

Sixteen dancers.

HARTFORD CHAMBER BALLET

308 Farmington Avenue
Hartford, Conn. 06105
(203) 525-9396

Michael Uthoff and Enid Lynn, Artistic Directors
Gary Lindsey, Tour Director

Under the producing aegis of the Hartford Ballet, this smaller company tours the small-cast works of its parent company to those communities which cannot accommodate or afford the larger group. Averaging seventy performances per year since its founding in 1974, the company presents a wide range of modern works by Uthoff, Enid Lynn, and Doris Humphrey, and maintains an educational program of master classes and lecture-demonstrations.

Ten dancers.

HOUSTON BALLET

Jones Hall
615 Louisiana Avenue
Houston, Tex. 77002
(713) 225-0275

Ben Stevenson, Artistic Director
Mary K. Bailey, Administrative Director

Since its establishment in 1968, this company has concentrated on full-length classics. Traditional productions of *Swan Lake, Sleeping Beauty,* and *Coppélia* are supplemented by the evening-long *Prodigal Son (in Ragtime)* by Barry Moreland, several modern pieces by company director Stevenson, and a sampling of such well-known contemporary choreographers as Doris Humphrey, Walter Gore, and Rudi van Dantzig. The company provides an extensive scholarship-apprentice program in conjunction with the Houston Ballet Academy, and offers the student apprentices regular performing opportunities.

Thirty dancers; fifty performances per year with live orchestra.

THE JOFFREY BALLET
130 West 56 Street
New York, N.Y. 10019
(212) 265-7300

Robert Joffrey, Artistic Director
Peter S. Diggins, Administrator

The City Center Joffrey Ballet made its first tour in 1956, as Robert Joffrey's Theatre Dancers, with a repertory of four Joffrey ballets and six dancers, one of whom was Gerald Arpino. Arpino is now Resident Choreographer and Associate Director of a company numbering fifty-one. Joffrey's twofold dedication, to the reconstruction and revival of the great works of the past and the presentation of the major works of the present, has engendered an eclectic repertory that encompasses Arpino, de Mille, Massine, Jooss, Robbins, Tharp, and more Ashton than any company but the Royal Ballet. Understandably, there is no "Joffrey style" of dancing, but the dancers' energy, enthusiasm, and chameleonlike adaptability validate even the most superficial pieces. Original works like Robert Joffrey's multimedia *Astarte* and Arpino's *Trinity* link classical ballet directly to contemporary subjects and the contemporary audience. The company has danced throughout Europe and in Russia, as well as at Wolf Trap, and on public television.

Fifty-one dancers.

JOFFREY II DANCERS
130 West 56 Street
New York, N.Y. 10019
(212) 265-7300

Sally Bliss, Artistic Director
Maria Grandy, Associate Director

Organized by Robert Joffrey in 1969 as the Joffrey Apprentice Company, and originally affiliated with the New York City Opera, this is now an independent company of sixteen dancers, aged sixteen to twenty, whose repertory includes the work of Arpino, Ashton, Tudor, Sally Bliss, Tom Pazik, and William Whitener (formerly of the Joffrey Ballet). Since it feeds constantly into the parent company (one-third of the present Joffrey Ballet danced here), important aspects of the dancers' training are adapting to various touring conditions and understudying roles, both in their own repertory and in the parent company's repertory as well, nearly all of which they have learned. They regularly offer master classes and lecture-demonstrations while on tour, and have appeared with Sarah Caldwell's Boston Opera Company and in the Delacorte Festival.

Sixteen dancers.

Top: **Cortège Parisien *(Feld)*, Eliot Feld Ballet. Bottom:** **Le Corsaire, *First Chamber Dance Company.***

KANSAS CITY BALLET
1208 Waltower Building
823 Walnut Avenue
Kansas City, Mo. 64106
(816) 421-1979

Ron Sequoio, Artistic Director
David T. Greis, General Manager

In 1957, while still director of the dance division of the Kansas City Conservatory of Music, Tatiana Doukodovska formed this company with the intention of presenting major classical works and introducing new and nationally known choreographers to the area. Along with excerpts from *Coppélia, Carnaval, Sleeping Beauty,* and *Nutcracker,* often staged by Doukodovska, the company now performs contemporary works by Eric Hyrst, by guest choreographers John Clifford, George Skibine, and Zachary Solov, and by faculty members of the Conservatory with which it is still affiliated. "Brown Bag" lunchtime performances in schools and municipal buildings are sponsored by the Civic Arts Council and include the traditional *Le Pas de Quatre* and Fokine's *Les Sylphides.* The company has also appeared with the Kansas City Philharmonic and outdoors as part of the Parks and Recreation Department's Theatre Under the Stars.

Sixteen dancers; guest artists Fernando Bujones, Veronica Tennant; lecture-demonstrations.

LOS ANGELES BALLET
11843 West Olympic Boulevard
Los Angeles, Calif. 90064
(213) 478-0107

John Clifford, Artistic Director
R. Derek Swire, General Manager

In 1974, John Clifford resigned as a principal dancer with the New York City Ballet to cross the country and establish this company. Its repertory now numbers fifty-five ballets; twenty-four are selections from the forty works Clifford has choreographed since the company's inception and ten are by Balanchine. Clifford would like the company to appeal to the broadest possible audience and to make a distinctly American contribution to an international art form. He has therefore focused the repertory on contemporary works and set some of his own pieces to the popular music of Gershwin and Ravi Shankar. The company has completed one local tour, which included twenty-five performances and three short residencies, and is planning another to the Midwest.

Twenty-five dancers.

Top: **Prodigal Son (in Ragtime) (Barry Moreland), Houston Ballet. Bottom: Schubert Waltzes (Heinz Poll), Ohio Ballet.**

MARYLAND BALLET
2510 St. Paul Street
Baltimore, Md. 21218
(301) 366-5800

Petrus Bosman, Artistic Director
Joseph Patterson, Business Manager

This company, the first professional ballet company in Maryland, was founded in 1959 by Kathleen Crofton, who also reorganized it to advantage in 1974. Its repertory combines classical works, like *Le Spectre de la Rose*, *Paquita* Act II (staged by Alexandra Danilova and Norman Walker), and *Napoli* divertissements, with contemporary ballets by Alvin Ailey, John Butler, Roland Petit, John Taras, and guest choreographer George Skibine. The subscription series features an annual *Nutcracker*, performed at the Lyric Theatre with the Baltimore Symphony Orchestra.

Eighteen dancers; principals Camille Izard and Sylvester Campbell were both award winners at the Third International Ballet Competition, Moscow.

MILWAUKEE BALLET COMPANY
536 West Wisconsin Avenue
Milwaukee, Wis. 53203
(414) 276-2566

Jean Paul Comelin, Artistic Director
Randall J. Voit, Company Manager

Established by Robert Boorse in 1970 to perform traditional and contemporary choreography, this company is now directed by Jean Paul Comelin, whose one-act ballets to Beethoven, Britten, Strauss, Ravel, and Albinoni provide a wide range of expression for the young dancers. His Associate Director, Marjorie Mussman, has also choreographed several modern works, as has company dancer Mark Diamond. Balanchine's *Pas de Dix*, Comelin's one-act *Nutcracker* and *Paquita*, and several Grand Pas de Deux make up the classical side of the repertory. The company's home is in the Milwaukee Performing Arts Center, but it also offers informal "beer and ballet" evenings in the cabaret atmosphere of Century Hall, in civic clubs, and in small dinner theatres.

Twenty-five dancers; guest artists Galina and Valery Panov; lecture-demonstrations, master classes, Young People's Performances.

MINNESOTA DANCE THEATRE
528 Hennepin Avenue
Minneapolis, Minn. 55403
(612) 335-7808

Loyce Houlton, Artistic Director
Diane Norman, Company Manager

The more than fifty ballets Loyce Houlton has created for this company form the core of its repertory, which also contains works by Ashton, Limón, and Tetley. Her own creations range widely in style and structure, from the historical survey of American dance called *Kaleidoscope: Spirit of America Dancing*, produced to honor the Bicentennial, to her annual, more classical *Nutcracker Fantasy*, and plotless explorations of music by Mahler and George Crumb. The company performs year-round in the Twin Cities and Midwestern states, and has appeared at Jacob's Pillow, at the Festival of Two Worlds in Spoleto, Italy, and at Minnesota's salute to nineteenth-century Russian art along with the Minnesota Orchestra and members of the Guthrie Theatre.

Twenty-six dancers; guest teachers Valentina Pereyaslavec, Brian Shaw, Mary Hinkson.

NEW YORK CITY BALLET
New York State Theater
Lincoln Center Plaza
New York, N.Y. 10023
(212) 877-4700

George Balanchine, Artistic Director
Lincoln Kirstein, General Director

When George Balanchine and Lincoln Kirstein established this company in 1948, they hoped to create and maintain a repertory, founded in the classical idiom, which would advance the public's appreciation of ballet while advancing the art itself. Today the company is internationally acclaimed for the musicality and adaptability of its dancers, and for its landmark repertory. Balanchine's multi-faceted works range in style from the nineteenth-century classicism of Petipa, on which he was reared in his native Russia, to the swift, streamlined angularity which is his own creation, an American style uniquely of and for the twentieth century. Besides his "practice clothes" ballets stand lavish extravaganzas like *Vienna Waltzes, Union Jack,* and the annual *Nutcracker.* Jerome Robbins's choreographic explorations of lyricism, jazz, humor, and theater complete the remarkable repertory. The company has appeared all over the world and on public television's *Dance in America.* The no-star roster lists dancers alphabetically, including Baryshnikov, Suzanne Farrell, Peter Martins, and Patricia McBride.

Ninety dancers.

Kirstein, Lincoln. *The New York City Ballet.* New York: Knopf, 1973.
Reynolds, Nancy. *Repertory in Review.* New York: Dial, 1977.
Taper, Bernard. *Balanchine.* 1963. Paperback, rev. and updated, New York: Macmillan, 1974.

NORTH CAROLINA DANCE THEATRE

7 Vintage Avenue
Winston-Salem, N.C. 27107
(919) 761-2190

Robert Lindgren, Director
Stan Ware, General Manager

Established in 1970 to bring professional ballet to the Southeast region of the United States, this company's subsequent tours of twenty states, its lecture-demonstrations, and its community activities can be considered the successful fulfillment of its original goal. Repertory ranges from Balanchine, Tudor, and Anton Dolin's setting of *Le Pas de Quatre* to ballets on American themes by Valerie Bettis, Charles Czarny, and Norbert Vesak, and abstract works by Ailey, Job Sanders, and Duncan Noble. In 1977, the North Carolina General Assembly passed a resolution of recognition and appreciation for the company's contribution to the artistic life of the state. The troupe is affiliated with the North Carolina School of the Arts in Winston-Salem, and has appeared at the American Dance Festival, Durham.

Fifteen dancers; fifty performances per year.

OHIO BALLET

354 East Market Street
Akron, Ohio 44325
(216) 375-7900

Heinz Poll, Artistic Director
Rod J. Rubbo, General Manager

Artistic Director Heinz Poll founded this company in 1968 as a classically rooted ensemble, without stars, that would focus on contemporary choreography. At present, twenty-six of his original ballets make up the core of the repertory which, over the years, has also included Paul Taylor's *Aureole*, Anna Sokolow's *Rooms*, Ruthanna Boris's *Cakewalk*, and Robert Joffrey's *Pas des Déesses*. The company gives annual outdoor performances at Akron's Cascade Plaza and has appeared with the Cleveland Orchestra and the Akron Symphony Orchestra. Along with its standard schedule of local touring, it has traveled to Jacob's Pillow, to the Delacorte Festival in New York, and to the inaugural season of the Spoleto Festival, USA, in Charleston, where it was one of two companies invited to perform.

Twenty-two dancers; fifty performances per year; lecture-demonstrations, single performances, residencies.

PACIFIC NORTHWEST BALLET

4649 Sunnyside Avenue North
Seattle, Wash. 98103
(206) 447-4750

Kent Stowell, Artistic Director
Timothy Duncan, Managing Director

While leaning heavily on ballets by Stowell, this company also encourages its dancers to choreograph and sponsors programs called "Summer Inventions" comprised of new works. The repertory consists of Balanchine's *The Four Temperaments, Serenade*, and *Concerto Barocco*, Stowell's *Coppelia* and his shorter pieces to Ravel and Stravinsky, and modern works by Choo San Goh, Benjamin Harkarvy, and Charles Czarny. In conjunction with the Seattle Symphony and Opera, the company also performs at the Seattle Opera House in the Schools' Cultural Enrichment Program.

PENNSYLVANIA BALLET

2333 Fairmount Avenue
Philadelphia, Pa. 19130
(215) 978-1400

Benjamin Harkarvy, Artistic Director

When Executive Director Barbara Weisberger founded this company in 1964, she hoped it would "create a climate in which ballet can develop" in Philadelphia. She borrowed the bulk of its early repertory, and a host of guest stars, from the New York City Ballet. Within two years of its founding, the new company was invited to dance in Philadelphia's Academy of Music where it has given annual performances ever since while steadily enlarging its repertory and enhancing the reputation of its fine ensemble. Balanchine is still the mainstay of the repertory, which also features Harkarvy, van Manen, John Butler, Lar Lubovitch, and a new full-length *Coppélia* staged by Petrus Bosman. The company has appeared on public television's *Dance in America*, and at Jacob's Pillow, the Delacorte Festival, and the Blossom Festival accompanied by the Cleveland Orchestra. It has also toured thirty-five states and Canada.

Thirty dancers.

PITTSBURGH BALLET THEATRE

244 Boulevard of the Allies
Pittsburgh, Pa. 15222
(412) 281-0360

Patrick Frantz, Artistic Director
Kay S. Cushing, General Manager

The first ballet company ever established in Pittsburgh, in 1970 this organization set its sights on building and educating a new audience while maintaining a wholly professional performance atmosphere for its dancers. To this end, Artistic Director Patrick Frantz has amassed a classical repertory consisting of full-length works, like *Romeo and Juliet, Coppélia,* and *Swan Lake,* and one-act ballets in a variety of contemporary styles by such choreographers as Balanchine, Anton Dolin, John Butler, Ruth Page, Frederic Franklin, and Frantz himself. In the last several years, he has commissioned fourteen new

works. The company dances nearly 100 performances a year, half of them on tour in the United States, Puerto Rico, and Canada, and offers regular lecture-demonstrations in schools and civic clubs. It has also danced for the employees of U.S. Steel in the corporation's own auditorium, and welcomed the university's football team, the Pittsburgh Panthers, as participants in a company class.

Thirty-six dancers.

SAN ANTONIO BALLET
212 East Mulberry Avenue
San Antonio, Tex. 78212
(512) 736-3794

Vladimir Marek, Artistic Director
Nancy Smith, Assistant Director

This chamber company limits its repertory to three full-length classics, one Fokine work, and several contemporary ballets. Individual acts, solos, and pas de deux are excerpted from the full-length works. In addition to lecture-demonstrations and school performances, special activities include free "Family Concerts" in local parks, malls, and Farmer's Markets, and numerous free performances during "Ballet Week in San Antonio."

Sixteen dancers; fifty performances per year, touring to surrounding states and Mexico.

SAN DIEGO BALLET
526 Market Street
San Diego, Calif. 92101
(714) 239-4141

Keith J. Martin, Artistic Director
Gary Lindsey, General Manager

Decidedly traditional in focus, this company presents such standard works as *Les Sylphides, Swan Lake* Act II, and *Le Pas de Quatre,* and less familiar selections such as Asaf Messerer's *Spring Waters* Pas de Deux and one act of *La Bayadère,* staged by David Holmes. Local choreographers have contributed to the contemporary branch of the repertory, as have Lew Christensen, John Pasqualetti, and Jean Paul Comelin, all guest choreographers from various regional companies. The company has performed at Jacob's Pillow and in the San Diego Opera lecture series. For performances of Keith Martin's full-length *Nutcracker* and four-act *Swan Lake,* the company employs an expanded roster of thirty-six.

Eighteen dancers; guest artists Galina and Valery Panov, Jillana; lecture-demonstrations, master classes, open rehearsals.

Top: "Theme and Variations" from Suite No. 3 *(George Balanchine), New York City Ballet.* Bottom: Symphonic Impressions *(Kent Stowell), Pacific Northwest Ballet.*

SAN FRANCISCO BALLET
378 18th Avenue
San Francisco, Calif. 94121
(415) 751-2141

Lew Christensen and Michael Smuin,
Artistic Co-Directors
Richard E. LeBlond, General Manager

The San Francisco Ballet prides itself on being the oldest ballet company in the United States. Organized as a unit of the San Francisco Opera in 1933, it began performing independently under Willam Christensen in 1937. It was also the first American ballet company to perform a full-length *Nutcracker,* in 1944, and the first to tour the Far East, in 1957. The repertory now features a representative sampling of works by Balanchine, Ashton, Robbins, and Cranko, alongside the choreographic efforts of company dancers Tom Ruud and John McFall, and of both artistic directors. Other popular full-length productions include founder Willam Christensen's *Coppélia* and *Swan Lake,* and Smuin's *Romeo and Juliet,* which was recently broadcast on public television's *Dance in America.* The company has toured Latin America, the Mideast, and Africa, and made its New York debut in 1965.

Forty dancers; principals Diana Weber, Tom Ruud, Betsy Erikson, Vane Vest; guest artists Galina and Valery Panov, Paolo Bortoluzzi; 150 performances per year.

WASHINGTON BALLET
3515 Wisconsin Avenue NW
Washington, D.C. 20016
(202) 362-1683

Mary Day, Director
Peter Grigsby, Company Manager

The roots of this company lie in the Washington School of Ballet, which Lisa Gardner and Mary Day established in 1944. Five years later, its dancers began appearing with the National Symphony Orchestra as the present company, founded in 1956, still does. The classical side of the repertory is devoted to Balanchine, to the one-acts, *Les Sylphides, Prince Igor,* and *Swan Lake* Act II in stagings by former Company Director Frederic Franklin, and to an annual *Nutcracker* by Mary Day and Martin Buckner. The contemporary side features ballets to Bartók, Mozart, and various Baroque composers by Resident Choreographer Choo San Goh, previously choreographer for his native Singapore Ballet and for the Dutch National Ballet. Rudy Perez, Louis Johnson, Salvatore Aiello, and Joffrey dancer Kevin McKenzie have also contributed modern works. The company has appeared at Jacob's Pillow, and on Washington public television in a performance of *The Unicorn, The Gorgon and the Manticore*, choreographed by Heino Heiden and taped at the National Cathedral.

Foreign Ballet Companies

AUSTRALIAN BALLET
11 Mt. Alexander Road
Flemington, Victoria 3031 Australia
(03) 335-1400

Dame Peggy van Praagh, Artistic Director
Peter F. Bahen, Administrator

Dame Peggy van Praagh started this national company in 1962 with forty-four dancers, forty-two of whom were Australian. Its repertory of Ashton, Cranko, and the full-length classics was modeled on that of the Sadler's Wells Ballet in England. Over the years, lavish spectacles like Cranko's *Eugene Onegin,* Nureyev's *Don Quixote,* and the Ronald Hynd-Sir Robert Helpmann *Merry Widow* have entered the repertory, as have shorter works by Hynd, Helpmann (long-time director of the company), Eugene Loring, and Jerome Robbins. The company's extensive touring throughout Australia includes annual seasons in each of its capital cities. After earlier tours to the Far East and Europe, the company made its North American debut at Expo '67 in Montreal, and its New York debut in 1971. Fully subsidized by national, state, and municipal funds, it sponsors an annual competition to support and encourage new Australian choreographers.

Fifty-five dancers; principals Marilyn Rowe, Kelvin Coe; recent guest artists Margot Fonteyn, Rudolf Nureyev, and Ray Powell.

BALLET OF THE 20th CENTURY
Théâtre Royal de la Monnaie
4, Rue Leopold
Brussels, Belgium

Maurice Béjart, Artistic Director
Anne Lotsy, Administrator

This company is best known for its grandiose ballets by founder and Artistic Director Maurice Béjart, which combine religious mysticism, theatrical extravaganza, and sensual fantasy in daring and inventive productions, often more strikingly staged than choreographed. By turning profound, sometimes philosophical subjects into glittering spectacles, Béjart hopes to make his work accessible to the largest possible audience. Music is by Mahler, Ravel, Boulez, Mozart, and Bach; performances are frequently danced in vast sports' arenas.

Seventy dancers; principals Jorge Dann, Daniel Lommel.

Como, William (ed.). *The Essence of Béjart.* New York: Danad, 1977.

Opposite: **Bolero *(Maurice Béjart)*, Ballet of the 20th Century. Maya Plisetskaya.**

BALLET RAMBERT
94 Chiswick High Road
London W4 1SH, England
(01) 995-4246

Dame Marie Rambert and John Chesworth,
Artistic Directors
Prudence Skene, Administrator

This company dates its existence from the premiere, in 1926, of Sir Frederick Ashton's first ballet, *A Tragedy of Fashion*. With its indefatigable founder Dame Marie Rambert as Artistic Director, it began life as a tiny classical company, nurturing the seeds of ballet in Britain by presenting the early works of Ashton and Tudor. Forty years after its founding, the decision was made to restructure the company and the repertory along more modern and experimental lines. Abandoning the classics to the Royal and Festival Ballets, Ballet Rambert drew new choreographers Norman Morrice, John Chesworth, and Christopher Bruce from its own ranks, and encouraged outsiders like Glen Tetley, Rudi van Dantzig, and Robert North to contribute to the repertory as well. More recently, the works of American choreographers Anna Sokolow, Lar Lubovitch, Cliff Keuter, and Louis Falco have added to the challenging, often controversial, character of this company's performances.

Fourteen dancers.

Percival, John. *Experimental Dance*. New York: Universe, 1971.
Rambert, Marie. *Quicksilver*. New York: St. Martin's, 1972.

BERLIN OPERA BALLET
Richard-Wagner-Strasse 10
1 Berlin 10, West Germany
030/34-38-1

Gert Reinholm, Artistic Director

Created in 1961 from the combination of the Berlin State Opera ballet company and Tatiana Gsovska's Berlin Ballet, this company has developed a rounded repertory of traditional classical ballets, varied pieces from an international group of modern choreographers, and specially commissioned works. Balanchine, MacMillan, Jooss, and van Manen figure prominently. Tudor's staging of *Giselle* is performed and, during a recent guest appearance, Valery Panov added his staging of *Nutcracker* and his original *Rite of Spring* to the company's repertory.

Fifty-three dancers; principals Eva Evdokimova, Vladimir Gelvan; guest artists Galina and Valery Panov.

Top: **Embrace Tiger and Return to Mountain (Glen Tetley), Ballet Rambert. Center: Spartacus (Yuri Grigorovich), Bolshoi Ballet. Bottom: Four Last Songs (Rudi van Dantzig), Dutch National Ballet.**

BOLSHOI BALLET
Bolshoi Theatre
Sverdlov Square
Moscow, U.S.S.R.

In 1773, the trustees of the Moscow Orphanage decided their charges should study ballet. The first public performance by these students, given three years later at the Petrovsky Theatre, now the site of the Bolshoi Theatre, began the long history of the Bolshoi Ballet. Today's company of 250 still performs Petipa's full-length *Don Quixote* which premiered there in 1869, as well as *Giselle*, Lavrovsky's *Romeo and Juliet,* and new stagings of *Nutcracker, Sleeping Beauty,* and *Swan Lake* by Yuri Grigorovich, ballet master since 1964. (*Swan Lake* also premiered at the Bolshoi in 1877, but was a failure in its earliest version by Julius Reisinger.) Grigorovich's modern, realistic ballets, *Spartacus, Stone Flower,* and *Ivan the Terrible* resemble choreographed epics; short on dance and long on drama, they are mixtures of heroic gestures, acrobatic movement, mime, and broad comedy. For these, the classically schooled dancers must enlarge their powerful technique to vitalize the spectacle, and must blend ballet and folk dancing convincingly. Ever since it first appeared in London in 1956, with the legendary Galina Ulanova, and in America in 1959, the company has been known for the way it infuses bravura technique with delicacy and emotional force.

Principal dancers include Maya Plisetskaya, Vladimir Vassiliev, Natalia Bessmertnova, Ekaterina Maximova, Mikhail Lavrovsky, and Ludmilla Semenyaka.

Two hundred and fifty dancers.

Cameron, Judy. *The Bolshoi Ballet.* New York: Harper and Row, 1975.

Demidov, Alexander. *The Russian Ballet: Past and Present.* New York: Doubleday, 1977.

DUTCH NATIONAL BALLET
Stadsschouwberg
Amsterdam, Holland
(020) 25-57-54

Rudi van Dantzig, Artistic Director
Anton Gerritsen, Administrative Director

Deriving from the fusion in 1961 of the Amsterdam Ballet and the Netherlands Ballet, this company was inspired by the preexisting Netherlands Dance Theatre to update its repertory of Diaghilev ballets and older classics (including Galleotti's *The Whims of Cupid* [1786], the oldest ballet still danced in its original form) with a variety of modern works. Jooss, Tudor, and sixteen Balanchine ballets now form one branch of its contemporary repertory; three resident Dutch choreographers, van

Dantzig, Hans van Manen, and Toer van Schayk, contribute frequently to the other branch. The company is completely subsidized by state and municipal funding. It made its New York debut in 1976 as the official cultural representative of the Netherlands to the Bicentennial celebrations.

Eighty-four dancers, principals Alexandra Radius, Han Ebbelaar, guest artist Rudolf Nureyev; 150 performances per year.

LES GRANDS BALLETS CANADIENS
5465 Queen Mary Road
Montreal, Quebec, Canada H3X 1V5
(514) 487-1232

Brian Macdonald, Artistic Director
Colin McIntyre, General Manager

First organized in 1955 by Ludmilla Chiriaeff, this company drew international attention with its colorful production of the rock ballet *Tommy,* created by Fernand Nault in 1970 to the rock opera of the same name by The Who. In 1974, *Tommy* was retired from the active repertory after 285 performances in Europe and North America. Nault's contemporary works to Orff and Stravinsky remain in the repertory, alongside more traditionally classical pieces like Lichine's *Graduation Ball* and Balanchine's *Theme and Variations.* Many of Brian Macdonald's ballets are also offered, modern and theatrical works to music by Beethoven, Paul Creston, and Stravinsky. Wholly subsidized by national, provincial, and municipal funds, the company has also appeared in South America, at Jacob's Pillow, at Expo '67 in Montreal and on Canadian television.

Fifty dancers.

KIROV BALLET
Kirov Theatre of Opera and Ballet
1 Theatre Square
Leningrad, U.S.S.R.

The renowned Maryinsky Theatre in St. Petersburg lies at the heart of Russia's national ballet heritage. Renamed the Kirov Theatre in 1935, it is now officially known as the Vaganova Choreographic Institute after its illustrious teacher, Agrippina Vaganova, but its resident company is the Kirov Ballet. Characterized by fluid arms, clearly defined line, movement emanating from the lower back or trunk, and exceptional elevation, the company style is elegant and aristocratic. It is seen to best advantage in full-length works, such as three which premiered here: *La Bayadère* (1877), *Sleeping Beauty* (1890), and *Nutcracker* (1892). Newer versions of the classics include

Overleaf: **Grosse Fuge (Hans van Manen), Netherlands Dance Theatre.**

Sergeyev's *Raymonda* and *Cinderella,* and Lavrovsky's *Romeo and Juliet,* which emphasizes drama even more than dancing. Other dramatic and literary subjects have been explored in Lavrovsky's *Hamlet,* Leonid Yacobson's *Spartacus* (danced without pointe shoes in the interest of historical accuracy), and Rostslav Zakharov's *The Fountain of Bakhchisarai,* a lavish rendering of Pushkin's poem. Nureyev, Makarova, Baryshnikov, and the Panovs have all defected from this 200-member company, thinning its principals' roster considerably but recalling the technical and dramatic strengths of the company every time they dance.

Two hundred dancers.

Demidov, Alexander. *The Russian Ballet: Past and Present.* New York: Doubleday, 1977.

LONDON FESTIVAL BALLET
Festival Ballet House
39 Jay Mews
London 8W7 2ES, England
(01) 581-1245

Beryl Grey, C.B.E., Artistic Director
David Rees, Administrator

Since its first performance in 1950, this company has traveled more frequently and extensively abroad than any other British company. Maintaining the classical character established by the Markova-Dolin company from which it emerged, the company concentrates its repertory on nineteenth- and twentieth-century masterpieces. Revivals of Massine, Bournonville, and Fokine (including the rarely seen *Schéhérazade*) alternate with Mary Skeaping's staging of *Giselle* and Nureyev's of *Sleeping Beauty* and *Romeo and Juliet.* Balancing these traditional works is contemporary choreography by Ronald Hynd and Barry Moreland, whose *Prodigal Son (in Ragtime)* was a recent popular attraction. The company's more than 250 performances a year are divided among three London seasons and fifteen weeks of touring.

Seventy-five dancers, principals Patricia Ruanne, Elisabetta Terabust, Kerrison Cooke, Nicholas Johnson, recent guest artists Rudolf Nureyev and Patrice Bart.

Braunsweg, Julian. *Braunsweg's Ballet Scandals.* London: Allen and Unwin, 1973.

NATIONAL BALLET OF CANADA
157 King Street East
Toronto, Ontario, Canada M5C 1G9
(416) 362-1041

Alexander Grant, Artistic Director
Gerry Eldred, Administrator

Sadler's Wells dancer Celia Franca founded this Toronto-based company in 1951, bringing to it her parent company's fidelity to classical technique and the performance of the nineteenth-century Romantic ballets. Over the years, she has also absorbed contemporary works into the repertory and made special efforts to encourage young Canadian choreographers. The repertory now features Nureyev's staging of *Sleeping Beauty* and Bruhn's of *La Sylphide, Swan Lake,* and *Coppélia.* Company members Ann Ditchburn, James Kudelka, and Constantin Patsalas have contributed modern ballets, as have Neumeier, van Dantzig, and van Manen. The only classical ballet company invited to perform at Expo '70 in Japan, this is also the first company in North America to dance Sir Frederick Ashton's *La Fille Mal Gardée.*

Sixty-four dancers; principals Karen Kain, Veronica Tennant, Peter Schaufuss, Frank Augustyn; 150 performances per year in Canada and on tour.

NATIONAL BALLET OF CUBA
Calcada between C and D
Bezado, Havana, Cuba

Alicia Alonso, Artistic Director
Jorge Luis Diáz, Administrator

The first professional ballet company in Cuba was founded in 1948 by Cuban ballerina Alicia Alonso and her husband, Fernando. Named the national company in 1959, it has since achieved its stated goals in bringing ballet to all sectors of the population and enriching the cultural life of the entire Cuban community. Alonso has herself staged productions of the classical works, *Coppélia, Les Sylphides, Giselle,* and *Le Pas de Quatre,* and invited Cuban choreographer Alberto Mendez and Spanish dancer Antonio Gades to celebrate the country's Latin American, Indian, black, and Spanish heritages in their choreography. One work, *Oedipus,* was collectively choreographed by the dancers, who personify an amalgamation of the country's diverse ethnic cultures. Having already toured Europe, Russia, and China, the company made its American debut in New York in 1978.

Ninety-four dancers; principals Alicia Alonso, Jorge Esquivel, Marta Garciá, Mirta Pla.

De Gamez, Tana. *Alicia Alonso: At Home and Abroad.* New York: Citadel, 1971.

NETHERLANDS DANCE THEATRE
Koningstraat 118
The Hague, Holland
(070) 88-16-00

Hans Knill, Artistic Director

Ever since its founding in 1959 by the American Benjamin Harkarvy, this company has concentrated on the creation and performance of contemporary choreography, and has limited its repertory exclusively to ballets by living choreographers. Featured among these are the Americans

Louis Falco, Jennifer Muller, Anna Sokolow, and Glen Tetley (who created the nude ballet *Mutations* for this company), and more recently the Dutchmen van Manen, Jaap Flier, and Resident Choreographer Jiri Kylian. The dancers' training emphasizes the modern techniques which such works require, and the company provides opportunities for young choreographers.

Twenty-four dancers.

PARIS OPERA BALLET
Théâtre National de l'Opéra
Place de l'Opéra
75009 Paris, France
266-50-22

Violette Verdy, Artistic Director

The continuous history of ballet at the Paris Opéra began in 1671 when the first opera-ballet, *Pomone*, was staged there. For centuries the recognized leader of all ballet activity in Western Europe, this company premiered the great Romantic classics *La Sylphide* (1832) and *Giselle* (1841). After a slow decline lasting more than 50 years, the company was revived through the efforts of Serge Lifar, who directed it between 1929–44 and 1948–58. Presently directed by former New York City Ballet principal Violette Verdy, the company still presents Romantic masterpieces, most recently reopening its smaller theatre, the Opéra-Comique, for a program featuring *Konservatoriet, Napoli* divertissements, and the Pas de Six from *La Vivandière.* At the Opéra, *Giselle, La Sylphide,* and Grigorovich's *Ivan the Terrible* revolve in repertory with eight Balanchine ballets (many of them from the 1975 New York City Ballet Ravel Festival), an original piece by Merce Cunningham entitled *Un Jour ou Deux,* and works by Bronislava Nijinska, Roland Petit, and Fokine. Massine's restaging of Nijinsky's *L'Aprés-Midi d'un Faune* has shared a program with Robbins's *Afternoon of a Faun.* Another American, Carolyn Carlson, regularly contributes modern ballets.

One hundred fifty-five dancers.

THE ROYAL BALLET
Royal Opera House
Covent Garden
London WC2 7QA, England
(01) 240-1200

Norman Morrice, Artistic Director
Peter Brownlee, General Manager

In 1931, Ninette de Valois's young company, the Vic-Wells Ballet, presented its first full-length ballet program at

Top: **Romeo and Juliet** *(Kenneth MacMillan), Royal Ballet. Bottom:* **The Nutcracker** *(Celia Franca), National Ballet of Canada.*

London's Old Vic Theatre. The troupe moved to the Sadler's Wells Theatre in 1933, to Covent Garden in 1946, and was named the Royal Ballet in 1956. Having joined the company in 1935, Frederick Ashton (now Sir Frederick) remained as resident choreographer through the years, and served as artistic director between 1963 and 1970. The lyric simplicity, elegance, humor, and detailed drama which characterize performances of the Royal Ballet are the enduring results of Dame Ninette's objective, overseeing eye and of the extraordinary emotional and technical demands of Ashton's ballets. The company first appeared in America in 1949, when Margot Fonteyn was recognized as one of the leading ballerinas of her time. Whether presenting Ashton or the nineteenth-century full-length masterpieces, opulent dramatic narratives by Kenneth MacMillan or contemporary works by Balanchine, Robbins, and Tetley, the company performs with a musicality and an unassuming British reticence that honors dances and dancing more than individual dancers. The company has toured the world's theaters and dance festivals, appeared on television and in films.

Eighty dancers; principals Anthony Dowell, Merle Park, Lynn Seymour; guest artists Natalia Makarova, Rudolf Nureyev.

Clarke, Mary. *The Sadler's Wells Ballet.* London: A. and C. Black, 1955.

De Valois, Ninette. *Come Dance with Me.* London: Hamish Hamilton, 1957.

Vaughan, David. *Frederick Ashton and His Ballets.* New York: Knopf, 1977.

————. *The Royal Ballet at Covent Garden.* London: Dance Books, 1975.

ROYAL BALLET OF FLANDERS
Kerkstraat 64
2000 Antwerp, Belgium
(031) 36.47.64

Jeanne Brabants, Director
Jan Vanderschoot, Administrator

Originally formed in 1923 as an adjunct to the Flemish Royal Opera House, this company became independent in 1969 and now comprises two distinct units, a "traveling group" of thirty-nine members and an "opera group" of fifteen which dances the divertissements in opera performances. Its repertory has grown to include classical and contemporary works of every style, period, and country, with a preponderance of modern ballets by John Butler, Ben Stevenson, director Brabants, and Resident Choreographer André Leclair. The company considers itself a vital part of today's Flemish culture. It has toured

Top: La Sylphide, *Royal Danish Ballet. Bottom:* Eugene Onegin *(John Cranko), Stuttgart Ballet.*

Europe and South America, and in 1978 made its first United States tour, appearing in sixty-five cities.

Fifty-four dancers.

ROYAL DANISH BALLET
Royal Theatre
Holmens Kanal 3
1060 Copenhagen K. Denmark

Henning Kronstam, Artistic Director
Kirsten Ralov, Associate Director

The Royal Danish Ballet is cherished, both at home and abroad, as the privileged custodian of August Bournonville's unique style and spirited repertory of ballets. In continuous existence since its establishment in 1748, it is today the oldest of the world's major troupes. During the years of his directorship, 1830–77, Bournonville evolved a fleet, light style which blended the purest elements of French Romantic classicism with traditional mime, naturalistic gesture, and delicate musicality of phrasing. Equally suited to men and women, its concentration on épaulement, batterie, and the lightest elevation makes the Danish male dancers supremely elegant, and the women among the most gracious and buoyant in the world. The credit for reviving such richly textured Bournonville ballets as *La Sylphide, Napoli, Konservatoriet,* and *The Guards of Amagar* belongs to Harald Lander, artistic director from 1932 to 1951. The company first appeared outside Denmark in London in 1954. Since then, it has toured regularly, offering a repertory that sets the modern ballets of Flemming Flindt, John Neumeier, Paul Taylor, and Murray Louis alongside its Bournonville treasures.

Seventy-two dancers.

ROYAL SWEDISH BALLET
Kungliga Theatre
Jakobs Torg 4
S-111 52 Stockholm, Sweden
(08) 22-17-40

James Moore, Artistic Director
Veit Bethke, General Administrator

The first professional ballet company in Sweden was established in 1773 when King Gustave III founded the Royal Opera. Ballet activity waned during the nineteenth century, but interest in the company revived with Antony Tudor's visit in 1949. Mary Skeaping accepted the post of Artistic Director in 1954, and set about rebuilding the classical repertory with her own *Giselle* and *Sleeping Beauty,* staged in versions as close to the originals as possible. She also commissioned new ballets from Swedish choreographers Ivo Cramér and the now internationally acclaimed Birgit Cullberg, who over the years created more than a dozen works for the company. Today's repertory also includes Bournonville, Massine,

Feld, Tetley, a full-length *Swan Lake,* and *Aurora's Wedding.* The Company has toured Germany, Italy, Scotland, Spain, France, China, and the United States.

Sixty-two dancers.

ROYAL WINNIPEG BALLET
289 Portage Avenue
Winnipeg, Manitoba, Canada R3B 2B4
(204) 956-1083

Arnold Spohr, Artistic Director
Edward A. Reger, General Manager

The oldest ballet company in Canada, this troupe was founded in 1938 by two Englishwomen, Gweneth Lloyd and Betty Farrally. It became fully professional in 1949 and received its "Royal" title four years later. Since its earliest days, it has consistently offered its dancers the chance to investigate contemporary expression while maintaining classical standards. Leaving the grander European style to larger companies, this one emphasizes the modern idiom, primarily through works by native Canadians Brian Macdonald and Norbert Vesak, and by Argentinian Oscar Araiz, whose ballets make up one-third of the repertory. Because of the company's compact size, each dancer is guaranteed frequent performances and regular opportunities to tackle soloist roles. The company has appeared in 374 cities in twenty-three countries.

Twenty-six dancers; principals Salvatore Aiello, Marina Eglevsky, Roger Shim.

STUTTGART BALLET
Postfach 982
7000 Stuttgart 1, West Germany
Telephone: 21951

Marcia Haydée, Artistic Director
Dieter Graefe, Administrative Director

Between his arrival in Stuttgart in 1960 and his tragic and sudden death at the age of forty-five in 1973, John Cranko transformed the Stuttgart Ballet from a minor appendage of the opera house into a major company of international repute. An equally international roster of nearly 100 dancers, led by the American Richard Cragun, the German Birgit Keil, the Danish Egon Madsen, and the Brazilian Marcia Haydée (now also artistic director), continues to perform the dramatic full-length works like *Romeo and Juliet, Taming of the Shrew,* and *Eugene Onegin* for which Cranko is best remembered. The large and varied repertory also includes traditional nineteenth-century classics (often in Cranko's own versions), his shorter plotless ballets, and the contemporary choreography of Kenneth MacMillan and Glen Tetley. The company has made several tours to the United States.

Ninety-five dancers.

Holberg Suite *(John Cranko)*, *Peninsula Ballet Theatre.*

Regional Companies

The following companies share several important characteristics: they are far more modest in size than the companies already described, and most have developed around a school or artistic director rather than a choreographer. Some tour and some do not, but all perform in places the large professional companies rarely, if ever, reach. The regional companies serve, therefore, to develop and educate audiences and to give student dancers the experience of performing without their having to commit their entire lives to dance. Many of the repertories are similar; often *The Nutcracker* is the most frequently performed ballet among them.

AUGUSTA BALLET COMPANY
2941 Walton Way
Augusta, Ga. 30904
(404) 733-5511
Ron Colton, Artistic Director

AUSTIN BALLET THEATRE
717B West 23 Street
Austin, Tex. 78705
(512) 478-9557
Stanley Hall, Artistic Director

AUSTIN CIVIC BALLET
3810 Speedway
Austin, Tex. 78751
(512) 454-0625
Eugene and Alexandra Slavin,
Artistic Directors

BALLET IMPERIAL OF CANADA
111-A Rideau Street
Ottawa, Ontario, Canada K1N 5X1
(613) 233-5724
Nesta Toumine, Director

BALLET OKLAHOMA
3014 North Paseo
Oklahoma City, Okla. 73103
(405) 521-1377
Conrad Ludlow, Director

BALLET ROYAL
Post Office Box 866
Winter Park, Fla. 32790
(305) 647-3010
Edith Royal, Artistic Director

BALLET TACOMA
902½ North Second
Tacoma, Wash. 98403
(206) 272-4219
Jan Collum, Director

**BRISTOL CONCERT
  BALLET COMPANY**
c/o Virginia Intermont College
Box 259
Bristol, Va. 24201
(703) 466-2401
Constance Hardinge, Artistic Director

CALIFORNIA BALLET COMPANY
8276 Ronson Road
San Diego, Calif. 92111
(714) 560-5676
Maxine Mahon, Artistic Director

CAPITOL BALLET COMPANY
1200 Delafield Place NW
Washington, D.C. 20007
(202) 882-4039
Claire Haywood, Doris Jones,
Co-Artistic Directors

CONNECTICUT BALLET COMPANY
1044 Chapel Street
New Haven, Conn. 06510
(203) 865-4936
Robert Vickrey, Robin Welch,
Artistic Directors

CORNISH BALLET
c/o Cornish School
710 East Roy Street
Seattle, Wash. 98102
(206) 323-1400
Karen Irvin, Director

CORPUS CHRISTI BALLET
5610 Everhart Avenue
Corpus Christi, Tex. 78411
(512) 991-8151
Larry Roquemore, Director

DALLAS METROPOLITAN BALLET
6815 Hillcrest
Dallas, Tex. 75205
(214) 361-0278
Ann Etgen, Bill Atkinson,
Artistic Directors

**DAYTON CONTEMPORARY
DANCE COMPANY**
3915 West Third Street
Dayton, Ohio 45417
(513) 268-5312
Jeraldyn Blunden, Director

DELTA BALLET OF NEW ORLEANS
1605 Cleary Avenue
Metairie, La. 70001
(504) 834-1748
Joseph and Maria Giacobbe,
Artistic Directors

DES MOINES BALLET COMPANY
2919 53 Street
Des Moines, Iowa 50310
(515) 255-2127
Mary Joyce Lind, Artistic Director

DULUTH BALLET COMPANY
c/o The Depot
506 West Michigan Street
Duluth, Minn. 55802
(218) 722-2314
Gilbert Reed, Artistic Director

FORT WORTH BALLET
3505 West Lancaster
Fort Worth, Tex. 76107
(817) 731-0879
Fernando Schaffenburg,
Artistic Director

GERMANTOWN DANCE THEATRE
5555 Germantown Avenue
Philadelphia, Pa. 19144
(215) 843-4797
Jean Williams, Artistic Director

GREATER HOUSTON CIVIC BALLET
9902 Long Point
Houston, Tex. 77055
(713) 468-3670
Margo Marshall, Artistic Director

**KRASSOVSKA BALLET JEUNESSE
OF DALLAS**
Post Office Box 30014
Dallas, Tex. 75230
(214) 821-4160
Nathalie Krassovska, Director

MARIN CIVIC BALLET
100 Elm Street
San Rafael, Calif. 94901
(415) 453-6705
Maria Vegh, Artistic Director

**METROPOLITAN BALLET
COMPANY OF BETHESDA,
MARYLAND**
4836 Rugby Avenue
Bethesda, Md. 20014
(301) 654-2233
Charles Dickson, Director

MIAMI BALLET
5818 South West 73 Street
South Miami, Fla. 33143
(305) 667-5543
Martha Mahr, Renee Zintgraf,
Robert Pike, Co-Directors

NEW JERSEY BALLET COMPANY
270 Pleasant Valley Way
West Orange, N.J. 07052
(201) 736-5940
Carolyn Clark, Artistic Director

OAKLAND BALLET COMPANY
2968 MacArthur Boulevard
Oakland, Calif. 94602
(415) 530-7516
Stephanie Zimmerman,
General Manager

OMAHA BALLET
5915 Maple Avenue
Omaha, Neb. 68104
(402) 551-7968
Thomas Enckell, Artistic Director

PASADENA DANCE THEATRE
25 South Sierra Madre Boulevard
Pasadena, Calif. 91107
(213) 792-0873
Evelyn Le Mone, Artistic Director

PENINSULA BALLET THEATRE
333 South B Street
San Mateo, Calif. 94401
(415) 343-8485
Anne Bena, Artistic Director

PRINCETON BALLET COMPANY
262 Alexander Street
Princeton, N.J. 08540
(609) 921-7758
Audree Estey, Artistic Director

SACRAMENTO BALLET
3839 H Street
Sacramento, Calif. 95816
(916) 452-1436
Barbara Crockett, Artistic Director

SAN JOAQUIN CONCERT BALLET
7632 Larkspur Lane
Stockton, Calif. 95207
(209) 477-4141
Dorothy Percival, Artistic Director

SAN JOSE DANCE THEATRE
16 Lyndon Avenue
Los Gatos, Calif. 95030
(408) 354-4231
Shawn Stuart and Paul Curtis,
Co-Directors

SOUTHERN BALLET OF ATLANTA
One-Half West Paces Ferry Road,
North West
Atlanta, Ga. 30305
(404) 233-5831
Pittman Corry, Director

**TACOMA PERFORMING
DANCE COMPANY**
7106 Sixth Avenue
Tacoma, Wash. 98406
(206) 588-9322
Jo Emery, Artistic Director

U.S. TERPSICHORE
c/o American Dance Foundation
2291 Broadway
New York, N.Y. 10024
(212) 799-5445
Richard Thomas, Barbara Fallis,
Directors

WICHITA FALLS BALLET THEATRE
2009 Huff
Wichita Falls, Tex. 76301
(817) 322-6675
Frank and Irina Pal,
Artistic Directors

Modern Dance, Contemporary Dance, and Avant-Garde Companies
By Robert J. Pierce

ALVIN AILEY AMERICAN DANCE THEATER
1515 Broadway
New York, N.Y. 10022
(212) 997-1950

Alvin Ailey, Artistic Director
Edward Lander, Executive Director

This is America's foremost modern dance repertory company. The twenty-seven member troupe presents dances by Ailey, Lester Horton, John Butler, Talley Beatty, Anna Sokolow, Louis Johnson, Paul Sanasardo, Brian Macdonald, Norman Walker, José Limón, Ted Shawn, Katherine Dunham, Donald McKayle, George Faison, Louis Falco, Jennifer Muller, Lar Lubovitch, Rudy Perez, Dianne McIntyre, and Eleo Pomare. This is a substantial quality list. The AAADT was founded in 1958 as an all black company and became integrated in the mid-sixties. Many of Ailey's works during this period revolved around themes of social unrest and the American black heritage. His most famous work, *Revelations* (1960), explores the motivations and emotions of American Negro religious music. It is his company's signature piece, and audiences frequently demand encores of its finale with good-natured insistence. In the 1970s, Ailey has become more eclectic and often creates abstract or impressionistic works for his own or other ballet companies. The strongest movement influences in his own work remain the Lester Horton and Martha Graham techniques, the American black movement vernacular, and the dynamics of African dances. Of late, a strong ballet orientation has also emerged in his choreography.

Twenty-seven dancers.

Cook, Susan, and Mazo, Joseph H. *The Alvin Ailey American Dance Theater.* New York: Morrow, 1978.

ALBUQUERQUE DANCE THEATER
805 Tijeras Avenue, North West
Albuquerque, N. Mex. 87102
(505) 242-2656

Pamela Knisel
Whitney Rau, Co-Artistic Directors

This company was founded in 1973 as an outgrowth of the Hooliwhar Dance Company, which had performed in New York City from 1970 to 1972. The founders were Paul Hindes, Whitney Rau, and Pamela Knisel. ADT is something of a choreographers' collective: each of the eight company members creates dances for the company, resulting in an understandably diverse repertory which includes both choreographed and structured improvisation pieces. The latter seem particularly apt for the outdoor performances in public spaces and parks which the company enjoys doing. Some indication of ADT's eclecticism is provided by the choice of accompaniment, which includes a Ramayana Monkey Chant as well as the music of Sousa, Chopin, and Hank Williams.

Eight dancers.

MANUEL ALUM DANCE COMPANY
200 West 72 Street
New York, N.Y. 10023
(212) 580-8107

Manuel Alum, Artistic Director
Ivan Sygoda, Director of Operations

Before forming his own company, which now numbers six, in 1970, Manuel Alum was a dancer with the Paul Sanasardo group. Alum choreographed for that company and was its Assistant Artistic Director before striking out on his own. Alum makes dances about ideas, dark moods, emotions, dramatic situations, or religious myths. *Palomas,* for instance, probably his best-known work, is about war. The Spanish title means doves, and the six women who perform the dance create images of these symbols of peace as well as images of horror and agony, fear, and of crippled or dead refugees. There are no actual characters, however, nor does the situation resolve itself. For Alum, it is enough to state the themes boldly and profoundly.

Six dancers.

TANDY BEAL AND COMPANY
2-1601 East Cliff Drive
Santa Cruz, Calif. 95062
(408) 462-0303

Tandy Beal, Artistic Director
Jon Scoville, Co-Artistic Director
Alan Savat, Administrative Director

This modern dance and theater ensemble, formed in 1971 by Tandy Beal, has a repertory that is exclusively hers. She was formerly a dancer with the Nikolais Dance Theatre. Her concern for sculptural shape and spatial values reflects this background. She is interested in both abstraction and drama. Some of her pieces are about pure motion and abstract forms, while others have been likened to monologues and are either pantomimes or dance-theater pieces. Jon Scoville composes much of the music for the company including jazz, percussion, and electronic scores.

Six dancers, two mimes.

Opposite: **Cellar (Alum), Manuel Alum Dance Company.**

BOTTOM OF THE BUCKET, BUT...DANCE THEATRE

95 Canterbury Road
Rochester, N.Y. 14607

Garth Fagan, Artistic Director
Sara Tornay, Management

1995 Broadway
New York, New York 10023
(212) 580-8696

This fourteen-member company was created in 1970. Its genesis lies in the series of dance classes that were initiated by Garth Fagan at the Rochester Educational Opportunity Center. A group of committed students at the REOC became the nucleus for the company. Fagan is originally from the West Indies, and his choreography is a combination of ethnic movement from that area, along with jazz and modern dance. A consistently recurring theme in Fagan's dances is the black experience, both universal and specifically American. Fagan's dances are also characterized by a high expenditure of energy.

Fourteen dancers.

TRISHA BROWN DANCE COMPANY

c/o Artservices
463 West Street
New York, N.Y. 10014
(212) 989-4953

Trisha Brown, Artistic Director
Artservices, Company Management

Although this six-woman company was only formed in 1970, Brown was one of the extreme avant-gardists whose work centered around Judson Church in New York in the mid-sixties. This group is now perhaps most noted for its use of everyday movement (like walking and running) and its refusal to seduce the audience with virtuosic technique, theatricality, or emotionalism. In the past, Brown has created works in which the dancers literally walked on the walls (assisted by ropes and castors attached to the ceiling), or gestured in canon from rooftops widely scattered over half a mile. Most of the dances her company performs today, however, are less outrageously conceptual. Her choreography is characterized by rigorous and, of late, complex structures and pure movement which has no meaning other than its own existence.

Six dancers.

Opposite: **Crazy Jane** *(Beal), Tandy Beal and Company.* **Top:** **The Mooche** *(Ailey), Alvin Ailey American Dance Theatre. Judith Jamison.* **Bottom:** **Water Motor** *(Brown), Trisha Brown Dance Company.*

CHICAGO MOVING COMPANY
2433 North Lincoln Avenue
Chicago, Ill. 60614
(312) 929-7416

Nana Solbrig, Artistic Director
Lauren Westover, General Manager

This is a repertory dance theater company which was founded in 1972. The principal choreographers, Nana Solbrig, John Magill, and Nolan Dennett, are also among the seven dancers in the troupe. Works by Bill Evans and Anna Sokolow are currently in the repertory, as are Charles Weidman's *Brahms Waltzes* and Dan Wagoner's *Penny Supper*. Occasionally, less well established but promising choreographers are invited to create dances. Among these have been Diane Germaine and Lonny Joseph Gordon.

Seven dancers.

LUCINDA CHILDS AND COMPANY
541 Broadway
New York, N.Y. 10012
(212) 431-7599

Lucinda Childs, Artistic Director

Lucinda Childs danced with James Waring and was a member of the avant-garde Judson Dance Theater in the mid-sixties. She has studied ballet with Merce Cunningham. She retired temporarily between the late sixties and early seventies while she acquired a master's degree in education, then returned to choreography. Her dances are minimal, repetitive, and primarily about structure, which she dissects for the audience's enjoyment. Her programs are like kinetic puzzles—the viewer's pleasure grows as he recognizes the changes, some of them minute, which occur as each movement is repeated. Her dances stress time, and the determined, constant flow of movement through time. The movement tends to be simple, forthright, and based on everyday activity such as walking, running, skipping, turning, and the like. The performance quality, of course, is anything but everyday. Floor patterns are very important. Rhythms are crucial. There is seldom any music and the dancers stay in unison by giving themselves up to the rhythms and sounds of their colleagues' feet (sometimes clad in sneakers) striking the floor. The dancing tends to be vertical, uninflected, with an unrelievedly fierce attack. The result is severe, and at the same time, curiously sensual, qualities which are equally apparent in Childs's own presence. Childs has also collaborated with the performance art-theatre-opera avant-gardist, Robert Wilson, in several of his works.

Top: **Transverse Exchanges** *(Childs)*, **Lucinda Childs and Company.** *Bottom:* **Mothers of Israel** *(Margalit Oved),* **Ze'Eva Cohen Solo Dance Repertory.**

ZE'EVA COHEN SOLO DANCE REPERTORY
Studio C-618
463 West Street
New York, N.Y. 10014
(212) 691-1568

Ze'eva Cohen, Artistic Director

This one-woman company was initiated in 1971. Ze'eva Cohen, who was born in prepartitioned Israel (Palestine), received most of her training there before coming to the United States to study at the Juilliard School. She danced with Anna Sokolow before deciding to perform as a soloist, dancing an entire program alone. Although she choreographed as early as 1968, her idea from the outset was to provide repertory programs on which several accomplished choreographers would be represented. Her active repertory today includes solo works by Anna Sokolow, Deborah Jowitt, Jeff Duncan, Frances Alenikoff, Peggy Cicierska, Elizabeth Keen, Kei Takei, James Waring, Margalit Oved, Art Bauman, John Gibson, and Lynn Dalley as well as by Cohen herself.

CONTEMPORARY DANCERS
Box 1764
Winnipeg, Manitoba R3C 2Z9, Canada
(204) 943-4597

Rachel Browne, Artistic Director
David Williams, Administrative Director

This Winnipeg company is Canada's oldest modern dance troupe. It was founded in 1964 by Rachel Browne and became a professional company in 1970. Contemporary Dancers tours frequently in North America, especially to a variety of American and Canadian dance festivals each year. This is a repertory company with works by such diverse choreographers as Norbert Vesak, David Earle, Paul Sanasardo, Cliff Keuter, Norman Morrice, James Clouser, James Maslow, Sophie Maslow, Norman Walker, Richard Gain, James Waring, and Rachel Browne. Company members are encouraged to choreograph for regularly scheduled Choreoconcert programs.

JAMES CUNNINGHAM AND THE ACME DANCE COMPANY
c/o Pentacle Management
200 West 72 Street, Suite 20
New York, N.Y. 10023
(212) 580-8107

James Cunningham, Artistic Director

The six dancers in this troupe must be accomplished actors as well as dancers since they are frequently required to act out dance-theater sketches, engage in monologues and dialogues, and even sing. The company was created in 1967 by James Cunningham, whose background is as much in drama as in dance. Cunningham has an incisive wit and is fond of parody. His works often satirize such famous ballets as *Swan Lake* and *Afternoon of a Faun*. He also points up the absurdities of everyday life with his barbed humor, and especially likes to poke fun at sexual stereotyping and role-playing. It is not unusual to find men portraying women and vice versa in his dances, and at times one doesn't discover the travesty until the end. His dances are constructed in a montage-like manner, and they are likely to veer this way and that in a series of zany episodes.

Six dancers.

MERCE CUNNINGHAM DANCE COMPANY
463 West Street
New York, N.Y. 10014
(212) 255-8240

Merce Cunningham, Artistic Director
Art Becofsky and Martha Lohmeyer, Administrators

No one working today, except, perhaps, Martha Graham, has had as tremendous an impact on modern dance as Merce Cunningham. As John Cage, the company's Musical Director, has written, Cunningham's choreography does not rely on the continuity provided by "linear elements, be they narrative or psychological, nor does it rely on a movement towards and away from a climax. As in abstract painting, it is assumed that an element (a movement, a sound, a change of light) is in and of itself expressive; what it communicates is in large part determined by the observer himself. It is assumed that the dance supports itself and does not need support from the music." In a Cunningham work, dancing, choreography, costumes, and decor coexist, rather than being mutually supportive. When Cunningham formed his company in 1953, this approach to dance was considered extremely radical. Some audiences still find it so, but Cunningham has nonetheless won an enormous popular following. Cunningham is famous for his collaborations with important artists like Frank Stella, Bruce Nauman, Jasper Johns, Andy Warhol, and Robert Rauschenberg; and with avant-garde composers including John Cage, Gordon Mumma, David Tudor, David Behrman, Morton Feldman, and La Monte Young among others. Cunningham has created a body of recognized masterpieces, including *Summerspace* (1958), *Winterbranch* (1964), *Rainforest* (1968), *Walkaround Time* (1968), and *Canfield* (1969). Although he is now in his sixties, Cunningham still creates works for himself and his company of fifteen dancers, and the quality of his artistic output has not declined.

Fifteen dancers.

Cunningham, Merce. *Changes: Notes on Choreography.* New York: Something Else Press, 1968.

Klosty, James (ed.). *Merce Cunningham.* New York: Saturday Review–Dutton, 1975.

LAURA DEAN/DANCERS AND MUSICIANS

15 West 17 Street
New York, N.Y. 10011
(212) 675-5484

Laura Dean, Artistic Director

After spending several months exploring movement basics by herself in a studio in California, Laura Dean returned to New York in 1971 to create dances solidly based on the repetition of a few basic movement ideas. *Circle Dance,* for example, was comprised solely of a shuffling step and spinning, and it went on for nearly half an hour. More recently, Dean's dances have become considerably more complex, but they still rely heavily on repetition. She composes her own music—having been strongly influenced by avant-garde composers Steve Reich and Philip Glass—and her seven dancers sing as well as dance, layering repetitive melodies over a steady, rapid pulse. The dancers keep this pulse in their bodies as they execute spinning, hopping, jumping, shuffling, or stamping steps. Much of this has the simplicity of folk dancing, and if there is an identifiable theme beyond the dancing and music themselves, it is one of community.

Seven dancers.

DOUGLAS DUNN AND DANCERS

c/o Artservices
463 West Street
New York, N.Y. 10014
(212) 989-4953

Douglas Dunn, Artistic Director
Kermit Smith, Business Manager

Douglas Dunn's company was formed in 1976 as he began working on *Lazy Madge,* a continuing project which he frequently adds to or changes. Although there is no improvisation involved, the structure is indeterminate. Each dancer has solo passages and there are group sections of dancing for two, three, four, or more dancers. During a performance, each dancer is free to choose what he wishes from the choreographed material, performing entire sequences or fragments or, if he chooses, not performing at all. His choice is, of course, affected by what his colleagues choose to do. Dunn is one of the most

Opposite: Dancing with Maisie Paradocks (J. Cunningham), James Cunningham and the Acme Dance Company. *Top:* Dance (Dean), Laura Dean/Dancers and Musicians. *Bottom:* Travelogue (M. Cunningham), Merce Cunningham Dance Company. *Overleaf:* Work in progress, Douglas Dunn and Dancers.

interesting choreographers to have emerged in the seventies. *Time Out,* a solo he made for himself in 1973, contained no movement other than vital life functions like breathing. In it, he placed himself atop an enormous labyrinth of a sculpture he had created and remained motionless for several hours each day, on display. *Gestures in Red* (1975) is an amazing, and long, solo which is about endurance as much as about intelligent dancing. Dunn was a member of the Merce Cunningham company and his movement style is Cunningham-based, modified by his own interests and loose-limbed style.

BILL EVANS DANCE COMPANY
704 19 Avenue East
Seattle, Wash. 98112
(206) 322-3733

Bill Evans, Artistic Director
Greg Lizenbery, Co-Director

This Seattle-based company, tours twenty-five weeks a year. The repertory is almost exclusively by Bill Evans, who has also staged works for other companies, including the 5 x 2 Plus Dance Company, Ballet West, Chicago Ballet, and Dance LA as well as the Repertory Dance Theatre of Utah, with which he danced and choreographed for eight years before forming his own company in 1975. Evans's dances are based in traditional modern dance values, and he creates both dramatic and lyrical abstract works. His style is a combination of sturdy modern dance elements and ballet, with a very broad range.

Ten dancers.

LOUIS FALCO DANCE COMPANY
c/o HI Enterprises
200 West 57 Street
New York, N.Y. 10019
(212) 247-4230

Louis Falco, Artistic Director
Juan Antonio, Associate Artistic Director
HI Enterprises, Company Management

Louis Falco was a dancer in José Limón's company before forming his own in 1968. His style is based on the Limón technique, transformed by a high, often wide-flung energy and a much more virtuosic approach. Falco's company are fine technicians, invariably attractive, and charged with a strong, if casual, sexual aura, qualities which account for some of the group's popularity. Falco also encourages his dancers to choreograph for the company. He frequently uses rock or quasirock scores, particularly those by Burt Alcantara and has collaborated with artists like Robert Indiana, Stanley Landsman, Michael Kamen, John Duff, Marisol, and William Katz, who have designed costumes and props for him.

Eight dancers.

VIOLA FARBER DANCE COMPANY
1841 Broadway
Room 808
New York, N.Y. 10023
(212) 757-0410

Viola Farber Slayton, Artistic Director
Robert M. Jaffe, Administrative Director

Viola Farber danced with Merce Cunningham's troupe from its creation until 1965. She started her own company, now numbering nine dancers, in 1968. Her aesthetic is consonant with Cunningham's; her movement style is an adaptation and elaboration of Cunningham technique. Her dances, which are usually abstract, are often percussive, and the energy level is sometimes extreme to the point of violence. Farber also has a fine sense of kinetic humor which frequently surfaces in her dances. She has used Beethoven and Poulenc as accompaniment but is better known for her collaborations with avant-garde composers, especially David Tudor and Alvin Lucier.

Nine dancers.

5 x 2 PLUS, A MODERN DANCE REPERTORY COMPANY
180 Riverside Drive
New York, N.Y. 10024
(212) 595-7328

Jane Kosminsky, Bruce Becker, Artistic Directors
Rena Shagan, Administrator

Although it now numbers five dancers, 5 x 2 was founded in 1972 as a two-member troupe by Jane Kosminsky and Bruce Becker, who performed solos and duets by a variety of modern dance choreographers. The concept of doing modern dance repertory—still relatively novel in the early seventies despite Alvin Ailey's success in the same area—proved so successful that the company and repertory possibilities were expanded. 5 x 2 performs Merce Cunningham's *Night Wandering,* Lester Horton's *The Beloved,* Tamiris's *Negro Spirituals* (Bruce Becker is her nephew), and James Waring's *Gallopade* as well as works by Paul Taylor, Anna Sokolow, Norman Walker, Bill Evans, and Pilobolus, among others. The company's choice of repertory is, as one can see, of high quality. Bruce Becker choreographs for the company while Jane Kosminsky generally does not. Both of their backgrounds are in modern dance. Becker trained with Norman Walker, May O'Donnell, and at the Batsheva School of Israel. Kosminsky's teachers also included Norman Walker, May O'Donnell, as well as Paul Taylor.

Five dancers.

ANNABELLE GAMSON, DANCE SOLOS

c/o Shaw Management
1995 Broadway
New York, N.Y. 10023
(212) 595-1909

Annabelle Gamson, Artistic Director

Although Gamson presents her own solo choreography, the most significant fact about her programs is that she also presents solos choreographed by Isadora Duncan and Mary Wigman. These dances are not new, but they are almost unknown to American audiences. Duncan last danced in the United States in 1922, and Wigman, the most important of the German modern dancers, performed here only three times, in the 1930s. Gamson learned the Duncan dances from Julia Levine, who danced in the companies of Anna and Irma Duncan, who were, in turn, taught them by Isadora herself. Gamson claims that it is easier to transmit these works from body to body than it would be to do the same for, say, *Giselle*, because the form and design of Isadora's dances are essentially simple. Gamson has likened them to folk dances in this respect. She does not, however, attempt to reproduce Isadora's legendary charisma, undoubtedly a wise decision. The Wigman dances were learned, from a film of Wigman dancing which was made in 1929, with the help of the American modern dance pioneer, Hanya Holm, who was a Wigman disciple. Gamson is the only dancer in this country performing Wigman choreography, but since she first started dancing Duncan's work, former Duncan associates have formed a company, the Isadora Duncan Centenary Dance Company, and a second is in the process of being created.

DAVID GORDON/PICK UP COMPANY

541 Broadway
New York, N.Y. 10012
(212) 966-1106

David Gordon, Artistic Director

David Gordon has danced with James Waring, Yvonne Rainer, the Judson Dance Theater, and The Grand Union. These are impeccable credentials in the New York avant-garde which centered on and developed out of Judson Church in the mid-sixties. The dances Gordon's company currently performs deal with structure, which the audience is expected to perceive or unravel, and with the qualities of perception as well as the correspondence between words and movement. In *What Happened*, all seven women speak and move at once, presenting a chaotic cacophony of words and movement to the audience. As the dance progresses, it becomes clear,

Top: **Caviar (Falco), Louis Falco Dance Company.**
Bottom: **Motorcycle/Boat (Farber), Viola Farber Dance Company. Ande Peck, Viola Farber.**

through repetition and sporadic synchronization, that each of the seven is relating similar or the same details of an accident, and the movement is a wry pantomimic accompaniment (a cackle and sidestep for "which," a downward gesture in front of the face for "avail"). The pleasure in watching the dance is in discovering, in time, how it is put together. *Not Necessarily Recognizable Objectives* contains a section in which Gordon dances, seemingly spontaneously, while dancers stand in a cluster making wryly critical remarks about Gordon's performance. This is followed by the members of the group performing the same movement material, each at his own pace, allowing the audience to discover it in depth while appreciating the subtle differences which exist among the bodies. This is intelligent, and perhaps even intellectual, dancing; certainly it challenges audiences.

MARTHA GRAHAM DANCE COMPANY

316 East 63 Street
New York, N.Y. 10021
(212) 832-9166

Martha Graham, Artistic Director
Ron Protas, Associate Artistic Director and General
  Director

This is the oldest extant modern dance troupe in the world, founded in 1926 and still directed by Martha Graham, who is now in her eighties. The repertory is exclusively by her. The movement style is based on the principle of contraction and release in the torso and is an extension of the simple act of breathing. Graham has influenced just about everyone in modern dance—her name is virtually synonymous with the term—and many in ballet as well. Her greatest successes have been dances which reveal the psychological and emotional states of a variety of often stark heroines, many based on mythological or literary sources. Graham once said she was obsessed with "making visible the interior landscape," that is, the landscape of the mind and emotions. It is perhaps her most famous quote, and it accurately characterizes her dances. Over the past few years, Graham has been diligently reviving many of her old masterpieces, including the 1930 solo, *Lamentation,* and the 1931 *Primitive Mysteries,* dances which, without her careful reconstruction, might have been lost.

Armitage, Merle. *Martha Graham.* 1937. Paperback, New York: Dance Horizons, 1966.
Graham, Martha. *The Notebooks of Martha Graham.* New York: Harcourt Brace Jovanovich, 1973.
McDonagh, Don. *Martha Graham: A Biography.* 1973. Paperback, New York: Popular Library, 1977.

Top: **Seraphic Dialogue (Graham), Martha Graham Dance Company. Bottom: National Spirit (Grossman), Danny Grossman Dance Company. Opposite: Bach Dances (Bill Evans), 5 x 2 Plus. Jane Kosminsky.**

DANNY GROSSMAN DANCE COMPANY

65 Empire Avenue
Toronto, Ontario, M4M 2L3, Canada
(416) 466-2108

Danny Williams Grossman, Artistic Director
Peter Sever, Business Manager

For ten years, between 1963 and 1973, Danny Williams Grossman was a dancer with the Paul Taylor company. He formed his own company—which now numbers twelve dancers—in 1974 and has established it as a significant troupe which tours North America. As Michael Crabb, the Canadian critic has written, "Grossman dances can be very serious indeed. Grossman has strong human concerns which come out in his work, but more often it is a light, sunny humour, a kinetic sense of fun, which permeates his repertoire."

Twelve dancers.

HARRY

c/o Trinity Dance Management
162 West 56 Street
New York, N.Y. 10019
(212) JU 2-1760

Senta Driver, Artistic Director

Although unusual, Harry is the name of a dance company formed in 1975 by Senta Driver, a former dancer with Paul Taylor who methodically stripped herself of all preconceptions about how one ought to move as a dancer and what dances ought to look like. Driver describes one of her first dances, *Memorandum* (1975) thus: "a solo work involving a prepared recitation of names in their appropriate foreign accents governed by rhythmic and tonal rules and accompanied by extremely plain repetitive movement, chiefly a heavy stride, no music, decor. The costume is a jumpsuit of pinstriped fabric cut like a business suit." The recited names are all of historically important dancers and all, except for Nijinsky's, of women. Driver's movement vocabulary continues to be restricted, but not only to heavy strides. She has added running, walking, lying down, skipping and jumping, and other, less everyday, movement possibilities. But her dances do not rely on dance virtuosity. There is no interest in established dance steps, line, beautiful bodies, or the defiance of gravity. Instead, she takes the weight and natural awkwardness of the human body and makes it art. Her most recent dances have been about extended rhythmic design and the limits of physical and emotional endurance. She comments—

Opposite: **Brahms Waltz by Isadora Duncan,** *reconstructed by Annabelle Gamson. Top:* **Recherché (Hauser), Nancy Hauser Dance Company. Bottom:* **Gallery (Senta Driver), Harry.**

sometimes wryly, sometimes hilariously—on performing and the nature of performance as communication.

Four dancers.

NANCY HAUSER DANCE COMPANY
504 Cedar Avenue South
Minneapolis, Minn. 55454
(612) 333-8269

Nancy Hauser, Artistic Director
Cissy Erwin, Company Manager

Nancy Hauser was one of the original members of modern dance pioneer Hanya Holm's company. Her own works are solidly built on Holm technique, which Hauser teaches with its founder in Colorado each summer. It is interesting to note that Holm is the American link to the famous German modern dancer, Mary Wigman, with whom Holm danced before coming to the United States. Hauser creates both abstract, "dancey" dances and dramatic ones. She has also augmented her repertory by inviting other choreographers to stage works for her company. Currently, the eight-member troupe performs Murray Louis's *Proximities* and Viola Farber's *Transfer* and also has pieces by Don Redlich and James Cunningham. Hauser formed her company in 1961, before the dance explosion resulted in a tremendous proliferation of companies from coast to coast.

Eight dancers.

ERICK HAWKINS DANCE COMPANY
78 Fifth Avenue
New York, N.Y. 10011
(212) 255-6698

Erick Hawkins, Artistic Director

Like his colleagues from the 1950s, Alwin Nikolais and Merce Cunningham, Erick Hawkins developed an original movement style coherent enough to be called a technique (see page 141) and attractive enough to students that today second-, third- and, in some cases, even fourth-generation choreographers use the basics of his technique in their own work. Hawkins's approach to dance is based on what he terms a "normative" technique, a movement vocabulary which appears to be effortless and free of any artificial tensions. Hawkins's dances utilize a smooth, largely undisturbed flow of energy. There is no dissonance in his choreography, only serenity and harmony. His dances have been described as chaste and meditative and are strongly influenced by Oriental art and ritual. He frequently collaborates with the artist Ralph Dorazio, who designs costumes and sets, and the composer Lucia Dlugoszewski, who often plays her own scores during performances. Hawkins, more than any other modern dancer, demands live accompaniment during performances. The troupe, was founded in 1951.

Ten dancers.

MARGARET JENKINS DANCE COMPANY
115 Wisconsin Avenue
San Francisco, Calif. 94107
(415) 838-7580

Margaret Jenkins, Artistic Director
Maryann K. Maslan, Business Manager

Of the former Cunningham company dancers who have gone on to create their own dance troupes and bodies of work, Margaret Jenkins seems to remain the most faithful Cunningham disciple. The movement style of her dances is based directly on Cunningham technique, modified somewhat by her own personal movement qualities which include finely developed legato phrasing and a calmer, rather less assertive presence than Cunningham's. Some of her dances are performed in silence; others have accompanying monologues or word and sound structures by Michael Palmer, with whom she collaborates. Jenkins enjoys pursuing various permutations of particular themes. *Copy,* for example, is "a dance divided into nine sections which explores various extensions of unison activity." The piece is illuminated alternately by the gray-blue glow of a battery of television sets, unshielded light bulbs, and slide projections so that the audience's perception of the same or similar movement material will be different in each section. *About the Space in between* is in two sections divided by a five-minute pause. The movement for both parts is the same, but the costumes and accompaniment change radically.

Eleven dancers.

JONES-LUDIN DANCES WE DANCE COMPANY
411 Hobron Lane
Honolulu, Hawaii 96815
(808) 955-5665

Betty Jones, Fritz Ludin, Artistic Directors

Betty Jones and Fritz Ludin formed their company in 1967 as a duo. The repertory includes works created by Jones and Ludin, as well as pieces by José Limón, Doris Humphrey, Murray Louis, Dan Wagoner, and others. Because of its commitments to European touring and to Hawaii, where the company is based, it has not toured the Mainland as frequently in the past few years as previously, although plans are under way for Mainland appearances in the future.

Seven dancers.

Opposite: **Here and Now with Watchers** *(Hawkins),* ***Erick Hawkins Dance Company.***

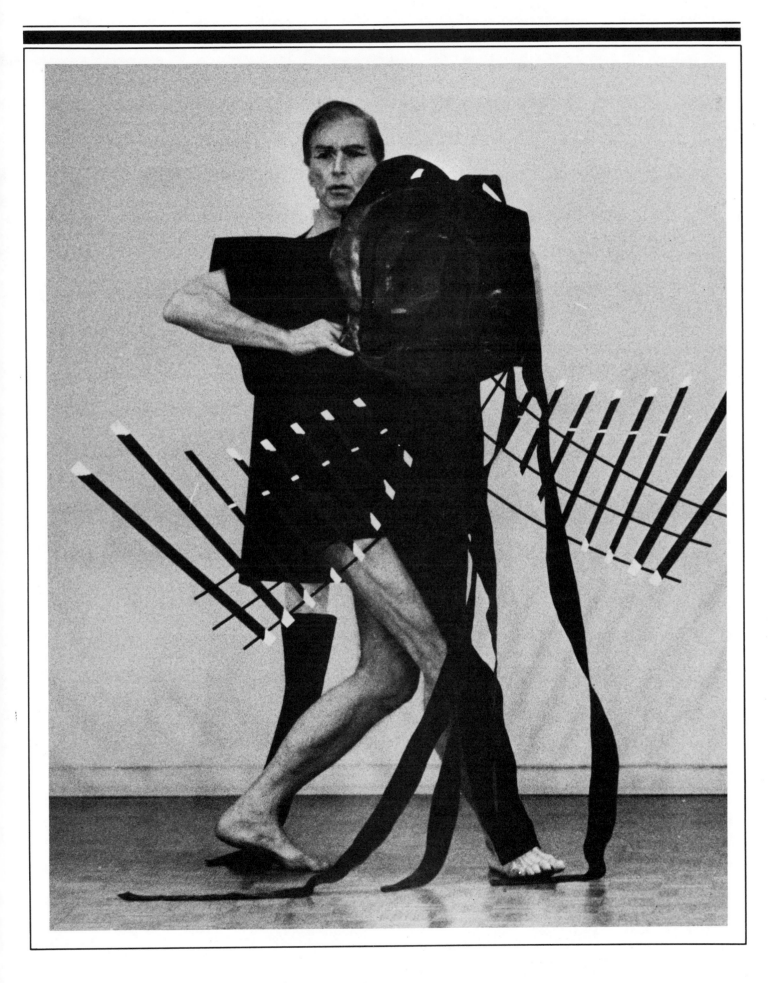

ELIZABETH KEEN DANCE COMPANY
439 West 21 Street
New York, N.Y. 10011
(212) 586-6300

Elizabeth Keen, Artistic Director
Jon Knudsen, Business Manager

Elizabeth Keen danced with the Tamiris-Nagrin and Paul Taylor dance companies before beginning to pursue her own choreographic interests in the early sixties. She has a finely developed, wry wit which she weaves into many of her dances. In *Poison Variations,* for instance, she presents a series of variations based on the idea of murder. The inspiration for the dance, and its main action, comes from the play within a play in *Hamlet.* The events in the dance are wicked and evil, yet so terribly clever that they evoke laughter. Keen's dances are generally fragmented and full of non sequiturs, all carefully plotted and crafted.

CLIFF KEUTER DANCE COMPANY
330 Broome Street
New York, N.Y. 10002
(212) 966-5260

Cliff Keuter, Artistic Director
Alan Kifferstein, Managing Director

Cliff Keuter formed his own company in 1969, after having danced with both the Tamiris-Nagrin company and Paul Taylor. In the past, he has explored two general types of choreography: a neo-Dada manipulation of bizarre props and costumes with movement structured in an assemblage manner, and movement-oriented pieces which explore the textural quality of emotions. His interests appear to be changing currently. *The Murder of George Keuter* (a cousin) is an outraged statement on the horror of senseless violence. *Field* is about family, community, and continuity. Recently, Keuter has set dances to the cantatas of Carl Orff, *Carmina Burana* and *Catulli Carmina.*

PAULINE KONER DANCE CONSORT
263 West End Avenue
New York, N.Y. 10023
(212) 249-4847

Pauline Koner, Artistic Director
Cecil C. Connor, Company Manager

Pauline Koner's career as a choreographer has spanned

Opposite: **Facets** *(Murray Louis), Jones-Ludin Dances We Dance Company.* **Top:** **A Time of Crickets** *(Koner), Pauline Koner Dance Consort.* **Center:** **The Forget-Me-Not** *(Keen), Elizabeth Keen Dance Company.* **Bottom:** **Air for the G String** *(Doris Humphrey), José Limón Dance Company.*

the last fifty years. She presented her first works in 1929 and has been closely associated with Doris Humphrey, the brilliant modern dance pioneer, and with the José Limón Dance Company for which she created several important roles in Limón works. Her Dance Consort, however, performs works she has created only since 1953, most notably *Cassandra*, a solo of agonizing guilt, and *The Farewell*, a danced eulogy to Doris Humphrey.

PEARL LANG DANCE COMPANY

229 East 59 Street
New York, N.Y. 10022
(212) 753-9646

Pearl Lang, Artistic Director
William Schorr, General Manager

Pearl Lang danced with the Martha Graham Dance Company for ten years prior to forming her own troupe in 1952, and she still dances occasionally as a guest artist with Graham. Her own movement style is based on the Graham technique—she has a fine reputation as a teacher of that technique—modified by her own softer, more lyrical performing style. Lang has made several dances based on her Jewish heritage, the most successful of which is *The Possessed* (1975). The dance is a full-length work—rare in modern dance—based on S. Ansky's famous play, *The Dybbuk*. Lang makes effective use of slide projections in the possession scenes, and she has incorporated fairly authentic Chassidic dances into the work. Lang's company now numbers fifteen, a figure unusually high for a modern dance company.

Fifteen dancers.

BELLA LEWITZKY DANCE COMPANY

3594 Multiview Drive
Hollywood, Calif. 90068
(213) 766-1058

Bella Lewitzky, Artistic Director
Darlene Neel, Manager

Bella Lewitzky received her early dance training from Lester Horton, the California choreographer whose importance in early modern dance is only now being recognized. Lewitzky formed her first performing concert group in 1951. Her present twelve-person company, however, dates from 1966. Lewitzky's style, while perhaps based on elements of Horton technique, remains unique. She was born in the California Mojave desert and believes that the qualities of that open, spacious Western territory are very clearly reflected in her dances.

Twelve dancers.

Moore, Elvi. "Bella Lewitzky." *Dance Chronicle* II, 1 (1978).

Inscape *(Lewitzky)*, Bella Lewitzky Dance Company.

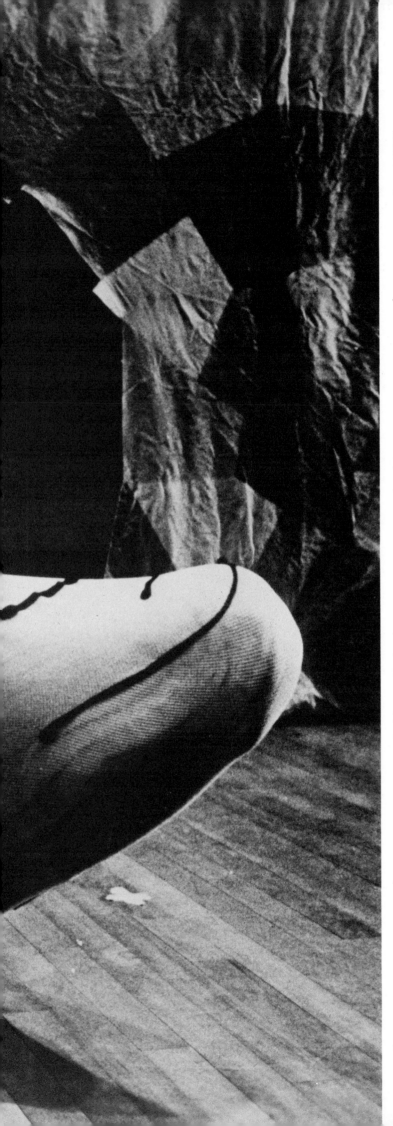

JOSÉ LIMÓN DANCE COMPANY
c/o HI Enterprises
200 West 57 Street
Suite 1310
New York, N.Y. 10019
(212) 247-4230

Carla Maxwell, Artistic Director

Created in 1946, this is the only modern dance company that has survived the death of its founder (in 1972). Today, the bulk of the repertory is still dances by Limón and by his mentor, Doris Humphrey (until her death, in 1958, the Artistic Director of his company). Most of these dances are masterpieces, but it is doubtful that any company can survive long as a museum. Consequently, choreographers both outside and within this sixteen-member troupe have been invited to stage works; the most notable contributors are Murray Louis, who has done two pieces, and Kurt Jooss, who taught his famous ballet, *The Green Table,* to the company. Limón's gesturally based movement style was built on the foundation of the Humphrey-Weidman technique. The overriding theme in most of Limón's works is the essential nobility of man. The basis of Doris Humphrey's style was the physical principle of fall and recovery regulated by a breath impulse, a giving into and a resisting of gravity, and an intensification of the simple act of walking. The basic philosophy which emerges from Humphrey's work is similar to Limón's. As the critic Deborah Jowitt has noted, "Through its many stylistic transformations, her theme remained the perfectability of mankind through the pursuit of noble ambitions." There is a strong and recent public interest in the heritage of modern dance, and several Humphrey works are being revived before they are forgotten. The Limón company is involved in this revivalist trend. Most recently, it staged Humphrey's 1938 masterwork, *Passacaglia,* and it is reasonable to expect that it will revive other Humphrey and Limón dances.

Sixteen dancers.

Cohen, Selma Jeanne. *Doris Humphrey: An Artist First.* 1972. Paperback, Middletown, Conn.: Wesleyan University, 1977.

MURRAY LOUIS DANCE COMPANY
33 East 18 Street
New York, N.Y. 10003
(212) 777-1120

Murray Louis, Artistic Director
Anthony P. Micocci, General Manager

Murray Louis was, for two decades, the most prominent dancer in the Nikolais Dance Theatre. Like many modern dancers, he has inherited the technique of his mentor, a

Chimera *(Louis), Murray Louis Dance Company.*

technique which was, in part, developed on Louis's body. The main difference between the styles of the two men is that for Nikolais movement is one part—and not necessarily the most important part—of an overall, multi-media, theatrical conception, while for Louis movement is the primary focus of his dances. Louis began creating dances for his own group as early as 1953, while still with Nikolais. His style has often been described as "quirky." He uses isolation—the articulation of individual body parts in an otherwise calm body—and an abrupt, unanticipated impulse, although he is also capable of more lyrical, sustained, somewhat balletic movement. Body configurations tend to be odd and asymmetrical, and sculptural shape, frequently deployed at the end of phrases as punctuation, is an important element in his work. Louis's dances may be narrative or abstract; he is witty and sometimes comic. Most often he creates pieces for his own troupe but has also worked with Nureyev and Friends, the Royal Danish Ballet, and the José Limón company, among others.

LAR LUBOVITCH DANCE COMPANY
c/o Columbia Artists Management
165 West 57 Street
New York, N.Y. 10019
(212) 397-6900

Lar Lubovitch, Artistic Director

Lar Lubovitch is a popular modern dance choreographer who has had a company since 1969. His background is in both modern dance (Anna Sokolow, Martha Graham, José Limón techniques) and ballet (Margaret Black, Leon Danielian, and Antony Tudor were his teachers). He has danced both in first-rate ballet and modern dance companies. As might be expected, his choreographic style blurs the traditional distinctions between the two genres. His works are characterized by high energy expenditure and a relentless intensity. He is fond of using familiar music by great composers like Handel and Stravinsky but has of late begun to use the evenly pulsing, repetitive music of avant-garde composers Philip Glass and Steve Reich. The use of this music has transformed his choreographic approach and the dances seem to ride the musical pulse as repetition or a range of small-scale movements presented in a montagelike series. It is perhaps too soon to suggest Lubovitch's style has permanently changed. This new direction, temporary or not, is nonetheless interesting.

Ten dancers.

MARYLAND DANCE THEATER
Dance Department
Building EE

University of Maryland
College Park, Md. 20742
(301) 454-4056

Larry Warren, Director
Elizabeth Ince, Artistic Advisor

This repertory company was established in 1971. Its twelve dancers include both professionals, some from the faculty of the University of Maryland, and select students. Members of the company who also choreograph for it are Larry Warren, Anne Warren, Diane Frank, Doris E. Madden, Joanie Smith, Alvin Mayes, and Sandra Pollocke. Outside choreographers who have been invited to stage works for the company include Dan Wagoner (*Penny Supper*), Bill Evans (*For Betty*), Anna Sokolow (*Moods*), and Don Redlich (*Cahoots* and *Air Antique*). The company also performs Doris Humphrey's masterwork, *Shakers*. As with many repertory companies that must be able to dance in a variety of styles, Maryland Dance Theater strives to avoid a company style, preferring instead a general approach to training which director Larry Warren terms "enlightened eclecticism"

Twelve dancers.

MEREDITH MONK/THE HOUSE
47 West 9 Street
New York, N.Y. 10011
(212) 691-5434

Meredith Monk, Artistic Director
Catherine Smith, Business Manager

Meredith Monk, who began to choreograph in 1963, is one of the most respected of the avant-garde choreographers. She studied dance at Sarah Lawrence College and with Ann Halprin, a San Francisco choreographer who exerted a strong influence on the New York avant-garde in the sixties. Monk is also a composer, and she creates the music for her own works. She is difficult to categorize because her works—she refers to some as "epic operas"—blur the distinctions between music, theater and dance. Most are meticulously designed mosaics which integrate music, usually played and sung by Monk, drama, media, environment, and dance. The movement in these mosaics is gesturally based and uses a fair amount of everyday derived activity. *The Plateau Series* exists in several versions and is one of the more abstract works Monk has done. It is anthropological and totemic, an evocation of humans in nature which includes images of wood chopping, the washing of clothes, combat, and the appearance of a demon. Monk has called it a poetry piece rather than a prose piece. One performance, presented in New York in 1978, juxtaposed a solo and group version. *Quarry* (1976) uses words, music, and movement to create a fragmented, dreamlike landscape of dimly and

vividly remembered images associated with World War II. *Paris, Chacon, Venice, Milan* is a striking juxtaposition of images associated with those places. *Vessel,* which occurred in three locations (a garage, a loft, a parking lot) over the course of two days, is, in some sense, about Joan of Arc. The final image of Joan's immolation, for instance, was transformed by Monk into a skittering dance across the parking lot, while a person welded something with an acetylene torch casting a huge, flickering, ominous shadow of Monk on the brick wall bordering the lot. The uniqueness of Monk's imagery—verbal, musical, or physical—is what makes her performances so riveting.

JENNIFER MULLER AND THE WORKS

131 West 24 Street
New York, N.Y. 10011
(212) 691-3803

Jennifer Muller, Artistic Director
Alan Dachman, Business Manager

This nine-dancer company was created in 1974, although Muller began choreographing in 1971 while still a member of Louis Falco's group. She created several works for his company before branching out on her own. Like Falco, Muller was a dancer in the José Limón company and her movement style is based on Limón technique, extended and distorted by a high expenditure of energy. Her dances, which are often centered around rituals, give the impression of hedonism, perhaps because the dancers so obviously take pleasure in their virtuosic movement and because the style is so sensual. The display of line is never as important as dynamics. Legs are kicked into the air rather than placed, bodies are constantly swooping into pliés in order to explode outwards, dancers frequently hurl themselves off-center and, consequently, off-balance. It is this calculated recklessness and apparent risk-taking, combined with the virtuosity of the dancers, which make Muller's work so viscerally exciting, although the quality of the choreography is a controversial subject, on which, so far, no clear-cut consensus has emerged.

Nine dancers.

DANIEL NAGRIN

550 Broadway
New York, N.Y. 10012
(212) 226-3551

Daniel Nagrin, Artistic Director

Top: **Education of the Girlchild** *(Monk),* **Meredith Monk/The House.** *Bottom:* **Nocturnes** *(Bertram Ross),* **Maryland Dance Theater.**

Daniel Nagrin began choreographing in 1942, was one of the directors of the Tamiris-Nagrin company, and has also headed his own company. Over the last few years, however, he has been performing alone. His concerts are frequently retrospectives of dances he has created over the past thirty or so years. The basis of Nagrin's style is often jazz dance of the forties and fifties, not to be confused with the slick Broadway or television dancing which is so frequently called jazz dance today. His programs generally feature several dance portraits of characters who bring to mind the popular culture of the forties and fifties, including Bogart-like heros *(Strange Hero),* or New Orleans, neo-Dixieland, funky jazz characters, or Spanish dancers, or the anti-hero Jewish Community Center bumpkin. He also performs solos which are stylistically minimal, outgrowths of the famous avant-garde Judson Church aesthetic of the sixties, as well as excerpts from his *Peloponnesian War,* which combines the non-narrative logic of his portraits with the repetition and simplicity of the avant-garde pieces. A Nagrin concert is likely to have an informal quality since Nagrin enjoys a cheerful (and informative) banter with his audience. Although no longer young—he has been performing for close to forty years—he is still an extraordinarily exciting dancer.

One dancer.

NEW ENGLAND DINOSAUR
103 Pleasant Street
Lexington, Mass. 02173
(617) 862-6688

Toby Armour, Artistic Director
Michael Mao, Manager

This Massachusetts-based four-dancer company is headed by Toby Armour, who has danced in the companies of Midi Garth, Paul Taylor, James Waring, and Aileen Passloff. She began choreographing in the early sixties and, although living in Boston, presented dances at the Judson Church, a center for avant-garde activity in New York during the mid-sixties. Her dances tend to be introspective, calm, self-possessed, and purposeful. They are also whimsical but maintain an unassailable dance logic. Armour choreographs in a fragmentary manner, juxtaposing a range of dynamics and rhythms in interesting contrasting ways. Her alert movement style is a combination of everyday movement, gesture, and Cunningham-based technique, rapidly shifting between small body articulations and movements with more largesse. What at first appears to be different kinds of movement in the same piece is really the development of

Opposite: **Come Bid the Pipers Calling** *(Newman),* **Gloria Newman Dance Theater.**

a limited range of options. Armour often performs alone, and she and her company tour the Northeast regularly.

Four dancers.

GLORIA NEWMAN DANCE THEATER
3845 East Fernwood Avenue
Orange, Calif. 92669
(714) 532-2818

Gloria Newman, Artistic Director
Charles M. Schoenberg, General Manager

Gloria Newman is a New Yorker who went visiting California and ended up staying. She formed her company, which now numbers ten dancers, in 1961. She has studied with a wide range of modern dance teachers, including Martha Graham, Merce Cunningham, Doris Humphrey, and José Limón. Her choreographic interests are similarly wide-ranging. She creates both abstract and dramatic works and enjoys exploring dance through a variety of approaches. *Magazine,* for instance, uses no music but is accompanied by the natural sounds of the dancing and by the dancers' speaking. *Orbits* pursues the relationships between dancers, and their individual relationships to space and the floor. The first section is earthbound, the second features a dancer who never touches the floor, and the third uses movement material which appears suspended in space. Newman's company performs dances by her and by other choreographers, including Anna Sokolow *(Rooms),* Donald McKayle *(Games),* and Elizabeth Keen *(Rushes* and *Parentheses).*

Ten Dancers.

NIKOLAIS DANCE THEATRE
33 East 18 Street
New York, N.Y. 10003
(212) 777-1120

Alwin Nikolais, Artistic Director
William Bourne, General Manager

Nikolais formed his company in 1951 and during the fifties was considered a member of the avant-garde, largely because he insisted on making abstract, non-emotional works, a choice which has become dominant in the seventies. Nikolais's dances are about sculptural shape and dynamics. He frequently disguises the shape of the human body with fantastic costumes and further obscures it with spectacular, phantasmagorical lighting and projections. He sees the dancer—the human—as inseparable from his environment. Nikolais creates all the elements in his multi-media works, even the electronic music which accompanies them. He has been called, justifiably, a theatrical wizard. His movement style has a tendency toward quick, abrupt, sporadic impulses and darting, flickering energy. The most striking quality in his dancers is their ability to isolate and articulate body parts. In works that emphasize the dancer rather than the environment, his style can seem extraordinarily effortless and virtuosic.

"Nik." *Dance Perspectives* 48, 1971.

PILOBOLUS DANCE THEATRE
Box 233
Washington, Conn. 06793
(203) 868-7244

Mark Ross, Manager

This company was created by four men who were, at the time, students at Dartmouth College in New Hampshire. Although they had studied dance there with Alison Chase, they had not been influenced by any of the established dance styles in the country. Indeed, their dances derived more from acrobatics and gymnastics. Sculptural shape was crucial. The men often created unusual configurations with their counterbalanced bodies and mutual leverage. The subjects of their works were fantastic (they took pleasure in imitating real or imaginary plants and animals) or playful (one dance seemed to be a riotous variety of pratfalls and collisions, perhaps in a gym, which was timed in split-seconds). In 1974, one of the men was replaced and two women joined the company, with predictable effect. For the first time, the intrinsic drama of male-female relationships became a viable choreographic subject for the group. From the beginning, the company has performed collectively choreographed dances. This is a unique approach to creation in dance. The dancer/choreographers are Alison Chase, Martha Clarke, Michael Tracy, Robert Pendleton, Jonathon Wolken, and Robert Barnett.

Six dancers.

PORTLAND DANCE THEATER
716 S.W. 16 Avenue
Portland, Ore. 97205
(503) 227-3840

Jann McCauley, Artistic Director
Maria Warshawski, General Manager

This six-member company was formed in 1970 and maintains a repertory created by its own dancers, who are encouraged to choreograph. The repertory also includes dances by significant choreographers outside the company including Daniel Nagrin, Don Redlich, and Dan Wagoner. This results in an eclecticism which embraces a variety of modern dance styles as well as elements of jazz and ballet. The musical accompaniment ranges from

Ravel and Haydn through the contemporary avant-garde composers Mumma and Subotnik, and even manages to cover the pop bases with Judy Garland and Judy Collins.

Six dancers.

KATHRYN POSIN DANCE COMPANY
c/o Pentacle Management
200 West 72 Street, Suite 20
New York, N.Y. 10012

Kathryn Posin, Artistic Director
Lance Westergard, Associate Director

Kathryn Posin danced with the companies of Anna Sokolow, Valerie Bettis, and Dance Theater Workshop before forming her own in 1970. Her style is a flashy, sometimes hard-hitting combination of modern dance and elements of ballet, jazz, and rock dance. She uses these idioms to provide a wide range of movement possibilities. Her thematic approach is equally eclectic. *Waves,* a muscular and sturdy dance, is what *New York Times* critic Anna Kisselgoff has aptly called "a nature and surf study." When Eliot Feld had it staged for his ballet company, it brought Posin national attention. Other works in her repertory include science-fiction pieces like *Nuclear Energy* which has sections based on the ideas of fission and fusion, *Light Years,* with jazz-rock accompaniment by John McLaughlin and the Mahavishnu Orchestra, and more traditional dances like *Bach Pieces.* A curious duet with a laundry basket seems to fit into no existing category.

DON REDLICH DANCE COMPANY
c/o Sheldon Soffer Management
130 West 56 Street
New York, N.Y. 10019
(212) 757-8060

Don Redlich, Artistic Director
Sheldon Soffer, Management

Don Redlich has directed his own company since 1966. The troupe presently numbers five dancers. The repertory—with the notable exceptions of *Rota,* created in 1975 by the distinguished early modern dance choreographer, Hanya Holm—is exclusively by Redlich, who creates diverse works. *Earthling,* for instance, is impressionistic, *Estrange* is dramatic, *Cahoots* is humorous, while *Traces* and *Passin' Through* are based on American folk material. Redlich has a fine facility for exaggerating American vernacular movement. He is also interested in character and mood studies.

Five dancers.

REPERTORY DANCE THEATRE
Building 509, University of Utah
Salt Lake City, Utah 84112
(801) 466-8607

Linda Smith and Kay Clark, Artistic Coordinators
Barry Bonifas, General Manager

This company was created in 1966 by a grant from the Rockefeller Foundation and matching funds from the University of Utah, as part of an early attempt by the Foundation to decentralize dance in the United States. (The rate of decentralization has in recent years increased dramatically, but New York continues to be the center of dance activity.) Repertory Dance Theatre was originally, and still is, in residence at the University, but it maintains its autonomy. Interestingly, it has been a democratically run company from the outset. Decisions are made by the entire company, and everyone is encouraged to choreograph. RDT also performs a repertory of works by important modern dance choreographers including José Limón, Lar Lubovitch, Donald McKayle, Lucas Hoving, Viola Farber, Paul Sanasardo, Jennifer Muller, and others. Most recently, the company has acquired Doris Humphrey's *Day on Earth* and *Water Study,* and has further plans to add further early modern dance masterpieces to the repertory. RDT also offers works by Bill Evans, who now has his own company in Seattle, and Tim Wengerd, who is now a dancer with the Martha Graham troupe. Both men are former members of RDT.

RIRIE-WOODBURY DANCE COMPANY
Post Office Box 11566
Salt Lake City, Utah 84147
(801) 328-1062

Shirley Ririe and Joan Woodbury, Artistic Directors
Susan Salazar, General Manager

This seven-dancer Salt Lake City company was founded in 1969 by Shirley Ririe and Joan Woodbury, who had worked together in their previous companies since 1951. Both have extraordinarily varied backgrounds, having studied, between them, most of the established modern dance techniques. Woodbury also studied with Mary Wigman in Germany on a Fulbright scholarship. Both have very strong ties with Alwin Nikolais and Murray Louis who, through the German-American modern dance pioneer, Hanya Holm, can also trace their movement lineage back to Wigman in Germany. Both Ririe and Woodbury choreograph for this company. Their works tend to be theatrical and to use a variety of unusual

Top: **Sue's Leg** *(Tharp), Twyla Tharp Dance Foundation (lecture-demonstration). Bottom:* **Whoops, Quivers and Flaps** *(Jann McCauley), Portland Dance Theater.*

lighting, film, and projections. Their wide choreographic range includes both entertaining and esoteric works. As with many dance companies outside New York, they invite other choreographers to stage works for them, including Murray Louis, Alwin Nikolais, Pilobolus, Cliff Keuter, and Steve Paxton.

Seven dancers.

ROD RODGERS DANCE COMPANY
8 East 12 Street
New York, N.Y. 10003
(212) 924-7560

Rod Rodgers, Artistic Director
Marilynn M. Smith, General Manager

This eleven-member troupe was created in 1964. Rodgers's earliest dance training, in his native Michigan, was in jazz and tap. He danced with several companies, most notably that of Erick Hawkins whose influence can still be seen in Rodgers's own work. Much of the movement style and thematic content of the dances in the company's repertory is based on Rodgers's black American heritage. Nonetheless, his most famous dance is probably the 1973 *Rhythm Ritual,* an abstract work in which the dancers create their own music with a variety of hand–held percussion instruments, thus effectively becoming dancer and musician in the same person.

Eleven dancers.

PAUL SANASARDO DANCE COMPANY
59 West 21 Street
New York, N.Y. 10010
(212) 989-6070

Paul Sanasardo, Artistic Director
William Weaver, President

Paul Sanasardo formed his own group in the early 1960s after having danced with the Dance Theatre of Washington and Anna Sokolow, with whom he shares an interest in themes of psychic pain, loneliness, and despair. His works are primarily emotional although the situations depicted are either interestingly ambiguous or at least partially abstracted. He seldom creates a work which has a clearly developed narrative line. His dances reflect his interest in pure dance values, virtuosic movement, and balletic line. He has recently begun choreographing for ballet dancers such as Lawrence Rhodes, Naomi Sorkin, and William Carter. He has also mounted dances for the Batsheva Dance Company of Israel and the Alvin Ailey American Dance Theater.

THE SOLOMONS COMPANY/DANCE
889 Broadway
New York, N.Y. 10010
(212) 242-5633

Gus Solomons, Jr., Artistic Director
Philip Moser, Management

Gus Solomons, Jr., is tall and very slender, with unusually long legs and arms. His body helps to make him a most interesting spatial dancer. As a child, he studied jazz and tap dance; later, he earned a degree in architecture from the Massachusetts Institute of Technology while continuing to study dance. Later still, he danced in the companies of Martha Graham, Pearl Lang, Donald McKayle, Joyce Trisler, and Merce Cunningham. He began choreographing in the early sixties and today dances only with his own company. The single strongest influence on him has been Cunningham, and one can perceive that choreographer's style in Solomons's works, which tend to be structurally complex. Solomons has a wonderful sense of wit, which is evident in the monologues he writes to accompany some of his dances and in the movement itself. Most recently, his company has been spending half its time in residence at a California college, and half in New York where it is officially based.

KEI TAKEI'S MOVING EARTH
19 Hudson Street
New York, N.Y. 10013
(212) 966-0562

Kei Takei, Artistic Director
Maldwyn Pate, Associate Director
Donald Moore, Company Manager

Takei has been choreographing in the United States since she arrived from Japan in 1967 to study at the Juilliard School on a Fulbright scholarship. Her movement style is based on natural, everyday movement, extremely intensified. Unlike most choreographers frequently categorized as avant-garde, Takei makes dances which are metaphors for the human condition. They are about hope pitted against human suffering, the meaning of life, endless time and inexorable process, the rhythms of the universe. In 1969, Takei created a short work called *Light.* It became known as *Light, Part 1* since, as months and years went by, other parts were created. Today there are fourteen sections to *Light.* This dance-epic has become Takei's lifework.

Twelve dancers.

PAUL TAYLOR DANCE COMPANY
550 Broadway
New York, N.Y. 10012
(212) 431-5562

Paul Taylor, Director
Robert Yesselman, General Manager

Opposite: **Statements of Nameless Root I (Gus Solomons), The Solomons Company/Dance.**

Paul Taylor, a tall, big-boned dancer with a gently imposing presence, performed briefly with Pearl Lang and Merce Cunningham before dancing with Martha Graham's company from the mid-fifties through the early sixties. He began choreographing in the fifties and was one of the most outrageous members of the avant-garde, creating, for example, a dance in which there was no dancing. During the sixties, he made dances for his own company, which was formed in 1961 and now numbers thirteen dancers, that were ambiguous in content. We are used to ambiguity now, but at the time some audiences had difficulty with works that left ends dangling tantalizingly. During this period, Taylor also emerged as a master satirist. *Agathe's Tale* (1967), *Churchyard* (1969), and *Big Bertha* (1969) reveal the lewd and depraved underpinnings of an otherwise apparently well-adjusted American sexuality. *From Sea to Shining Sea* (1965) is a bitter look at a morally corrupt and embattled Republic. *Cloven Kingdom* (1976) suggests that the human race may decorate itself with evening gowns and tuxedos, but the simian qualities of our past lie just beneath the veneer of civilization. Ever since he created *Aureole* in 1962— unequivocally a masterpiece—Taylor has returned frequently to its refined and vibrant neo-classicism. His most recent works, choreographed after he ceased dancing a few years ago, have been increasingly in this vein. Taylor's movement style is based on Graham technique, adapted to his own interests and body. Deborah Jowitt, dance critic for the *Village Voice,* has written about this style that *Aureole* "can almost be viewed as a primer of Taylor dancing; in it you can see the chains of ground-skimming leaps; the parallel feet,...the archaic Graham poses with jutting hips which give the dancers the look of frolicking satyrs; the flyaway hands; the swinging, twin-armed gestures, the fluent knots. And above all, the buoyancy."

Thirteen dancers.

Hodgson, Moira. *Quintet: Five American Dance Companies.* New York: Morrow, 1976.

TWYLA THARP DANCE FOUNDATION
38 Walker Street
New York, N.Y. 10013
(212) 966-2590

Twyla Tharp, Artistic Director
Roddy O'Connor, Administrator

This company, which was formed in 1970, has grown to eleven dancers. Tharp began creating dances in 1965 and is considered perhaps the most innovative and important figure to emerge in dance in the past decade. She has choreographed for companies other than her own, most

Opposite: **Light, Part 10 *(Takei), Kei Takei's Moving Earth.***

notably for American Ballet Theatre and the Joffrey Ballet, where her *Deuce Coupe* first brought her widespread national attention and acclaim. Tharp's own company exists exclusively as a vehicle for her choreography. Her dances combine elements of modern dance, jazz dance, and ballet as well as social dances from this century. Her use of space and rhythm is unconventional, and her highly complex and structured formality is offset by a very personal and appealing style.

Eleven dancers.

TORONTO DANCE THEATRE
95 Trinity Street
Toronto, Ontario, M5A 3C7, Canada
(416) 362-7761

Peter Randazzo, Patricia Beatty, David Earle, Artistic Directors

This is one of the most important of the Canadian modern dance companies. It was founded in 1968 by Peter Randazzo, Patricia Beatty, and David Earle, who remain today the three artistic directors. Virtually the entire repertory of over fifty works has been created by this threesome. Each has a strong background in Graham technique. Randazzo danced with both Graham and the José Limón company; Beatty spent five years dancing with Pearl Lang, a Graham disciple; and Earle danced with Limón as well as with the National Ballet of Canada. Each of the eighteen dancers in the Toronto Dance Theatre has studied Graham technique extensively, and many have strong ballet backgrounds. The company's choreography shows a strong Graham influence, not only in the movement style, but often in thematic content as well. While this profile raises the question of artistic derivation, it is important to remember that this is not an American company but a Canadian one, and that outside the United States the overwhelming tendency is to base a modern dance company firmly on the Graham aesthetic.

Eighteen dancers.

DAN WAGONER AND DANCERS
20 East 17 Street
New York, N.Y. 10003
(212) 929-1018

Dan Wagoner, Artistic Director

Dan Wagoner founded his company in 1969. Like many choreographers today, he has been influenced by Merce Cunningham's non sequitur, pure dance approach, although Wagoner's performance background is with Martha Graham and Paul Taylor. His dances primarily convey mood, although there are fragments of dramatic or emotional material woven into them. If there is a recurring theme in his work, it is one of community. The energy level of his performances can be tremendously high as his dancers assault the air around their bodies, capriciously veer off into various movement non sequiturs, and unexpectedly abort phrases, driven by strong rhythms. Wagoner dancers make you think of wind-up toys that have been overwound and are running amok, an image reinforced by Wagoner's emphasis on the articulation of legs and torso while the arms are relatively passive. Wagoner also makes dances that are quiet and introspective, sometimes with a melancholic quality about them. He was born in West Virginia and went to college there, and his dances display an ingratiatingly downhome, country–boy charm.

Seven dancers.

WHAT TO READ

Very few books have been written about the dance companies in this section. Most of the information about them is contained in newspaper and magazine articles, which usually disappear the day or week after they are published. Two general books about modern dance, which discuss some of the companies included here, are both by Don McDonagh (both are available in paperback). *The Rise and Fall and Rise of Modern Dance*, 1970 (paperback, New York: New American Library, Mentor, 1977) and *The Complete Guide to Modern Dance*, 1976 (paperback, New York: Popular Library, 1977).

Right: **Polaris** *(Taylor), Paul Taylor Dance Company.*

MIMES

By Barbara Newman

BLACK LIGHT THEATRE OF PRAGUE

c/o Pragonkoncert
1 Maltezske Nam.
Prague 1, Czechoslovakia

Jiri Srnec, Director

This mime company chooses to emphasize props rather than performers, lighting the stage in such a way that objects like cups, sheets, and cutout letters of the alphabet seem to move by their own volition while the people maneuvering them remain obscured. This arrangement produces a series of surreal cartoons, broad in outline and limited in subject, but intriguing and often funny because of their visual implausibility. The company has toured widely in the United States and in Eastern and Western Europe.

Eleven performers.

ADAM DARIUS

104 Monarch Court
Lyttelton Road
London N2, England
(01) 458-1072

Darius is a mime, a dancer, and a choreographer. Originally trained in classical ballet, he has developed a personal mime style that combines elements of dance, acting, and acrobatics with traditional miming gestures. In contrast to the austere performances of someone like Marceau, whose formalized movement studies are most often presented in silence, Darius uses elaborate lighting effects and varied musical accompaniment to enhance the theatrical life of the various characters he creates. His subjects have included *The Dreamer, The Addict,* a contemporary Christ-figure *(Death of a Scarecrow),* clowns, and even Marilyn Monroe. He is the first American mime to have appeared in Russia, and has toured in thirty countries on five continents, appeared at the Festival of Two Worlds in Spoleto, Italy, and starred in a mime film, *Stigmata.* Darius recently founded The Mime Centre in London for the comprehensive training of mime students.

Darius, Adam. *Dance Naked in the Sun.* London: Latonia, 1973.

LOTTE GOSLAR'S PANTOMIME CIRCUS

c/o Sheldon Soffer Management
130 West 56 Street
New York, N.Y. 10019
(212) 757-8060

Lotte Goslar, Artistic Director

Having already established herself as "one of the world's great clowns" and as "a cross between Isadora Duncan and Fanny Brice," Goslar founded her first mime troupe, and her first school in 1954 in Hollywood. Since then, she and her company have toured the entire world presenting zany comedy sketches and gentle spoofs fashioned out of her own original blend of dance, theater, and mime. Her solo piece *Grandma Always Danced* is her lighthearted version of the seven ages of man; group works include *For Humans Only* and a circus sketch, featuring a lion and a clown, with an elaborate libretto by Bertolt Brecht. Goslar has also contributed pieces to the Hartford and Joffrey Ballets. Her company has appeared at Jacob's Pillow, at the Delacorte Festival, and at international dance festivals in dozens of countries.

Six to eight dancers; lecture-demonstrations, master classes and discussions in mime, ballet, modern dance, and related arts.

CLAUDE KIPNIS MIME THEATRE

13 East 16 Street
New York, N.Y. 10003
(212) 989-2916

Claude Kipnis, Artistic Director
John Philip Luckacovic, Manager

A student of Marcel Marceau, Claude Kipnis stylizes gesture to connect the visible to the invisible and to draw full-fledged characters out of tiny mannerisms. He has portrayed everything from astronauts and government officials to simple villagers and the mythical creatures in Moussorgsky's *Pictures at an Exhibition.* His group has appeared in extensive North American tours, with the Boston Opera in Bartók's *Miraculous Mandarin* and Schoenberg's *Moses and Aaron,* at Chicago's Ravinia Festival, and at Jacob's Pillow. In addition to creating solo and group works for the stage, television, and lecture-demonstrations, Kipnis founded a mime school in Israel in 1962 and performed for President Ford.

Eight dancers.

Kipnis, Claude. *The Mime Book.* New York: Harper and Row, 1974.

MARCEL MARCEAU

c/o Columbia Artists Management, Inc.
165 West 57 Street
New York, N.Y. 10019
(212) 397-6900

Arguably the greatest and certainly the most influential and widely seen mime of the twentieth century, Marceau

Opposite: Marcel Marceau.

studied in Paris with Etienne Decroux and first performed in the mime company of another Decroux student, Jean-Louis Barrault. As a solo performer, he has created style exercises and satires on every conceivable subject, from sculptors to tea parties to the ages of man, which he captures with perfect lucidity in a brief exercise entitled *Youth, Maturity, Old Age and Death.* His famous character Bip, the clown in the striped shirt and battered top hat who first appeared in 1947, is now as immediately identified with him as the Little Tramp is with Chaplin. Bip is a silent Everyman whose misadventures with nature, human behavior, and technology have moved and amused audiences around the world, both on stage and on television. In 1949, Marceau founded his own mime company, La Compagnie de Mime Marcel Marceau, which is still a rigorous proving ground for aspiring young mimes. In recognition of his art, the French government has awarded Marceau its highest honor, the Chevalier de la Légion d'Honneur.

MUMMENSCHANZ

c/o Arthur Shafman International Ltd.
1560 Broadway
New York, N.Y. 10036
(212) 873-1559

Andres Brossard, Floriana Frassetto, Bernie Schurch,
Artistic Directors

This three-member Swiss troupe explores the stages of man's evolution and the forms of his communication by investing amoebas, animals, and fanciful creatures of all sorts with instantly identifiable emotions and social mannerisms. Covering their faces with cardboard masks and their bodies with leotards, the performers employ mime and simple, focused movement, both to create a situation and to comment on it, revealing the essential qualities of humanity without ever portraying humans. Handmade props and masks, whose style has been compared to Paul Klee and Hieronymous Bosch, highlight the naïveté, wit, and insight of their short sketches. The company has toured throughout Europe, the United States, and the Orient.

Three dancers.

POLISH MIME BALLET THEATRE

c/o Pagert
Plac Zwyciestwa 9
Warsaw, Poland

Henryk Tomaszewski, Artistic Director

The company Henry Tomaszewski founded in Poland in 1955 cannot realistically be called a mime troupe. Though

Opposite: Lo (Chiang Ching), Chiang Ching Dance Company.

its work draws on both ballet and pantomime, its final form more closely resembles the modern dance of Alwin Nikolais. It is theatrical, often acrobatic, elaborately costumed, dramatically lit, sometimes narrative and sometimes purely evocative. Short pieces like *Labyrinth, Nightmare,* and *Jacob and the Angel* are abstract in form rather than enactments of their titles. The longer *Jaselka* retells familiar Biblical stories through colorful Polish folk dances, while *Faust* is an erotic love duet. Many works are original, both comic and serious; many are based on novels or stories. The company has performed throughout Europe and Israel, in the major cities of the United States, and at the first International Mime Festival in West Berlin.

Twenty-three dancers.

Ethnic Dance Companies

Most ethnic companies offer lecture-demonstrations, teaching residencies, and other educational services in addition to performing.

MARIA ALBA SPANISH DANCE COMPANY

c/o Performing Artservices
463 West Street
New York, N.Y. 10014
(212) 989-4983
Spanish

ALLNATIONS DANCE COMPANY

Performing Arts Foundation, Inc.
500 Riverside Drive
New York, N.Y. 10027
(212) 678-5030
Chuck Golden, Artistic Director
Multi-racial, wide range of ethnic dances including Scottish, Irish, Filipino, Korean, Spanish, Indian, Israeli

AMAN FOLK ENSEMBLE

1438 Gower Street, Room 371
Hollywood, Calif. 90028
(213) 464-7225
Leona Wood, Artistic Director
Balkan, Middle Eastern

BALLET HISPANICO OF NEW YORK

167 West 89 Street
New York, N.Y. 10024
(212) 362-6710
Tina Ramirez, Artistic Director
Wide range of Hispanic styles

CHIANG CHING DANCE COMPANY

32 Jones Street
New York, N.Y. 10014
(212) 989-1644; (212) 243-0360
Chinese

CHUCK DAVIS DANCE COMPANY
c/o Bess Pruitt Associates, Inc.
819 East 168 Street
Bronx, N.Y. 10459
(212) 589-0400
Chuck Davis, Artistic Director
African, Afro-American

AGNES DE MILLE'S HERITAGE DANCE THEATRE
c/o Jean Dalrymple
130 West 56 Street
New York, N.Y. 10019
(212) 246-7820
Agnes de Mille, Artistic Director
Evening-long lecture-performance tracing history of dance, concentrating on America

José Molina Bailes Españoles.

IBRAHIM FARRAH NEAR EAST DANCE GROUP
200 West 72 Street
New York, N.Y. 10023
(212) 580-8107; (212) 595-1896
Ibrahim Farrah, Artistic Director
Near Eastern

FELIX FIBICH DANCE COMPANY
1639 West Lunt
Chicago, Ill. 60626
(312) 761-3779
Felix Fibich, Artistic Director
Folk, mostly Israeli

JOSE GRECO COMPANY
c/o Royce-Carlton, Inc.
868 United Nations Plaza
New York, N.Y. 10017
(212) 355-7931; (212) 355-7433
Jose Greco, Artistic Director
Spanish, mostly lecture-demonstrations

ARTHUR HALL'S AFRO-AMERICAN DANCE ENSEMBLE
2544 Germantown Avenue
Philadelphia, Pa. 19133
(215) 225-7565
Arthur Hall, Director
Afro-American

INDRANI AND HER DANCERS AND MUSICIANS OF INDIA
c/o Frank Wicks
Dance in Maine, Inc.
117 Maine Street
Brunswick, Me. 04011
Indrani, Artistic Director
Wide range of Indian styles

REGINALD AND GLADYS LAUBIN
Grand Teton National Park
Box 4
Moose, Wyo. 83012
(307) 733-2690
American Indian, lecture-demonstrations

MATTEO ETHNOAMERICAN DANCE THEATER
c/o HI Enterprises, Inc.
200 West 56 Street
New York, N.Y. 10019
(212) 877-9565
Matteo, Artistic Director
Carola Goya, Associate Director
Wide range of ethnic styles including Spanish, Indian, Burmese, Japanese, Javanese, Polynesian

JOSE MOLINA BAILES ESPANOLES
c/o Arthur Shafman International Ltd.
1560 Broadway
New York, N.Y. 10036
(212) 873-1559
Jose Molina, Artistic Director
Spanish

LOLA MONTES AND HER SPANISH DANCERS
1529 North Commonwealth Avenue
Hollywood, Calif. 90027
(213) 664-3288
Lola Montes, Artistic Director
Spanish

Opposite: N'tore Dance, *Chuck Davis Dance Company.*

MORCA, FLAMENCO IN CONCERT
1349 Franklin Street
Bellingham, Wash. 98225
(206) 676-1864
Teodoro Morca, Artistic Director
Spanish

MARIANO PARRA SPANISH DANCE COMPANY
336 Central Park West
New York, N.Y. 10025
(212) 866-8520
Mariano Parra, Artistic Director
Spanish

PHILIPPINE DANCE COMPANY OF NEW YORK
c/o Herman Rottenberg
500 Riverside Drive
New York, N.Y. 10027
(212) 678-5000
Reynaldo G. Alejandro, Artistic Director
Filipino

LUIS RIVERA SPANISH DANCE COMPANY
232 East 26 Street
New York, N.Y. 10010
(212) 689-0921
Luiz Rivera, Artistic Director
Spanish

THE TAMBURITZANS
Duquesne University Tamburitzans
1801 Boulevard of the Allies
Pittsburgh, Pa. 15219
(412) 281-9192
Walter W. Kolar, Director
Nicholas Jordanoff, Artistic Director
East European folk dance

HISTORICAL DANCE AUTHORITIES AND COMPANIES

Fairly recently, in line with the increased interest in dance history and research, several companies have developed that are devoted to authentic (rather than theatricalized) reconstructions of dances of the past, mostly of the Baroque and Renaissance periods. Old dance manuals, paintings, and old forms of notation are among the resources used to stage these dances (see also page 194-199, 230).

BAROQUE DANCE AND MUSIC
c/o Wendy Hilton, Director
98 Riverside Drive
New York, N.Y. 10024
(212) 247-3169

Opposite: Baroque Dance (reconstruction).

BAROQUE DANCE ENSEMBLE
241 Alamo Avenue
Santa Cruz, Calif. 95060
(408) 427-3526
Dr. Shirley Wynne, Director

CAMBRIDGE COURT DANCERS
37 Princess Road
West Newton, Mass. 02165
(617) 332-4064
Dr. Ingrid G. Brainard, Director

DUPONT CONSORTIUM
P.O. Box 19451
Washington, D.C. 20036
(202) 387-6569
Frank Roberts, Director

NEW YORK BAROQUE DANCE ENSEMBLE
280 Riverside Drive, No. 5H
New York, N.Y. 10025
(212) 663-5995
Ann Jacoby and Catherine Turocy, Co-Directors

RENAISSANCE DANCERS OF THE CONSORTIUM ANTIQUUM
70 Karol Lane
Pleasant Hill, Calif. 94523
(415) 937-1356
Angene Feves, Dance Company Director

JULIA SUTTON
c/o The New England Conservatory
290 Huntington Avenue
Boston, Mass. 02115
(617) 262-1120

ASSOCIATIONS SERVING PERFORMING COMPANIES

Association of American Dance Companies
162 West 56 Street
New York, N.Y. 10019
(212) 265-7824
Newsletter; *Poor Dancer's Almanac;* New York branch, New York Dance Alliance, publishes *The New York Dance Calendar,* distributed to all TDF Dance Voucher members (see page 251).

National Association for Regional Ballet, Inc.
1860 Broadway
New York, N.Y. 10023
(212) 757-8460
Doris Hering, Executive Director
Newsletter; Craft of Choreography conferences; regional ballet festivals

II.
Dance and You: A Guide to Classes

BALLET
By Henley Haslam

 allet is classical theatrical dancing which originated in the court festivities of Renaissance Italy and was then brought to France, where it prospered under Louis XIV. In the mid-seventeenth century in Paris, Louis founded the first school for the training of dancers, which explains why the terminology of ballet classes throughout the world is French. The technique of ballet is based on the five positions of the feet, the outward rotation of the legs known as "turn-out," which provides freedom of movement in any direction, and the concept of performing even the most difficult movements with apparent ease and grace. Discoveries during the Renaissance in anatomy and physics were reflected in the development of ballet technique, which challenges the body beyond its normal capabilities.

A ballet class is carefully designed to prepare the body for the physical demands dancing imposes on it. Classes begin with a series of exercises to warm up the muscles; students hold onto a barre to help maintain balance and correct placement of the body. The barre exercises, variations on bending and stretching, include small movements of the legs which gradually get bigger and faster as the leg is lifted from the floor. After the barre, the class moves into the center of the room for more complicated exercises to which arm and head movements are added. These are executed slowly to develop balance, strength, and the line of the body. Allegro footwork follows, with small beats, jumps, and turns done at a quicker tempo. The last part of class, grand allegro, consists of sequences of steps combining big jumps, leaps, and turns which cover large areas and put the demands on the body's strength, endurance, and control.

The basic principles and rules of ballet have remained constant, but over the years differences in quality, temperament, and emphasis have created different methods of teaching, producing styles with different "accents." The most prevalent methods today are the Russian, Cecchetti, R.A.D. (Royal Academy of Dancing), Soviet, Bournonville, and "American." A brief description of each follows, along with supplementary information.

Russian refers to the training in Imperial Russia before the Revolution, which was largely spread in the 1920s–1940s by dancers of the Diaghilev, de Basil, and Blum Ballets Russes who settled throughout the world and opened schools when their performing careers ended. It is a system of training which stresses carriage, épaulement, flowing arm movements, and expressiveness.

Karsavina, Tamara. *Classical Ballet: The Flow of Movement.* New York: Macmillan, 1962.
————. *Theatre Street.* 1930. New ed., New York: Dutton, 1961.
Kirstein, Lincoln and Stuart, Muriel. *The Classic Ballet, Basic Technique and Terminology.* 2nd ed., New York: Knopf, 1976.

Cecchetti refers to a method based on the teachings of Enrico Cecchetti (1850–1928), an Italian dancer, ballet master, and teacher whose pupils were noted for their strength, brilliant footwork, and technical virtuosity. He emphasized a strictly routinized program of explicit exercises, organized into a daily practice schedule. Adagio and allegro work are neatly balanced. An organization was formed in London to perpetuate his method, and there is a Cecchetti Council of America which offers a graded system of teaching and a series of examinations to evaluate progress of students.

Cecchetti Council of America
c/o Jane Caryl Miller
770 Greenhills Drive
Ann Arbor, Mich. 48105

Beaumont, Cyril W. and Idzikowski, Stanislas. *Manual of the Theory and Practice of Classical Theatrical Dancing (Cecchetti Method).* 1922. Paperback, New York: Dover, 1975.
Craske, Margaret and Beaumont, Cyril W. *The Theory and Practice of Allegro in Classical Ballet (Cecchetti Method).* London: Beaumont, 1946.
Craske, Margaret and de Moroda, Derra. *The Theory and Practice of Advanced Allegro in Classical Ballet (Cecchetti Method).* London: Beaumont, 1956.

R.A.D. The Royal Academy of Dancing, founded in London in 1920 is not a school, even though it has a three-year teacher training course, but a system of teaching based on a number of syllabi which contain elements of other traditional schools of training as well as some national dance, character, and mime. There is a system of examinations both for students and teachers. The objectives are to improve the standard of ballet dancing, both for professionally oriented students and those not interested in a career, and to promote the correct teaching of classical ballet. The United States branch of the R.A.D. can be contacted to locate R.A.D. teachers.

Miss Elaine Keller, Executive Secretary, R.A.D.
8 College Avenue
Upper Montclair, N.J. 07043
(201) 746-0184

An International Summer School is operated for professional ballet teachers.

Opposite: Ballet. Fifth position on pointe and (inset) first, second and fifth positions on the whole foot. The turnout, shown here, is basic to all ballet technique.

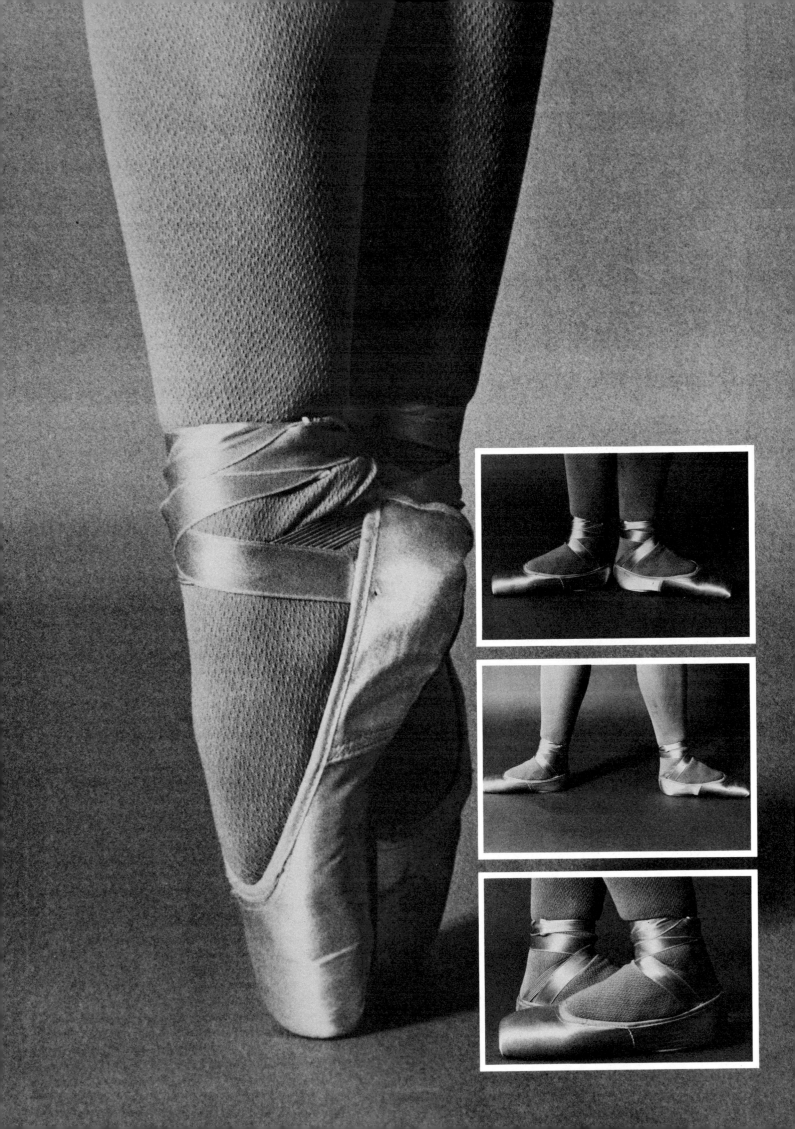

R.A.D. Summer School
48 Vicarage Crescent
London SW 11 3LT, England

Soviet, the system of teaching in the Soviet Union, is based on a syllabus developed in accordance with the methods of Agrippina Vaganova (1879–1951), a Russian dancer and teacher. Dancers trained in this comprehensive system (which usually takes eight years to master) are generally known for their precision, strength, and breadth of technique. The system stresses the creation of a virtuoso technique through development of attack, suppleness, and the use of the arms and épaulement, with movements coming "from the body." Characteristics of the system are the strength and flexibility of the back, and very high leg extensions, particularly in arabesque. The beginning exercises contain a great number of repetitions of very basic movements that become enormously complex in the advanced exercises.

Messerer, Asaf. *Classes in Classical Ballet.* New York: Doubleday, 1975.
Vaganova, Agrippina. *Basic Principles of Classical Ballet.* Paperback, New York: Dover, 1969.

Bournonville denotes a series of exercises by the Danish teacher and choreographer August Bournonville (1805–1879) that were preserved by some of his pupils after his death and used as the basis of training in the Royal Danish Ballet School. Barre and center combinations for each day of the week were set to specific music. For some years now, even in Denmark, the exercises have been incorporated into more internationally influenced training. The final result is dancers with a Bournonville style: male dancers with excellent batterie (beats) and elevation, and female dancers with lightness and charm.

Classes in Bournonville are taught in Denmark and are included in the Ballet West Summer Course.

International Ballet Seminar
Aaboulevard 32
2200 Copenhagen N
Denmark

Registrar,
Ballet West
P.O. Box 8745
Aspen, Colo. 81611

Bruhn, Erik, and Moore, Lillian. *Bournonville and Ballet Technique.* London: A. C. Black, 1961.

American. "The variety of individual approaches to teaching produces a variety of methods of teaching." This quote from Asaf Messerer sums up the teaching in the majority of American ballet schools. Teachers have taken what they feel to be the best from the many different influences on ballet training in the United States and evolved their own teaching method and style.

WHAT TO READ

For background and history:
Anderson, Jack. *Dance.* New York: Newsweek, 1974.
Lawson, Joan. *Classical Ballet: Its Style and Technique.* London: A. C. Black, 1960.

For general reference:
Chujoy, Anatole and Manchester, P. W. *The Dance Encyclopedia.* New York: Simon and Schuster, 1967.
Grant, Gail. *Technical Manual and Dictionary of Classical Ballet.* Paperback, New York: Dover, 1967.

For intermediate and advanced students, beginning adults:
Loren, Teri. *The Dancer's Companion.* New York: Dial, 1978.

For adult beginners:
Hammond, Sandra Noll. *Ballet Basics.* Palo Alto: Mayfield, 1974.

Below: Ballet. Partnering (also called supported adagio). **The** grand pas de deux *in both* The Sleeping Beauty *and in* The Nutcracker *finish with the famous*

fish dive (third from left).
Opposite: In the Cecchetti changement, the knees are bent slightly at the height of the jump.

Some Information and Definitions for the Beginning Ballet Student or Enthusiast

Equipment

Ballet studio. Usually a large empty room containing only a piano or record player. One wall is usually covered with mirrors, which add to the feeling of space and give the dancer a means of checking certain technical points. The floor, of utmost importance, is ideally wooden and resilient, with a surface that is not sticky or slippery. A covering of special linoleum is often put over the wood.

Barre. A railing around the walls of a ballet studio, usually of wood or metal, which is placed a little above waist height. A barre can also be a portable one that stands in the middle of a room (see page 209). "Doing a barre" refers to the warm-up exercises done at the beginning of a class, when the student holds the barre for stability.

What to Wear

Leotard. The basic uniform for class. It resembles a one-piece bathing suit and is made of a stretchable fabric that fits snugly to permit freedom of movement and show the outline of the body, thus helping the teacher to notice

faults and give corrections. (Men often wear a T-shirt instead of a leotard.)

Tights. The covering from foot to waist, also made of a lightweight stretchable fabric, usually worn under a leotard. For ballet class, tights are often pink for women, gray or black and of heavier weight for men.

Dance belt. An item for men to wear under tights, stronger than an athletic supporter and necessary for class.

Leg warmers. Heavy tights, usually footless and knitted of wool or orlon, worn over ordinary tights by more advanced dancers to keep muscles warm. (Plastic or rubber sweat pants are also worn as leg warmers, but there is some question as to whether this causes or encourages arthritis.)

Rehearsal skirt. A skirt of jersey or chiffon, short or mid-thigh in length, sometimes worn by advanced or professional dancers in rehearsal or class. (Should not be worn by beginning students as it hides the line of the hips and legs.)

Tutu. The typical ballet skirt made of many layers of tarlatan or nylon net. A classical tutu is short, a Romantic tutu falls to between calf and ankle (see page 219).

Ballet shoes. The basic shoe worn for ballet class, usually made of kid, leather, or canvas, which should fit like a glove. These shoes are specially made for flexibility and protection and should have elastic sewn toward the back of the shoe to keep it on the foot. A leather shoe gives more support to the foot than a canvas one, but it stretches more with use. The "Russian" shoe has a stronger, less flexible sole that provides even greater protection and support and is preferred by many male dancers, but its construction can make it more difficult to point the foot. Ballet shoes are not made to fit the left or right foot, so the life of the shoes can be prolonged by switching them.

Pointe shoes (Toe shoes). Satin slippers that have a glue-hardened toe and a strongly reinforced sole to support the arch of the foot when the dancer is standing on the tips of the toes. (A small amount of lamb's wool may be worn around the toes to protect them.) Pointe shoes must be fitted with great care. They vary with each manufacturer and are made on different lasts and with various shapes of the toe box. For example, Capezio, a leading American manufacturer of pointe shoes, makes the following:

Pavlowa: a strong shoe to give support to the beginner.

Nicolini: a lighter shoe with the standard tapered toe, for use as the dancer becomes technically proficient.

Assoluta: the lightest shoe with the standard tapered toe, for a more advanced dancer.

Ultimo: a flatter shoe with a medium–broad toe.

Top: Ballet. **Passé** *(also called* retiré*) showing épaulement.*

Opposite: Ballet. Attitude. Center: Bournonville style; upper right: R.A.D. style (with variant arms); lower left: Soviet style.

Contempora: an extra broad shoe with a squared-off toe.

Miscellaneous

Adagio (Adage). A combination during a ballet class executed slowly and designed to develop balance, grace, and a sense of line. Also, a slow part of a classic pas de deux performed by a ballerina and her partner. An adagio class is a class in the principles and practice of partnering.

Allegro. Small jumps, beats, and leaps done at a lively tempo during the later part of a ballet class.

Aplomb. Equilibrium; the sense of the center line of the body.

Character class. A class in the theatrical forms of dance based on the national dances of various Middle and Eastern European countries; such a class stresses rhythmic work and is usually done in boots or shoes with small heels.

Épaulement. Carriage of the shoulders and upper body in relation to the hips and lower torso.

Men's class. A ballet class for men which develops strength and endurance through the practice of the leaps, jumps, beats, and turns usually done by men on stage.

Révérence. A bow or curtsey, usually done at the end of a ballet class.

Rosin. An adhesive substance, in small lumps or powdered form, usually found in a box in a corner of a studio, which helps prevent the soles of the shoes (or the tip of pointe shoes) from slipping.

Variation. A solo performed in a ballet or divertissement. A variations class is one in which some (usually well-known) variations are taught.

Some Manufacturers of Dancewear and Supplies

Capezio
755 Seventh Avenue
New York, N.Y. 10019
(212) 245-2130
(shops in approximately twenty cities in United States)

Danskin, Inc.
1114 Avenue of the Americas
New York, N.Y. 10036
(212) 869-9800

Frederick Freed Ltd. of London
108 West 57 Street
New York, N.Y. 10019
(212) 489-1055

Herbet Dancewear
902 Broadway
New York, N.Y. 10010
(212) 677-7606

Parklane Hosiery
1540 Union Turnpike
New Hyde Park, N.Y. 11040
(516) 328-7400

Selva & Sons, Inc.
47-25 34 Street
Long Island City, N.Y. 11101
(212) 786-1234

Taffy's
710 Beta Drive
Cleveland, Ohio 44143
(216) 461-3360
(stores in Atlanta, Boston, Cleveland, Dallas, Salt Lake City)

Ballet class taught by Alfredo Corvino at The Juilliard School, New York.

Children

Children can gain great benefits as well as great pleasure from good dance training, whether or not a career is the goal. Dance involves and challenges the mind as well as the entire body, and an exhilarating sense of achievement can be felt as control of the body is attained. Dance training develops mental alertness and a strong, flexible, well-coordinated body. It can encourage self-confidence and musical awareness. Increased circulation is just one of the health benefits. Some orthopedic problems, such as weak ankles, can be minimized by dance training, but a doctor should be consulted first.

Because of the demands placed on the body, the academic study of classical ballet should not begin until a child is approximately eight–ten years old. Before then, children are not equipped physically or mentally for the intense effort and concentration required. Between the ages of four and seven, children love to move and respond to music, but this is not necessarily indicative of great talent or an immediate reason for formal instruction. By participating in some form of creative dance or pre-ballet class during these years, young children can derive a sense of accomplishment from learning to follow instruction, using their energy and expressiveness in a creative way, and working in a group situation. A pre-ballet class will include an introduction to balletic movement which is not too strenuous, touching on the positions of the arms and the use of the pointed foot. A creative dance class will stress more freedom of movement and self-expression. Both types of class can strengthen the body and improve coordination. Young children also benefit from and respond well to Dalcroze Eurhythmics, a system that helps develop a sense of rhythm by translating sounds into physical movement.

A beginning ballet student, perhaps age eight, usually starts with one or two classes a week. If a performing career is the goal, classes should be increased to three times a week around age ten, and daily classes should begin by thirteen. Becoming a professional ballet dancer requires a great deal of time and dedication, both from a young student and the family. The progress of a student is definitely affected by motivation and interest, and as it is the student who must do the work in class, it is the student's own interest and not that of the parent that makes the difference. If motivation for a career is not evident, the tendency is to give a child a few years of study and stop the training by age eleven or twelve. The longer a child studies dance, the greater the physical benefits will be, and these are especially important during the teens.

The most important factor in reaping the benefits of good dance training is the choice of a teacher. Performing experience or academic degrees do not guarantee a good teacher, especially not a teacher of children. A well-qualified teacher will have a thorough knowledge of technique and an understanding of anatomy and the fundamentals of movement. He will be able to make the classwork interesting and enjoyable and give the corrections that are such an important part of a class in a constructive and encouraging manner. There should be an atmosphere of discipline in which attentive students can work hard without feeling tension or strain. There should be a division of classes into levels of proficiency, and inclusion in any class should be based on age, ability, and previous training. Music is an integral part of a class, for the ear is being trained as much as the muscles. Live music is preferable, but if records are used they should be of good quality, and time should not be wasted operating the record player. Appropriately dressed and neatly groomed students are often indicative of caring on the part of the teacher. Regular attendance should be encouraged and promptness required.

Since it is not desirable to change teachers often during the period when a child is getting the extremely important fundamentals, care should be taken in the selection of a teacher. Observing a class, talking to the teacher, and talking to others who have studied at the school or who have children enrolled—all are good ways to get the "feel" of a teacher and school. The time put into making a good choice will be repaid by the rewards.

WHAT TO READ

DeMille, Agnes. *To a Young Dancer.* Boston: Little Brown, 1962.

Glen, Edwina Hazard. *The Wonderful New Book of Ballet.* Chicago: Rand McNally, 1962.

Gray, Felicity. *The Children's Picture Book of Ballet.* New York: Pitman, 1955.

Harris, Lewis. *The Russian Ballet School.* New York: Atheneum, 1970.

Isadora, Rachel. *Max.* New York: Macmillan, 1976.

Krementz, Jill. *A Very Young Dancer.* New York: Knopf, 1977.

Streatfield, Noel. *A Young Person's Guide to Ballet.* New York: Frederick Warne, 1975.

General books containing many photographs on ballet and particular companies are excellent for children. Most technique books are not, for children learn better directly from their teacher and might find books on the subject confusing.

WHERE TO STUDY

The following list is a selection of schools around the United States, giving the main methods that have influenced the teaching staff. (If nothing is mentioned, the method is assumed to be "American.")

II. Dance and You: A Guide to Classes

Alabama
Ballet UAB
1000 South 12 Street
Birmingham, Ala. 35205
(205) 934-5744
(Russian)

Arizona
Phoenix School of Ballet
4530 North 7 Street
Phoenix, Ariz. 85014
(602) 279-0777

Arizona Academy of Dance
95 East Southern Street
Tempe, Ariz. 85281
(602) 966-9751
(R.A.D.)

California
Ballet Petit
457 Foothill Boulevard
La Canada, Calif. 91011
(213) 790-5321

Lila Zali Ballet Center
1863 South Coast Highway
Laguna Beach, Calif. 92651
(714) 494-7271

Pacific Dance Center
514 High Street
Palo Alto, Calif.
(415) 323-2623

Le Mone Ballet Center
25 South Sierra Madre Boulevard
Pasadena, Calif. 91107
(213) 792-0873

Crockett Dance Studio
3839 H Street
Sacramento, Calif. 95816
(916) 452-1436

Marguerite Phares School of Dance
4430 Marconi Avenue
Sacramento, Calif. 95821
(916) 482-0278

Dance Spectrum Center
3221 22 Street
San Francisco, Calif. 94110
(415) 824-5044

Pacific Ballet Center
1519 Mission
San Francisco, Calif. 94103
(415) 626-1351

San Francisco Ballet School
378 18 Avenue
San Francisco, Calif. 94121
(415) 751-2141

Peninsula Ballet Theatre School
333 South B Street
San Mateo, Calif. 94401
(415) 343-8485

Colorado
Colorado Ballet Center
5305 East Colfax Avenue
Denver, Colo. 80220
(303) 377-8086

Connecticut
Hartford Ballet School
308 Farmington Avenue
Hartford, Conn. 06105
(203) 525-9396

Delaware
Academy of the Dance
209 West 14 Street
Wilmington, Del. 19801
(302) 656-8969

Florida
Martha Mahr School of Ballet
137 Giralda Avenue
Coral Gables, Fla. 33134
(305) 446-5238

Joni Messler School of Dance
1501 N.W. 16 Avenue
Gainesville, Fla. 32605
(904) 372-9898

Pofahl Studios
1325 N.W. 2 Street
Gainesville, Fla. 32601
(904) 373-1772

Royal School of Dance
717 West Smith Street
Orlando, Fla. 32804
(305) GA 2-2603

Miami Conservatory
5818 S.W. 73 Street
South Miami, Fla. 33143
(305) 667-5543
(Russian)

Georgia
Atlanta School of Ballet
3215 Cains Hills Place, NW
Atlanta, Ga. 30305
(404) 237-7872

Augusta Civic Ballet School
2941 Walton Way
Augusta, Ga. 30904
(404) 733-5511

Marietta School of Ballet
322 Cherokee Street
Marietta, Ga. 31201
(404) 428-6356

Illinois
Ellis-DuBoulay School of Ballet
17 North State Street
Chicago, Ill. 60602
(312) 236-4456

Stone-Camryn School of Ballet
185 West Madison Street
Chicago, Ill. 60602
(312) 332-8244

DuPage Dance Academy
124½ West Park Avenue
Elmhurst, Ill. 60126
(312)279-1445

Kansas
School of Dance Arts
1310 Hubbard Street
Great Bend, Kans. 67530
(316) 793-7110
(Soviet)

Barbara's Conservatory of Dance
2410 Huntoon Avenue
Topeka, Kans. 66604
(913) 357-7670

Topeka Ballet
315 West 4 Street
Topeka, Kans. 66603
(913) 232-5281

Dance Foundation of Kansas
211 North Broadway
Wichita, Kans. 67218
(316) 267-3701

Kentucky
Academy of the Louisville Ballet
200 East Oak Street
Louisville, Ky. 40203
(502) 637-3316

Louisiana
Giacobbe Academy of Dance
6925 Veterans Boulevard
Metairie, La. 70001
(504) 889-0940

Leclercq Ecole de Ballet
3211 Taft Park
Metairie, La. 70002
(504) 855-2352

Maryland
Maryland Ballet Center
2510 St. Paul Street
Baltimore, Md. 21218
(301) 366-5800
(R.A.D.)

Wally Saunders Dance Studio
5910 Reistertown Road
Baltimore, Md. 21215
(301) 764-9566

Maryland School of the Ballet
4923 St. Elmo Avenue
Bethesda, Md. 20014
(301) 657-4253

Metropolitan Academy of Ballet
4836 Rugby Avenue
Bethesda, Md. 20014
(301) 654-2233

Prochotsky Ballet Center
7939 Norfolk Avenue
Bethesda, Md. 20014
(301) 654-1121
(Soviet)

Bolshoi Ballet School
4609 Willow Lane
Chevy Chase, Md. 20015
(301) 652-3336
(Soviet)

Massachusetts
Boston School of Ballet
19 Clarendon Street
Boston, Mass. 02116
(617) 338-8034

Cambridge School of the Ballet
15 J. R. Sellers Street
Cambridge, Mass. 02139
(617) 864-1557

Berkshire Ballet School Cantarella
210 Wendell Avenue
Pittsfield, Mass. 01201
(413) 442-1307
(Cecchetti)

Michigan
Severo School of Ballet
1610 South Woodward
Birmingham, Mich. 48011
(313) 642-8141

Marjorie Hassard School of Ballet
13015 West 7 Mile Road
Detroit, Mich. 48235
(313) 861-2824

Evelyn Dreason Dance Studio
31315 West 13 Mile Road
Farmington Hills, Mich. 48018
(313) 626-1893

Rose Marie Floyd Studio of Ballet
939 North Main Street
Royal Oak, Mich. 48067
(313) LI 7-5319

Doris Marsh—
School of Classical Ballet
6410 Normandy Avenue
Saginaw, Mich. 480603
(517) 792-1400
(Cecchetti)

Mississippi
The Jackson Ballet
Mississippi Arts Center
Pascagoula Street
P.O. Box 1787
Jackson, Miss. 39205
(601) 948-5768

Missouri
Alexandra School of Ballet
68 East Four Seasons Plaza
Chesterfield, Mo. 63017
(314) 469-6222

Westport Ballet
300 Westport Road
Kansas City, Mo. 64111
(816) 531-4330

Ballet Arts Academy
7620 Wydown Boulevard
St. Louis, Mo. 63105
(314) 727-1705

Nathalie Le Vine Academy of Ballet
11607 Olive Boulevard
St. Louis, Mo. 63141
(314) 872-7165

Nebraska
Omaha Academy of Ballet
3915 Cuming Street
Omaha, Neb. 68131
(402) 555-8130
(R.A.D.)

Omaha Ballet
5915 Maple Street
Omaha, Neb. 68104
(402) 551-7968
(Cecchetti)

New Jersey
Monmouth School of Ballet
772 River Road
Fair Haven, N.J. 07701
(201) 842-8404
(R.A.D.)

Verne Fowler School of Dance
173 Essex Avenue
Metuchen, N.J. 08840
(201) 549-4584

School of the Garden State Ballet
45 Academy Street
Newark, N.J. 07102
(201) 623-1033
(Soviet)

Helena Baron School of Ballet
757 Buchanan Court
Paramus, N.J. 07652
(201) 445-6795

New Jersey School of Ballet
270 Pleasant Valley Way
West Orange, N.J. 07052
(201) 736-5940

New York
Roberson School of Ballet
30 Front Street
Binghamton, N.Y. 13905
(607) 772-0660
(Soviet)

André Eglevsky School of Ballet
20 Unqua Road
Massapequa Park, N.Y. 11762
(516) 541-2714
(Russian)

Enid Knapp Botsford School of
Dance, Inc.
3646 East Avenue
Rochester, N.Y. 14618
(716) 586-4605
(Soviet)

New York City

(There are too many good schools in
New York City to list them all. The list
is therefore limited to the schools of
the three major companies. For the

many other schools, see the ads in *Dance Magazine.* A recent publication may also be of help in locating ballet and other schools: O'Reilly, Barbi Leifert. *Manhattan Dance School Directory.* New York: Dekker, 1978.)

American Ballet Center (Joffrey)
434 Avenue of the Americas
New York, N.Y. 10011
(212) 254-8520

American Ballet Theatre School
3 West 61 Street
New York, N.Y. 10023
(212) 586-3355

School of American Ballet (New York City Ballet)
144 West 66 Street
New York, N.Y. 10023
(212) 877-0600

North Carolina
Bounds Dance Studio
121 South Estes Drive
Chapel Hill, N.C. 27514
(919) 942-1088

Academy of Dance Arts
105 South Hawthorne Road
Winston-Salem, N.C. 27103
(919) 724-9041

Ohio
School of Cleveland Ballet
1375 Euclid Avenue
Cleveland, Ohio 44115
(216) 621-3633

Schwarz School of the Dance
140 North Main Street
Dayton, Ohio 45402
(513) 223-1542
(Russian)

Oklahoma
Academy of Ballet
3000 Pershing Boulevard
Fair Park
Oklahoma City, Okla. 73107
(405) 946-5566
(Russian)

June Runyon School of Ballet
9525 East 47 Place
Tulsa, Okla. 74135
(918) 622-6852

Tulsa School of Ballet
3315 East 33 Street
Tulsa, Okla. 74135
(918) 742-5425
(Russian)

Pennsylvania
Marcia Weary/
Central Pennsylvania Youth Ballet
925 West Louther Street
Carlisle, Pa. 17013
(717) 249-3959

Pennsylvania Academy of Ballet
131 North Narberth Avenue
Narberth, Pa. 19072

30 West Baltimore Avenue
Media, Pa. 19063
(215) 664-3455
(Soviet)

Pennsylvania Ballet School
2333 Fairmount Avenue
Philadelphia, Pa. 19130
(215) 978-1427

Rhode Island
Barrington Ballet Studio
303 Sowams Road
Barrington, R.I. 02806
(401) 245-6117
(Russian)

Braecrest School of Ballet
Sherman Avenue
P.O. Box 155
Lincoln, R.I. 02865
(401) 723-9391
(Russian)

The Dance Academy
5 Hennessey Avenue
North Providence, R.I. 02911
(401) 353-6320
(Soviet)

Myles Marsden Studio
730 Warwick Avenue
Warwick, R.I. 02888
(401) 781-5922
(Russian)

South Dakota
Judith Szakats Ballet Studio
226 South Main Avenue
Sioux Falls, S.D. 57102
(605) 336-7370

Tennessee
Bristol School of Ballet
628 Cumberland Street
Bristol, Tenn. 24201
(703) 669-6051

Texas
Austin Academy of Ballet
3810 Speedway Street
Austin, Tex. 78751
(512) 454-0625

Dallas Ballet Academy
3601 Rawlins Street
Dallas, Tex. 75219
(214) 526-1370

Dallas Metropolitan Ballet School
6815 Hillcrest Avenue
Dallas, Tex. 75205
(214) 361-0278

Nathalie Krassovska School
of Classical Ballet
5731 Richmond Avenue
Dallas, Tex. 75206
(214) 821-4160
(Russian)

Schaffenburg Ballet Academy
2968 Park Hill
Fort Worth, Tex. 76109
(817) 927-5469

Houston Ballet Academy
2615 Colquitt Avenue
Houston, Tex. 77098
(713) 524-9417

Houston Dance Center
2018 West Gray Avenue
Houston, Tex. 77019
(713) 522-1903

Wichita Falls Ballet Theatre
2009 Huff Avenue
Wichita Falls, Tex. 76301
(817) 322-6675

Utah
Ballet West
P.O. Box 11336
Salt Lake City, Utah 84147
(801) 364-4343

Virginia
Academy of the Tidewater Ballet, Inc.
3222 Tidewater Drive
Norfolk, Va. 23509
(804) 622-4822

Academy of the
Virginia Beach Ballet
620 Village Drive
Virginia Beach, Va. 23458
(804) 425-0994

Washington
Academy of the Classic Ballet
4144½ University Way, NE
Seattle, Wash. 98105
(206) 634-1463

Seattle Dance Center
2320 First Avenue
Seattle, Wash. 98121
(206) 624-7702

Washington, D.C.
Washington School of Ballet
3515 Wisconsin Avenue NW
Washington, D.C. 20016
(202) EM 2-4462

West Virginia
Dance Theatre School
403 City Avenue
Beckley, W.Va. 25801
(304) 253-9111

American Academy Ballet
213 Knight Building
901 Quarrier Street
Charleston, W.Va. 25301
(304) 342-6541
(Cecchetti)

Wisconsin
Milwaukee Ballet School
536 West Wisconsin Avenue
Milwaukee, Wis. 53203
(414) 276-2566

Wyoming
Rehearsal S/D
3540 East 18 Street
Casper, Wyo. 82601
(307) 265-8499
(Cecchetti)

For additional listing of schools in the
United States, see *Dance Magazine
Annual.*

*Above: Children's ballet class at The New Ballet School,
New York. Pages 130-31:* Passé *(or* retiré *), contrasting
the pulled-up carriage of the classical ballet technique
with the off-centered weight often seen in modern* *dance. Pages 132-33: Side extension. Modern dance
(Humphrey technique) and ballet* (relevé à la seconde). *Pages 134-35: Arabesque. Ballet (left) and modern
dance.*

MODERN DANCE
by Dawn Lille Horwitz

Modern dance, sometimes called American dance or contemporary dance, is, to a large degree, the child of twentieth-century America. Isadora Duncan, its spiritual inspiration, stated that she could not, even in her wildest imagination, envision the goddess of liberty dancing in pointe shoes. In this spirit, modern dance began by rebelling not only against footwear and confining costumes but against the artificiality of classical ballet. Modern dance, as it developed during the late 1920s in the United States, stressed movement itself as the basic experience. Since each individual's movement could only come out of his own body and mind, this new form of dance often represented the personal and emotional experiences of its creators.

Technically it involved a greater use of the torso on a horizontal rather than a vertical plane, and new varieties of tilting, twisting, and bending movements. The legs were sometimes rotated outward, as in ballet, sometimes not. The feet could be pointed or flexed. Movement was not necessarily light, upward, beautiful, and effortless, as in ballet, but was instead strong, downward, and sometimes even ugly as the effort involved in producing it was revealed. Whereas traditional ballet stressed the beauty and ethereal qualities of the human situation, the pioneers of modern dance felt that the time had come to portray the human situation as it really was. Another area where modern dance differed radically from ballet was in the use of the floor. One not only sat or lay on it while warming up the body but incorporated it into many movements of a dance.

Contrary to the beliefs of those who feel that modern dance is purely "interpretive"—with everyone becoming a raindrop or a butterfly—there is a technical approach to training the modern dancer. However, because this art form was developed by several dancer/choreographers, there exist today several modern dance "techniques." The major ones are discussed briefly below. It should be remembered that the ultimate goal of each technique is to develop an instrument (the human body) that is capable of expressing any and all aspects of human behavior.

WHAT TO READ

Anderson, Jack. *Dance.* New York: Newsweek, 1974.

Cohen, Selma Jeanne. *The Modern Dance: Seven Statements of Belief.* 1966. Paperback, Middletown, Conn.: Wesleyan University, 1969.

Lloyd, Margaret. *The Borzoi Book of Modern Dance.* 1949. Paperback, New York: Dance Horizons, 1970.

Martin, John. *Introduction to the Dance.* 1939. Paperback, New York: Dance Horizons, 1965.

Graham Technique

Martha Graham once said that she did not set out to destroy ballet—she just went her own way! The technique that has evolved from her exploration emphasizes an inner state and often moves inward or toward the center of the body. There is great intensity in the short, broken, often percussive and angular movements. To many, the terms "contraction" and "release" are synonymous with the Graham technique. A contraction, which is usually initiated in the pelvis, involves exhaling the breath and making the entire torso concave. A release calls for inhaling and lengthening the torso.

Classes in the Graham technique begin with the students seated on the floor, going through a prescribed set of warm-ups which incorporate the contraction and release. The class then stands, begins pliés (bendings of the knees), and gradually progresses to combinations which move through space. This technique follows a set pattern, and the same basic combinations are repeated in each class, increasing in length and complexity as the student becomes more proficient.

The famous Graham "falls" are really a means of moving from an upright position to a lying position on the floor. They can be done at any speed; a beginners class might do a fall in eight counts and the advanced in one. The Martha Graham Center of Contemporary Dance in

Above: Modern Dance. Graham technique. Standing contraction. Opposite: Graham technique. Floor warm-up contraction (inset); floor warm-up release.

Modern Dance. Graham technique. Back fall.

New York City considers itself the only bona fide, accredited school teaching the Graham technique.

WHAT TO READ

Graham, Martha. *The Notebooks of Martha Graham.* New York: Harcourt Brace Jovanovich, 1973.
McDonagh, Don. *Martha Graham.* 1973. Paperback, New York: New American Library, Mentor, 1973.

Humphrey-Weidman Technique

Since the Humphrey-Weidman technique originated with two individuals, Doris Humphrey and Charles Weidman, it has often been difficult to pinpoint which aspect of it originated with whom. When questioned before his death, Charles Weidman said he himself could not always ascertain what was pure Humphrey and what was pure Weidman, but he did feel he had added to a great many of Humphrey's movements in an attempt to make the technique stronger and more masculine.

Doris Humphrey wanted to discover how the human body moved when it was in a "natural" state. From her observations of natural equilibrium, she developed a dance technique based on the body's "fall and recovery." The further a person leans from a balanced, centered position, the more likely he is to "fall." Once he regains his balance, he has "recovered" from the danger of falling. In Humphrey's view, all movement lies somewhere between these two extremes, along what she called "the arc between two deaths." Her essentially lyrical technique stresses outward movements that defy gravity and are resolved whenever the body returns to a balanced position. She emphasized the breath as the controlling force behind changes of weight and movement.

A Humphrey-Weidman class begins with the students standing, bouncing their torsos as if testing gravity, and moves on to circular swinging movements of the limbs and the entire body and more percussive movements that seem to bounce or rebound off space. The stretches on the floor also incorporate circular movements, as do the exercises at the barre. Falls to the floor are spiral in shape, both going down and coming up.

WHAT TO READ

Cohen, Selma Jeanne. *Doris Humphrey: An Artist First.* 1972. Paperback, Middletown, Conn., Wesleyan University, 1977.
Humphrey, Doris. *The Art of Making Dances.* 1959. Paperback, New York: Grove, Evergreen, 1962.
Stodelle, Ernestine. *The Dance Technique of Doris Humphrey.* Princeton, N.J.: Princeton Book Co., 1978.

Limón Technique

Since José Limón was trained by and danced with Humphrey and Weidman, it is not surprising that the Limón technique was greatly influenced by them. To the Humphrey-Weidman technique Limón added his own accents and rhythms, many of which derived from his Mexican-American background, and tense, sometimes angular movements. If Weidman added a masculine touch to Doris Humphrey's technique, Limón made their approach to movement even more masculine and strong.

The format of a Limón class is based on that of a Humphrey-Weidman class. The students begin standing, with swings and natural bounces, then go on to sitting stretches and barre work, before ending with longer combinations across the floor. Although Limón technique is often lyrical, it also contains much of the dynamic strength that Limón displayed as a performer.

Cunningham Technique

Although Merce Cunningham studied ballet and danced with Martha Graham, his technique differs from both

Modern Dance. Humphrey technique. Half fall.

Opposite: Modern Dance. Side hip thrust (used in several techniques).

radically but incorporates elements of each. It is strong, balanced, and rhythmic, requiring the dancers to make quick shifts of weight and frequent, fast changes of direction and focus as they move in floor patterns that cover a wide area of space. His primary concern is the constant interplay between time and space, and the infinite combinations and possibilities that result.

Classes begin in the center of the floor with torso warm-ups that gradually spread to include every part of the body and culminate in falls to the floor. Both his warm-ups and his traveling combinations train the body, especially the torso, to move in isolated sequences, with one part following the other.

WHAT TO READ

Klosty, James, ed. *Merce Cunningham.* New York: Saturday Review-Dutton, 1975.
"Time to Walk in Space." *Dance Perspectives* 34, 1968.

Hawkins Technique

Many have described Erick Hawkins's choreography and technique as "sculptural" and others have compared his stillness and minimal movement to the dance forms of the East. What follows is his own description of his teaching philosophy:

"An individual's name attached to a technique is a misnomer. By definition, Hawkins technique implies incompleteness, limitation and eccentricity. . . . There is only one thing to be known if one is searching for the bedrock of knowledge. That is what can be known by all knowers and therefore has some universal validity. This is something that we call scientific. This aspect of knowledge needs to make the distinction . . . between 'First Order Fact' and 'Second Order Fact.' A first order fact is something that one cannot have an opinion about, such as that men and women are physiologically different. A second order fact is something that can be argued, such as whether men are better than women. . . .

"The first requirement of a correct dance training is to train the novice only in the brightest, ascertainable, correct laws of moving according to scientific principles —that is, according to nature. On this first level of the dance art there can be little room for personal interpretation. In my teaching on the first level my goal is to teach a novice only what is scientifically true and can be proven. I am working toward a general theory of modern dance—of dance.

"Then we come to the use of the correctly trained body, to what movements you do, what spiritual ideas you have, what psychological goals you have, what aesthetic visions you have for works of art in dance. These questions are in the area of second order facts. One therefore has choice

and inevitably must choose what one does. In technical training of dancers in a school there arise questions of philosophic aims in the very kinds of movements one thinks valuable to teach and learn. At this point I choose to make dance movements that in no way, if possible, contradict any of the spiritual wisdom I have been able to learn from any other being. That is why, after my early training in classical ballet, I knew that . . . if I wanted to find my own life and not live it through older forms . . . I would have to find what I thought about the world and not shape my art about what others thought or follow their patterns."

Horton Technique

The following description of the technique of Lester Horton was written by James Truitte, principal dancer, teacher, and choreographer with the Lester Horton Dance Theater and presently teaching in the Dance Division, University of Cincinnati College-Conservatory of Music:

"The classroom objectives stressed in the Horton technique are: competence in movement, use of communicative possibilities in dance, correctness of posture and performance. Technical competence is based upon a wide tempo range, strength, endurance and the flexibility associated with a developed sense of movement design.

"The most outstanding and unique aspect of the Horton technique is that it does not label a dancer with a discernible style. A dancer trained in the Horton technique could not be picked out of a group from the manner in which he or she moved. Horton maintained the creativity and individuality of each dancer in his company. He did not want to stamp his personal style on his dancers, but instead he wanted them to creatively develop within his technique.

Opposite: Modern Dance. Stag leap. Top right: Transitional movement (preparing for lunge).

"Another facet of the technique is its objectivity and logical approach. It probes the anatomy deeply to get beyond physical limitations—fortifying, stretching, strengthening and developing the body. It works from the joint outwards, and every muscle is stretched and used. It uses all possible planes and levels of movement, all aspects of tempo range, rhythmical patterns and accents, and produces a variety of emotions. Another feature of the technique is that it produces long thigh muscles and flexible, but strong lower backs.

"Many of the Horton studies are called fortifications. The body is fortified and developed to move as a well trained instrument, ever responsive to different techniques and choreographers. In addition to the fortifications such as stretch, resiliency, endurance, suppleness and isolations, classes include studies based on locomotive actions, rhythms, qualities of movement based on dramatic sources, and improvisations on the above."

WHAT TO READ

Warren, Larry, et al. "The Dance Theater of Lester Horton." *Dance Perspectives* 31, 1967.

Warren, Larry. *Lester Horton: Modern Dance Pioneer.* New York: Dekker, 1977.

Louis-Nikolais Technique

Alwin Nikolais began his career as a musician and puppeteer. He studied dance with Hanya Holm and Truda Kaschman, both of whom have a background in German modern dance technique, and with Weidman, Humphrey, and Graham. He creates as a choreographer/musician/designer.

Students who work with him or study in his school learn to approach the stage much as a painter or sculptor would, seeing the human form as merely another shape or object in space, and learning to experiment or improvise with it.

Murray Louis was trained mostly by Nikolais. Students who have studied under Louis report an emphasis on exploring every part of the body and its possibilities, with a stress on isolated movement in each limb. Technique classes at the Louis-Nikolais studio begin with a series of stretches which explore and expand the range of the body. Classes in improvisation are also offered.

WHAT TO READ

"Nik." *Dance Perspectives* 48, 1971.

WHAT TO WEAR

The most important aspect of modern dancers' clothing is the lack of any foot covering—they dance barefoot. Women wear leotards and tights without feet, men the same or else T-shirts and tights (plus a dance belt). In recent years modern dancers have started wearing the same woolen or acrylic "warm-ups" on their legs, ankles, or torsos as their ballet counterparts.

WHERE TO STUDY

The cursory listing of modern dance teachers and centers given below is meant merely as an indication that classes are available throughout the United States. A teacher's training, if it has been mainly in one technique, is indicated. However, it must be remembered that modern dancers, much more than ballet dancers, although influenced by their own training, often teach a blend of several techniques. Hence the term "eclectic" in many instances.

A more detailed listing of modern dance classes in New York City can be found in the following book:

O'Reilly, Barbi Liefert. *Manhattan Dance School Directory.* New York: Dekker, 1978.

Left: Modern Dance. Angular dramatic pose with parallel feet (compare foot positions on page 119). Opposite: Attitude (compare positions on page 123).

II. Dance and You: A Guide to Classes

Arizona
Profile for Dance
23 South Morris Avenue
Mesa, Ariz. 85202
(602) 834-3131
(Eclectic)

California
Bella Lewitzky
3594 Multiview Drive
Los Angeles, Calif. 90068
(213) 766-1058
(Lewitzky)

Margaret Jenkins Dance Studio
1590 15 Street
San Francisco, Calif. 94103
(415) 863-7580
(Cunningham)

San Francisco Ballet School
378 18 Avenue
San Francisco, Calif. 94121
(415) 751-2141
(Limón)

Xoregos Performing Company
70 Union Street
San Francisco, Calif. 94111
(415) 989-3167
(Eclectic)

Colorado
Munt-Brooks Dance Studio
1527½ Champa Street
Denver, Colo. 80202
(303) 893-5775
(Their own, influenced by Holm, Weidman, and Graham)

Connecticut
The Ernestine Stodelle
Studios of Dance, Inc.
855 North Brooksvale Road
Cheshire, Conn. 06410
(203) 272-9377
(Humphrey)

Hartford Conservatory
834-846 Asylum Avenue
Hartford, Conn. 06105
(203) 523-9068
(Eclectic)

Delaware
Dolores Pye Josey
1402 Drake Road, Green Acres
Wilmington, Del. 19803
(302) 478-6796
(Eclectic)

District of Columbia
Dance Project, Inc.
2445 18 Street NW
Washington, D.C. 20009
(202) 462-1321
(Eclectic)

The Dance Exchange
1443-45 Rhode Island Avenue
Washington, D.C. 20005
(202) 797-7029
(Eclectic)

Washington Dance Center
4321 Wisconsin Avenue, NW
Washington, D.C. 20016
(202) 686-9847
(Eclectic)

Florida
Fusion Dance Company
4542 SW 75 Avenue
Miami, Fla. 33155
(305) 264-0661
(Eclectic)

Georgia
Atlanta School of Ballet
3215 Cains Hill Place NW
Atlanta, Ga. 30305
(404) 237-7872
(Horton)

Iowa
Dieman-Bennett Dance Theatre
of the Hemispheres
117 Third Avenue, SE
Cedar Rapids, Iowa 52401
(319) 362-0529
(Eclectic)

Kansas
Lawrence Arts Center
3412 West Ninth Court
Lawrence, Kans. 66044
(913) 843-5532
(Eclectic; Improvisation)

Michigan
Newman Dance Theater
1475 Lake Lansing Road
Lansing, Mich. 48912
(517) 482-1597
(Eclectic)

Mississippi
The Jackson Ballet
Mississippi Arts Center
Pascagoula Street

Jackson, Miss. 39205
(601) 948-5768

New Mexico
Eleanor King
865 Don Diego Avenue
Santa Fe, N. Mex. 87501
(505) 988-1924
(Humphrey-Weidman)

New Jersey
Carol Payne Fisch
Whole Theatre Company
188 Union Street
Montclair, N.J. 07042
(201) 744-0180
(Graham)

School of the Garden State Ballet
45 Academy Street
Newark, N.J. 07102
(201) 623-1033
(Eclectic)

Maureen Deakin Modern Dance Studio
10 Broad Street
Red Bank, N.J. 07701
(201) 291-2228
(Eclectic)

New York
Alvin Ailey American Dance Center
Minskoff Theater Building
1515 Broadway
New York, N.Y. 10036
(212) 832-7250
(Eclectic)

Clark Center for the Performing Arts
939 Eighth Avenue
New York, N.Y. 10019
(212) 246-4818
(Eclectic)

Merce Cunningham
463 West Street
New York, N.Y. 10014
(212) 691-9751
(Cunningham)

Viola Farber
1841 Broadway
New York, N.Y. 10023
(212) 757-0410
(Farber)

Martha Graham School
of Contemporary Dance

316 East 63 Street
New York, N.Y. 10021
(212) 838-5886
(Graham)

Erick Hawkins School of Dance
78 Fifth Avenue
New York, N.Y. 10011
(212) 255-6698
(Hawkins)

Louis-Nikolais Dance Theatre Lab
33 East 18 Street
New York, N.Y. 10003
(212) 777-1120
(Louis-Nikolais)

New Dance Group Studio
254 West 47 Street
New York, N.Y. 10036
(212)245-9327
(Eclectic)

May O'Donnell
439 Lafayette Street
New York, N.Y. 10003
(212) 777-0744
(O'Donnell)

Ohio
James Truitte
University of Cincinnati
 College-Conservatory of Music
Cincinnati, Ohio 15221
(Horton)

Schwarz School of the Dance
140 North Main Street
Dayton, Ohio 45402

(513) 223-1542
(Eclectic)

Cleveland Modern Dance Association
3756 Lee Road
Shaker Heights, Ohio 44128
(216) 283-5335
(Eclectic)

Pennsylvania
Philadelphia College
 of the Performing Arts
313 South Broad Street
Philadelphia, Pa. 19107
(215) 732-1038
(Eclectic)

Rhode Island
Dance Collective
266 Weyhosset
Providence, R.I. 02903
(401) 421-1858
(Eclectic)

Texas
Jerry Bywaters Cochran
3541 Villanova Street
Dallas, Tex. 75225
(214) 361-5360
*(Eclectic, although
 Graham influenced)*

Houston Dance Center
2018 West Gray Street
Houston, Tex. 77019
(713) 522-1903
(Hawkins)

Utah
Ririe-Woodbury Dance Company
P.O. Box 11566
Salt Lake City, Utah 84147
(801) 328-1062
(Eclectic)

Washington
Dance Theatre Seattle—School of the
 Bill Evans Dance Co.
704 19 Avenue East
Seattle, Wash. 98112
(206) 322-3733
(Bill Evans technique)

Martha Nishitani Modern Dance School
4205 University Way NE
Seattle, Wash. 98105
(206) 633-2456
(Eclectic)

West Virginia
Vicki Dils Modern Dance
P.O. Box 1712
Parkersburg, W.Va. 26101
(304) 295-4302
(Eclectic)

Wyoming
Dancers Workshop of Jackson Hole
 at the Center
145 North Cache
Box 218
Wilson, Wyo. 83014
(307) 733-3426
(Eclectic; A dance co-operative)

Modern dance class taught by Kazuko Hirabayashi at The Juilliard School, New York.

ETHNIC DANCE
By Matteo

In contrast to the popular terms such as ballet, modern, jazz, and tap, the term "ethnic" (multi-racial) dance has come into use only within the past thirty years. In spite of its fairly recent emergence, this term, in a universal sense, represents the oldest forms of dance in the world. The ramifications of its use are many, causing scholars, performing artists, and dance enthusiasts considerable dispute. On the one hand, it can be argued that the sophisticated traditional theater dances which have stood the test of time are the truly ethnic dances; another viewpoint, however, holds that any and all indigenous folk dances of the world (from which many of the classical forms have evolved) are also members of the ethnic dance family. Such folk dances are the treasures which comprise the dance culture of a country, often having their origins in rituals or celebrations of planting, harvesting, weddings, funerals, recreation, and occupations; as such, they unerringly reflect the "ethnos" (national character) of their people. They are also conditioned by the climate of a country, the clothing and type of footgear worn, the type of ground or floor performed on, religious beliefs, and indigenous racial characteristics.

Now that ethnic dance is coming into its own, serious consideration and respect for it and long overdue recognition in this country were given even further impetus by America's Bicentennial celebration, which stimulated a sense of ethnic heritage and racial identity by harking back to ancestral roots.

Spanish Dance

Among the most popular and widely taught forms of ethnic dance to have graced the concert stages and nightclub floors of the United States for the past fifty years are those of Spain. Like the language, Iberian in origin, Spanish dance has undergone many changes in many locales. Unfortunately, the popularity of flamenco has resulted in the overshadowing of other Spanish dance styles. But in fact, the dance heritage of Spain is so rich that four schools exist, each unique: the classical, regional, flamenco, and neoclassic-contemporary theater forms.

Classical

Danced in eighteenth-century (or earlier) costume to music of the period such as the *bolero, panaderos,* or *seguidillas manchegas,* this type of dance is seldom seen today. It is performed in *zapatillas* (balletlike slippers) and reflects the aristocratic and patrician society of that time. It is virtuosic, demanding the same training, skill, agility, and management of the body as classical ballet, and uses many of the same glissades, entrechats, brisés

volés, sissones, pirouettes, and leaps; the performer simultaneously plays the castanets, the mastery of which is a full course of study in itself.

Regional

There is an infinite variety of regional or folk dances in Spain, of which only a small portion have ever been seen by the general public. Many of these dances, stemming from Greek, Phoenician, Celtic, and Moorish origins, employ strange steps, patterns, and props, such as wooden shoes, water pitchers, flower arches, maypoles, stilts, swords, kerchiefs, etc., none of which are generally thought of as being Spanish. The accompanying instruments range from bagpipes to fife and drum, conch shells, and many varieties of castanets—which, incidentally, are not indigenous to Spain. Even *lo mas tipico* (most typical) of regional dances, the jota, has many varieties that come from numerous sections of Spain, each one different in style and tempo. The type from the province of Valencia (known as the Orange Grove of Spain) is slow and easy, not jumped, whereas that of Aragon (the most popular) is very lively and exuberant, literally springing from the soil with challenging kicks, leaps, and turns.

Flamenco

More than just a style of dancing, flamenco embodies and reflects a way of life. Unlike other Western dance, it requires the dancer to have a thorough knowledge of many forms of *cante* (singing), upon which it is founded. Flamenco dance was born of an Oriental people; it is most likely of Hindu origin. Overexaggeration, gimmicks, and tricky steps at breakneck speed, which evoke applause and audience hysteria, do not make good flamenco dance. The true performance is the result of the mood which grips the dancer. As soon as it becomes a standardized "routine," it risks boredom. Contrary to popular belief, flamenco should not be presented as an extroverted tour de force with disheveled hair and pistol-like heel stamping. It can and should be cool, with self-contained intensity. Arms, hands, and body movements should curve and spiral, revealing the Eastern origins.

Neoclassic-Contemporary

In contrast to the guitar-accompanied flamenco style, one of the most beautiful and creative branches of Spanish dance is the form that evolved in the late 1920s. Early pioneers, such as La Argentina and Argentinita abroad and Carola Goya in America, presented numerous solo dance concerts to the piano music of Spanish composers of the day—Albéniz, Granados, Halffter, Turina, etc., in delightful and dramatic interpretations. Complete ballets or danced stories (much like those in our Broadway musicals) were popular for more than twenty-five years.

Opposite: Charles Moore.

This golden era of true Spanish concert dance was enhanced by a full range of orchestrated Iberian music. Since then, the guitar has become, for better or worse, the most ubiquitous form of accompaniment in America.

Spanish dance in its full array of styles has been dormant now for many years, but history has a way of repeating itself, and perhaps the ignorant notion that flamenco dancing *is* Spanish dancing will soon be corrected. For to believe this is to know only one-fourth the truth.

Indian Dance

The dances of India open up a world of extraordinary beauty, refinement, and expressive power. They can be divided into three groups—the tribal, the folk, and the classical; classical or theater dance as we know it today is referred to as *natya* (a Sanskrit term meaning both dance and drama). The dancer must conform to probably the most complete and exacting, if not the oldest, codified technique existing. The best known and generally accepted schools of classical dance in India are Kathakali (Katha—story; Kali—play); Dasiattam (Dasi—servant; Attam—dance), known as Bharata Natyam, the style most generally seen and studied in this country; Kathak (Kattika—storyteller); and Manipuri. Several other traditional classical styles of more recent appearance in this country should not be overlooked, such as Kuchipudi, Orissi, Chhau, Yaksha Gana, and others.

The various dance styles in India are in essence the art forms of its many religions, and to the serious, disciplined student, the dance is a religion. Infinitely more demanding than any Western form, it requires the student to study and master minutely detailed movements of the body, limbs, and head. There are thirty-four *hasta mudras*

Matteo teaching Sanskrit to class in Bharata Natyam, Jacob's Pillow, Lee, Mass.

(single hand positions) and even more double ones, nine *pranas* ("lives of the hands" or movement qualities), ten movements of the waist, five of the chest, seventeen arm positions, eight shoulder movements, seven foot positions on the ground, twenty-four leg movements, twenty-one manners of walking, twenty-four types of turns, nine leaps. Movements for the eyes must be scored or choreographed, as nothing is left to chance—there are six positions for the eyelids, seven for the eyebrows, thirteen for the mouth, eight kinds of looks, and thirty-five glances. This highly sophisticated and codified technique of dramaturgy is found in all classic forms.

Kathakali

The dance-drama par excellence of Kerala is exclusively performed by males, whose training over a period of five to seven years begins each day before dawn with excruciating massages and exercises. Performances, with elaborate costumes and a makeup that takes over two hours to apply, last well into the night and early morning. Generally speaking, good characters have green faces, evil have red.

Kathakali tells ancient tales in which the grand themes of battle, love, and religious fervor are portrayed by heroes, gods, and evil characters. The movements are violent and expansive, the drums piercingly shrill, rapid, and staccato in complicated rhythmic cycles. The dancers must know by heart vast amounts of Hindu mythology and be able to converse in elaborate pantomime as demons, princes, and monkeys, all through the language of *mudras*, for which there is a complete grammar. Facial muscles are so minutely controlled that a Kathakali dancer can appear to cry on one side of the face and to laugh on the other. Kathakali is meant to be presented in a grove or courtyard and not inside a theater. The audience is seated in front on a matted floor and the singers and drummers stand immediately behind the dancers. Since the play, usually a story or scene from the classics, is a nocturnal entertainment, the entire dance-drama is lighted by a four-foot-tall brass lamp, which burns coconut oil throughout the performance.

Bharata Natyam

A Bharata Natyam performance is a solo dance recital that is designed to hold the attention of an audience for two or three hours. There is hardly any decor and seldom any change of costume. Its very name represents the purest form of Indian dance tradition. "Bharata" as used in this form of dance is said to be composed of the first syllables of each of its three main elements: *bha*va (mood), *ra*ga (melody, song), and *ta*la (rhythmic timing).

"Natya" means a combination of both dancing and acting, and because gesture and facial expression are part and parcel of the whole dance, the Indian makes no differentiation between the words "actor" and "dancer."

They are, unlike those terms in our Western theater, synonymous and require the peforming artist to be an expert in both *nrtta* (pure dance movements) and *nrttya* (dramatic expression). The performer must master the extremely complex intricacies of the rhythms (which often escape the general audience). His rapport with the drummer, who must follow the dancer's ankle bells, gives the impression of two musicians playing in perfect rhythm. In addition, the singer's lyrics and the cymbal player's rhythm (*talem*) present another set of sounds, all beautifully coordinated.

Great technical brilliance can be achieved by an accomplished dancer, as her feet beat these intricate patterns, synchronized with the syllables of both drummer and singer; she employs various bends and turns of the body, graceful designs of the arms and hands while advancing and retreating, unfolding one sequence after another of pure dance. As an actress, the same performer must master the art of *abhinaya* (dramatic expression), whereby she may tell a traditional tale of Krishna or Shiva and still imbue it with new ideas and personal interpretation. The very essence of Bharata Natyam is stated in the ancient Sanskrit: "For where the hand moves, there the glances follow; where the glances go, the mind follows; where the mind goes, the mood follows; where the mood goes, there is the flavor (*rasa*)."

Manipuri

It was due to Rabindranath Tagore, poet laureate of India, that the beauty of Manipuri dance, in isolated Assam, came to light and was later accepted as one of India's major dance styles. Manipuri dance has, over the years, developed a character entirely different from any other in India. Unlike Bharata Natyam of the south, with its *ardhamandali* (demi-plié) basic posture, or the erect stance of the northern Kathak form, or the splayed knees (open second position) of the Malabar Kathakali dancer, Manipuri is based on a natural, soft, easygoing position of the feet and flowing sinuous movements of the arms and hands.

The Lai Haraoba, a dance-drama meaning "Invoking and Providing Pleasure for the Gods," is the oldest Manipuri dance form and is the basis of all Manipuri dancing. It tells of the creation of man, birth, youth, adult life, and marriage, and of the arts and learning. The *ras lila* depicting the loves and joys of Radha and Krishna, is an exciting and elaborate spectacle dear to the hearts of the people. Although its theme occurs frequently throughout all India's dance styles, the actual *ras lila* performance is rarely seen since it is only performed at a specific sacred time and season. As all Manipuri people, young and old, dance, dancing is a constant reminder of God's ways of forming their world.

The style of the dance most generally seen is very different from its sister dance styles and can best be described as a delicate swaying of the torso, with gentle footwork which barely strikes the earth. It is known for its ease, alluring grace, and limpid rhythms, and is always danced in a circular or half-circular form. Unlike Bharata Natyam and Kathak, Manipuri technique appears simple, the movements are uncomplicated and the *bols* (dance symbols) easy to learn. But, as the art lies mainly in the dancer's grace, such dancing requires intense training, immense patience, and hard work to master the subtleties of these seemingly easy movements.

Kathak

Kathak originated in the temples of Rajasthan and Uttar Pradesh as an art of storytellers called Kathaks, who with song, facial expression, and gesture language interpreted episodes from mythology. During the course of its evolution, Kathak slowly migrated from the temple to the royal court and to the theater. The dance is performed by both men and women.

The technique as seen outside India in solo concerts is one of virtuosity with emphasis on endurance and the incredible speed of the feet. In fact, many Kathak dancers claim to know over 100 *parans* (a series of immensely intricate and rhythmically complex steps). These *parans* are considered to be the most complicated rhythmic units in all Indian dance. When linked together in a system of mnemonic syllables called *bols*, they can reach astounding lengths, which, once started by the drummer, must in turn be recognized by the dancer and then performed by both musician and dancer in perfect unison. The dancer must end in a sudden, immobile pose not unlike that of flamenco. The clusters of sounds showered by Spanish castanets and the provocative movements and quick turns

Matteo teaching children The Lord's Prayer *using hand gestures* (hasta mudras) *from Bharata Natyam. Overleaf: Matteo in pose from Bharata Natyam (classical dance of South India).*

of flamenco dancers are not too far removed from their Kathak predecessors. The dancers' feet in Kathak are percussion instruments that alternately slap, tremble, and stomp, producing rhythmic pulsations in the several pounds of metal bells strung in layers about each ankle. In the basic *hastak* (pose), the right arm is extended to the side, level with the shoulder, the left hand is held high above the head, and the feet cross with the right toes placed on the floor slightly behind the left foot. The dancer keeps the rhythm by gently touching his bent index fingers to his thumbs while holding the other fingers straight.

The program begins with an invocation that first gives obeisance to the gods and then greets the audience. At North Indian courts, where the dance was patronized by Muslim rulers, this salutation was directed to the emperor and members of the court and done in a more decorative and sensuous manner.

Even though the technique (compared to the other Indian forms) seems somewhat limited and fragmentary, with its abstract use of gestures and dramatic expressions, one finds excitement in the *chakkras* (multiple rapid spins) followed by a sudden halt, and in the complexity of rhythms in rapid sequence which dancer and musician end simultaneously on the final beat, leaving an erudite audience fatigued from following them. These artistic demands are probably why Kathak dance is referred to as "mathematics made into art." Excitement transports the knowing audience, and the dancer is hypnotized by his own rhythmic variations. The general public only sees an exhibition of virtuosity, but, as in all Indian dancing, the dancer has acquired a discipline to help him seek his oneness with the rhythm of the universe.

Jean-Léon Destiné in Voodoo Dance *(Haitian).*

Black Dance

Black dance in America today is a splendid example of continuity and change in African dance, and of Afro-American adaptation. To the uninformed or casual onlooker, African dance as performed in a non-theatrical setting may look manifestly primitive and repetitious. In viewing Africa's dance, one must realize not so much how as why the black dances as he does. African dance cannot be "only entertainment." It represents social, cultural, political, and economic behavior, expressed in dramatic terms, and consists of many types and styles, depending on the part of that immense continent from which it emanates, and even more on the occasion for which it is performed. Is it in celebration of birth, death and burial, ancestor honor, possession, hunting, occupation, recreation, worship? Each dance has a heritage that reflects the ideas of its location. When a house is built, the Lobi people of Ghana dance Bobina, expressing communal love in working together. The Ashanti reenacts past military glories by performing his Fontomfrom. The Fante style performed by the Akan people of Ghana is noted for its rapid footwork, while the Ashanti employ movements of arms and hands. The Dagbani undulate the upper torso. Eastern and Western Nigeria vary, in that in the former, gentle use of the hip distinguishes it from the Ijaw's flashy footwork.

Black dance in America, although thousands of miles from its origins and altered by alien customs and traditions, retains an unmistakable African influence, particularly evident in such dances as the Turkey Trot, the Eagle Rock, and Ballin' the Jack, which had their roots in Africa. Even the popular tap dance, although originating in the Irish clog, became American when imbued with an inimitable African style. And who gave birth to American jazz? Africa's children.

After ballet, modern, and folk dance, black dance is today one of the most widely taught dance forms in colleges and universities. Its academic acceptance introduced and established the now popular term "ethnic dance" as an equal to other forms in the dance curriculum.

During the past thirty years, many scholars and performing artists have pioneered black dance in the concert field, mounting colorful authentic African spectacles and ceremonies for metropolitan audiences. Katherine Dunham received her early training in Chicago and later developed her own approach to movement, incorporating African and Caribbean influences (which she had studied both as a dancer and as a qualified anthropologist). She was a sensuous personality, with a flowing style, and a teacher for many years in New York, where her technique is still taught at the Alvin Ailey American Dance Center and at the Clark Center for the Performing Arts. Other fine performing artists such as Pearl Primus, Charles Moore, Arthur Hall, Chuck Davis,

Jean-Léon Destiné, and Alvin Ailey are today giving unstintingly of their teaching talents. The field of dance is indebted to these blacks in their efforts to rediscover the dance heritage of their fatherland and set it in theatrical terms, for in doing so America is also discovering an aspect of Africa's beauty heretofore unknown. The power of their dance cannot be overestimated.

The panorama of ethnic dance in America is a broad one. It varies from the lovingly organized non-professional performing groups which function weekly and even nightly, giving local theatrical presentations of their dances from many homelands, to the highly organized and subsidized groups such as the Tamburitzans of Duquesne University and the Brigham Young International Folk Dancers of Utah, which travel and perform abroad annually. Scattered throughout the nation are Slavic, Scottish, Latin American, Basque, Irish, Philippine, Polish, Scandinavian, Middle Eastern, Chinese, Japanese, American and East Indian ethnic groups, all of which have their own, often highly competitive, dance groups and training centers within their own and neighboring communities.

WHAT TO READ

Ivanova, Anna. *The Dance in Spain.* New York: Praeger, 1970.

La Meri. *Total Education in Ethnic Dance.* New York: Dekker, 1977.

Lawson, Joan. *European Folk Dance: Its National and Musical Characteristics.* New York: Pitman, 1972.

People's Folk Dance Directory. P.O. Box 8575, Austin, Tex. 78712. Issued weekly.

Vatsyayan, Kapila. *Indian Classical Dance.* New Delhi.

Warren, Lee. *The Dance in America.* Englewood Cliffs, N.J.: Prentice-Hall, 1972.

Zarina, Xenia. *Classic Dances of the Orient.* New York: Crown, 1967.

The Asia Society, 133 East 58 Street, New York, N.Y. 10022 (212/371-4758), should be contacted for its brochure listing excellent monographs on Asian dance.

The Foundation for Ethnic Dance, Inc., 17 West 71 Street, New York, N.Y. 10023 (212/877-9565) maintains an information and consulting service for students and professionals.

For in-depth research, The Dance Collection, Lincoln Center, New York, has an international collection of dance books, periodicals, films, photographs, and memorabilia.

WHERE TO STUDY

In spite of this nationwide mosaic of ethnic dance activities, the question of where to study does not have an easy or all-inclusive answer. There is at present no one institution that can offer various levels of training even in the major forms of ethnic dance. Many dedicated and reputable teachers are to be found in several areas of the country, mainly on the East and West coasts, such as Teodoro Morca of Bellingham, Washington; Lola Montes and Carmen Mora of Los Angeles, and Rosa Montoya and Teresita Osta of San Francisco who teach Spanish idioms; Balasaraswathi School of Music and Dance, Berkeley, California, where the classical dance of India is taught; Dieman Bennett Dance Theater of Cedar Rapids, Iowa, teaching Spanish and East Indian dance; La Meri of Hyannis, Mass., who teaches privately; Mariquita Flores and Mariano Parra of New York who also offer classes in Spanish dance; Sahomi Tachibana, Charles Moore, Ritha Devi, Taneo, Ibrahim Farrah, Renaldo Alejandro, Matteo who in respective order teach Japanese, Dunham technique, several styles of classical Indian dance, Polynesian, Middle Eastern, Philippine, and multiracial ethnic forms. Consulates of various countries are often knowledgeable and helpful in locating visitors with dance training who may be nearby and willing to teach.

An area of recent development for the serious student of ethnic dance is a degree program in dance ethnology now being offered in several larger universities, such as New York University, U.C.L.A., University of Hawaii at Manoa, Honolulu. During the summer, short courses featuring well-known visiting ethnic dance specialists, usually on a beginner's level, are taught at Jacob's Pillow, Lee, Mass., Harvard University, and The American Dance Festival at Durham, North Carolina, among others.

La Meri and Peter di Falco (Spanish).

JAZZ DANCE
By Billie Mahoney

What is it?

Jazz dance as we know it today grew out of "popular" dance and spread, in various forms, to television, nightclubs, the Broadway stage, and films. It is many things; it borrows from many styles and techniques of dance, and even the exponents of jazz dance may be hesitant to describe it. In the early 1950s, the leading teachers shied away from the term "jazz" unless they were specifically teaching those steps made popular in the ballrooms in the first half of the century. Instead, classes might be called either free-style, dance for musical comedy, Afro-Cuban, or primitive. New York jazz classes began when the dancers and choreographers actually working on Broadway and in films brought the movement into a classroom, and devised warm-up exercises and stretches to prepare the body for its specific demands. Dance wasn't really taught—the class was more of a "jam session" where the professionals got together and danced, following their "leader," and the non-pros who dared just hung in there.

Theatrical jazz dance probably started when George Balanchine choreographed "Slaughter on Tenth Avenue" for the Broadway show *On Your Toes* in 1936. He was assisted by the black tap dancer Herbie Harper, who introduced rhythm dancing to blend with the ballet. About this time, Jack Cole added jazz rhythms to East Indian dancing for his variety act, called Jack Cole and His Dancers. Many refer to Cole as the "father of jazz dance." With a background in Denishawn, he created a technique derived from Humphrey-Weidman, with innovations based on East Indian and Latin dance, all brought together with American swing music.

During the 1940s, his work in film musicals, both as performer and choreographer, was outstanding. In 1944, he organized the Dance Workshop at Columbia Studios which functioned until 1948, performing in nightclubs and theaters. The members of this dance group included Gwen Verdon, Carol Haney, Matt Mattox, Rod Alexander, Alex Romero, Buzz Miller, and George and Ethel Martin. Many of today's jazz teachers, as well as prominent performers and choreographers of the musical theater, were influenced by Cole.

The jazz craze hit New York City in the early 1950s, and there were three major forces—Gennaro, Gregory, and black dance. Peter Gennaro, who had a New Orleans and Chicago background, was dancing the "Steam Heat" number in *Pajama Game* (1952; choreography by Bob Fosse) with Jack Cole dancers Carol Haney and Buzz Miller. His style was light, quick, loose, and flexible, with articulate footwork. In a rehearsal studio, Gennaro taught classes which began with a warm-up at the barre, with pliés and various ballet-based leg exercises to the front,

side, and back, developing into a series of "jazz" movements, followed by across-the-floor combinations. Accompaniment was usually provided by a jazz pianist.

In another studio not far away, Jon Gregory was conducting stimulating and exciting classes—"just like a Broadway show." Gregory had staged a few dance sequences for film and his distinctive style of movement, dictated by his strong, six-foot-four-inch frame, had professional dancers flocking to his classes. With a limited formal dance background, Gregory did not teach a particular technique. His two-hour classes, accompanied by records of the current jazz favorites—Kenton, Dorsey, Shaw, Ellington, and some of the then not so well-known artists—began with a sort of *port de bras* (a series of arm gestures) to "Night Train," followed by a few movement transitions across the floor. In less than a quarter of an hour the class would be doing the pre-choreographed combinations that were his trademark. These included spectacular leaps and falls that burst out of unorthodox spins. The repetition of such combinations definitely developed technical strength and stamina. When an exciting recording was found, Gregory would create a new combination to the eager applause of the class, which would then be added to the class repertory. Although much of the work was sensuous and provocative, Gregory would allow little or no pelvic movements in his combinations, achieving his effects through actions of the knees. For years his personal style appeared uncredited in the popular media, and even today his work would be considered avant-garde.

During this period, Katherine Dunham and the Dunham Dancers were appearing in films and on Broadway, and her school was producing dancers and teachers who taught primitive, Afro-Cuban, Haitian, and other ethnic forms. Perhaps the best-known teacher was Syvilla Fort, who continued to be an influence for many years. She presented still a different kind of class, accompanied by one or more drummers on congo drums, bongos, and timbals. The drummers would set up a rhythm, and a step pattern was done across the floor on the diagonal, with movements isolated in various parts of the body—shoulders, hips, pelvis. The tempo would build to a near-frenzied pitch, sending the dancers into flying leaps across the room.

The events that were to formalize jazz classes occurred in 1955. Jon Gregory had left New York to become dance director at Twentieth Century-Fox and to choreograph in Las Vegas, where he still has a school, and Peter Gennaro was beginning to work with Jerome Robbins on *West Side Story*. Matt Mattox arrived in New York and started teaching the classes that, with those of Luigi, would dominate the field over the next decade. His Cole-based

Opposite: **Slaughter on Tenth Avenue (Balanchine), 1936. Tamara Geva, George Church, Ray Bolger.**

class was at the time accompanied by a bongo drummer. It started with floor stretches, then moved to center-floor isolations and on to improvised combinations. His strict and disciplined classes featured his own clean, strong technique and his sometimes percussive, sometimes fluent liquid movement.

The same year, a short-lived Broadway show had brought West-Coast dancer Eugene "Luigi" Louis to New York. Luigi had a distinctive style, emphasizing the line of the body with arms lifted, chest high, and head thrown back. (He developed this after an automobile accident had left the muscles in half of his face paralyzed.) Accompanied by a solo drummer on snare, bass drum, and cymbals, Luigi began his classes with standing center floor stretches and *port de bras* incorporating the whole body, followed by floor stretches, sitting and lying, then pliés and kick-outs. His warm-up included highly stylized, continuously flowing movements for the whole body which developed the line and style required for the combinations that followed. These ran the gamut from slow blues to lyrical to fast Latin movements. Although Ohio-born Luigi had not worked with Jack Cole, he had partnered a former Cole dancer, Nita Beber, and there were traces of Cole in his early work.

By the 1960s, *West Side Story* had made its impact throughout the country, and dance teacher conventions

Top: "Steam Heat" from The Pajama Game, *1954 (film, 1957). Bottom: Jazz Oxford.*

were hiring jazz teachers to bring the new dance to the hinterlands. The movement spread. Soon, every local dance studio, community center, Y, and weight-reducing salon had added "jazz" classes to its schedule. And in the 1970s many college dance programs added jazz dance to the curriculum, with some discretion. Many summer dance workshops take jazz as seriously as ballet and modern dance.

There are certain characteristics that distinguish jazz from other forms of dance. An earthy quality and a distinctive use of space is achieved by moving at a low level, in deep plié. Although the Afro-primitive work (sometimes used by Jack Cole) uses the flat foot, the transference of weight generally develops *through* the feet, with quick steps on the high half toe. Feet are either parallel or slightly turned-out, in a natural manner. Isolated movements in various body parts are common, such as shifts and rotations. It is rare for the torso to move in one piece. With the advent of rock-and-roll and discotheque music, progressions of movement through the body and pelvic movements have become common-place. A good jazz teacher will emphasize strength initiating from the front of the pelvis, which should be drawn in and made shallow.

Louis Horst described jazz dance as urban—the dance of the city. It has an immediacy of communication and an energy and dynamic power not common in other dance forms. Marshall McLuhan has written, "Jazz of itself tends to be a casual dialogue form of dance quite lacking in the repetitive and mechanical forms of the waltz."

Whether jazz dance is the disciplined dance of the musical theater, or the dances done by "the people" popularized in the ballrooms (Savoy, Palladium, Roseland), remains a matter of controversy. In the early days, dancers were told to "forget technique—just dance." Today the serious jazz dancer is more likely than not accomplished in ballet and modern dance, with training in tap, ethnic forms, and even acrobatics.

The American Dance Machine (4 East 75 Street, New York, N.Y. 10021; Lee Theodore, Artistic Director) was established by Lee Becker Theodore* to keep alive the outstanding choreography of the American musical theater. It presents concerts comprised of such show-stopping numbers as "Quadrille" from Michael Kidd's *Can Can* (1953) and "Rich Kid's Rag" from Bob Fosse's *Little Me* (1962). The repertory also includes dances by Danny Daniels, Agnes de Mille, Gennaro, and Carol Haney, to name only a few. To prepare young dancers to perform this choreography, the American Dance Machine Training Facility offers classes in ballet, tap, and Dunham technique, with occasional master classes by such luminaries as Gwen Verdon (one-time assistant to Jack Cole) and Peter Gennaro. The historical dances of the

---

*Lee Becker danced the role of Anybodies in *West Side Story* on Broadway and in film.

musical theater are taught in Theodore's classes, each devoted to the dances of a decade—the 20s, 30s, 40s, etc. The ballroom dances which influenced jazz dance are offered in such classes as Cuban/Latin, Swing/Jazz, and Disco/Hustle.

The Pepsi Bethel Authentic Jazz Dance Theatre (156 Fifth Ave., New York, N.Y. 10010; Pepsi Bethel, Artistic Director) performs dances from minstrelsy to those of the ballroom era, such as The Shim Sham, Big Apple, Slow Drag, and Lindy Hop. Bethel learned dancing "from the streets and from the ballrooms" and later studied modern dance with Hanya Holm, which brought form to his teaching and choreography.

While these two companies present either proven choreography of the past or favorite traditional dances with considerable success, other jazz companies formed by highly successful jazz teachers, have made a minimum impact performing their own work in concert. Perhaps there is more pleasure and excitement in dancing with them than in having to sit still and watch. Jazz has been most successful when coupled with songs—when used to enhance a dramatic scene, as an interlude, or as a show opening or closing.

Jazz Class

The development sketched here indicates that no set format can be attributed to "the" jazz class. It is highly individualized, and each teacher has his particular way of moving. The musical accompaniment will inspire the teacher. While some prefer to use tape recordings or records for accompaniment, live music can add excitement. Whichever the case, jazz music is a must for jazz class. The class is generally divided between exercises which warm up the body, increase flexibility, and build strength, and patterns across the floor or creatively improvised combinations which really get you dancing.

Classes for the non-professional should be something to enjoy, whether or not a high technical level is achieved. A creative and innovative teacher will teach an exciting class that is an exhilarating experience even for the rank beginner. The most difficult task for the beginning jazz dancer is getting rid of inhibitions.

Once you are comfortable with your own body, no matter what shape it is in, and allow yourself to move, a whole new world of freedom will open up to you. The jazz class can free the spirit, clear the mind, and make the world outside the studio seem a better place. It can be a very healthy outlet for pent-up frustrations and emotions —yes, good therapy! You can get "hooked" on a good jazz class. It becomes something your body must have and feels sluggish without, something you enjoy.

Jazz dance is a very personal medium. Each teacher may project an entirely different personality, which will affect the atmosphere in the classroom, which, in turn, will affect your response. You want a class that will bring the most out of you, free you to move, inspire you to work your hardest. Some teachers will get results through intimidation and harsh demands, others through coaxing. Whichever spurs you on is right for *you.*

WHAT TO WEAR

The jazz "look" is important in helping one to move as a jazz dancer. Pink tights and ballet slippers, or the ankle-cropped tights and bare feet of the modern dancer just don't give the same results as dark tights with jazz shoes, or thin white anklets with sneakers, or jazz pants—even with bare feet. There is something about the "feel" of the "look" that puts you into low level with parallel feet. There is nothing so incongruous as feet in ballet slippers trying to act jazzy!

Jazz attire has changed over the years and the cue today is usually taken from the instructor, who may wear jazz pants or leotard and tights. If the teacher dances barefoot, you may do so, but if the teacher wears jazz shoes or sneakers, get yourself a pair. Luigi wore high-heeled boots from a show to teach a class one day, and soon jazz classes were filled with high-heeled boots and tights. The Jack Cole Latin look, fringed pants ending just below the knee and laced up to just below the navel with a shirt tied high on the chest exposing a long bare torso, was prevalent in Matt Mattox classes in the late 50s. After *West Side Story,*

Jazz class.

pants and dungarees became popular, although they do not provide enough freedom of movement. Dancers began designing their own pants, and stretch pants were worn for a while. Capezio has manufactured jazz pants in recent years that are tight over the thigh, and flare at the ankle. These are fine for those who can afford them, but the majority of professional dancers wear leotards pulled high above the thigh socket to emphasize the long line of the legs, and then perhaps heavy ankle socks with their jazz shoes or sneakers.

In the jazz class, unless hair is short, it is pulled back off the face, but not necessarily confined as in the ballet class. This applies to men as well as women. Even though individuality is sought, hair that flops over the face when the body tilts is a definite distraction.

The Capezio jazz oxford with a low rubber heel and stitched sole is recommended. A sole that is glued on will pull loose with the first toe drag. To prevent slipping, the shoemaker can attach a thin rubber sole to the front part of the shoe. Soles should be white or brown; a black rubber sole will mark the floor. Jazz shoes come in black or white soft leather and should be fitted like a glove, since the leather will stretch after a few wearings. With the shoe on, point the toe straight down, pressing into the floor. If you can get your finger into the shoe behind your heel, the shoe is too big. The correctly fitting jazz shoe could be as much as two sizes smaller than your street shoe, but be sure it is also wider.

An inexpensive thin-soled sneaker will serve as well for the beginner. The shoe should fit firmly over a *thin* stocking or dance tights, and it should be understood that it will take a few wearings to loosen its fabric enough to shape to your foot. If your shoes are uncomfortable in the beginning, only wear them during part of the class until you break them in. The thin sole is important because your feet should be able to "feel" the floor. The thick-soled sneaker is for the tennis courts, not for the dance studio. Also, sneakers that are worn on the street should not be worn in class.

WHAT TO READ

Fischer-Munstermann, Uta. *Jazz Dance & Jazz Gymnastics.* Ed. and intro. Liz Williamson. New York: Sterling, 1978.

Stearns, Marshall and Jean. *Jazz Dance.* New York: Macmillan, 1968.

Opposite: **Chicago (Fosse), 1975. Chita Rivera and Gwen Verdon. Pages 160–61: West Side Story (Robbins), 1957. Pages 162–63: Dancin' (Fosse), 1978.**

WHERE TO STUDY

In addition to teaching at their own or other schools, most jazz teachers listed here also teach at summer dance workshops throughout the country and are available for master classes and residencies.

American Dance Machine
  Training Facility
4 East 75 Street
New York, N.Y. 10021
(212) 879-5750

Pepsi Bethel
Clark Center for the Performing Arts
939 Eighth Avenue
New York, N.Y. 10019
(212) 246-4818

Phil Black Dance Studio
1630 Broadway
New York, N.Y. 10019
(212) 247-2675

Danny Daniels' Dance America
310 Wilshire Boulevard
Santa Monica, Calif. 90401
(213) 395-7331-33

Peter Gennaro
Igor Youskevitch School of Ballet
846 Seventh Avenue
New York, N.Y. 10019
(212) 245-9684

Gus Giordano Dance Studio
614 Davis Street
Evanston, Ill. 60201
(312) 475-9442; 251-4434

Jon Gregory Talent Center
1211 East Charleston Boulevard
Las Vegas, Nev. 89104
(702) 382-2092

Nat Horne
American Dance Center
1515 Broadway
New York, N.Y. 10036
(212) 997-1980

Luigi Jazz Center
36 West 62 Street
New York, N.Y. 10023
(212) 247-1995

Billie Mahoney
Theatre Teachers Alliance
Act 48 Studios
209 West 48 Street
New York, N.Y. 10036
(212) 541-9518

Jo Jo Smith
Jo Jo's Dance Factory
1733 Broadway
New York, N.Y. 10019
(212) 586-2940

Joe Tremaine Jazz Center
Moro-Landis Building
10960 Ventura Boulevard
North Hollywood, Calif. 91604
(213) 980-3336
and
1267 North Hayworth
Los Angeles, Calif. 90046
(213) 654-0947

Liz Williamson
Suite 5T
1270 Fifth Avenue
New York, N.Y. 10029
(212) 348-7318
Sundays: 2182 Broadway
  New York, N.Y. 10024

TAP DANCE
By Billie Mahoney

Tap dance involves manipulating the feet so that metal plates attached to the bottom of the shoes strike a hard surface in a variety of ways, creating a kind of music by spelling out rhythms. It is America's own development, a blending of the Irish jig and English clog dancing with African rhythms, and it all came about on the streets of New York during the nineteenth century when Irish immigrants exchanged steps with freed Negro slaves.

Tap dance developed throughout the minstrel era when challenges between black and white dancers were a source of entertainment. The greatest of these competitions was between William Henry Lane, the free-born Negro known as Juba, "king of all dancers," and the Irishman John Diamond, acclaimed as the greatest dancer of the jig.

Juba at Vauxhall Gardens. Etching (ca. 1849).

Tap dance emerged full-blown in vaudeville and musical comedy during the early part of the twentieth century, thanks to such stars as George M. Cohan, Pat Rooney, and Harland Dixon, and, from black musical comedy, such greats as Eddie Rector, John Bubbles, and Bill "Bojangles" Robinson.

With the advent of talking pictures, tap dance was considered a natural for the new movie musicals, and the first tap dance to music on film was performed by Joan Crawford in 1929. Later, in 1933, she was Fred Astaire's first screen dancing partner.

Acknowledged as the all-time great, Astaire was the star dancer in film musicals for more than twenty-five years, partnering such leading ladies as Ginger Rogers, Eleanor Powell, Judy Garland, and Ann Miller, to name only a few. Among the other dancing men of the movies, each with a distinctive style of his own, were Gene Kelly, Donald O'Connor, and James Cagney.

In his *Follies* of 1907, Florenz Ziegfeld introduced the tap-dancing chorus line doing unison tap, which became a mainstay of the musical comedies and revues that were to follow. This type of production was further developed in the movie extravaganzas choreographed by Busby Berkeley in the 1930s; on stage, the world-famed Rockettes at Radio City Music Hall, thirty-six precision tap dancers, have been one of New York's major tourist attractions for over forty years.

Although little or no tap was seen on Broadway from 1943 to 1971—from the time Agnes de Mille used ballet in *Oklahoma!* to further the story line until the revival of *No, No, Nanette,* which brought Ruby Keeler, the darling of the Busby Berkeley films, back to the stage—tap was much alive in the hinterlands. It would have been unthinkable for the dance teacher conventions (such as Dance Masters of America, Dance Educators of America, the National Association of Dance and Affiliated Artists, and Danny Hoctor's Dance Caravan) to hold sessions without tap and musical comedy dancing as the main attractions. America's folk dance was kept alive in local dance studios and in public schools in some parts of the Southwest it has always been part of the curriculum.

Tap dance is now being taken seriously as part of America's cultural background, but, as an art form, it has not progressed much beyond the 1950s when Paul Draper performed his ballet-integrated tap work to classical music on the concert circuit. In the early 1950s, Morton Gould composed his *Tap Dance Concerto* for Danny Daniels. It was later performed by Michael Dominico with major symphony orchestras.

In 1963, with the surge of interest in nostalgia, a group of old-time tap artists was assembled to perform at the Newport Jazz Festival. Encouraged by the enthusiastic audience response, they came to Broadway as *The Hoofers* for a successful run in 1969, and since that time these performers have been more active than before, teaching, performing, and assisting in documentaries to preserve their art.

On television, the most prominent tap dancer for more than a decade has been Arthur Duncan, who can be seen each week on the Lawrence Welk Show. Over the years, Duncan has changed his style of pure hoofing*; while not sacrificing his clean articulate footwork, he now sometimes adds a musical comedy flair, more often than not introducing his dance with a song.

In *The Book of Tap,* Jerry Ames states that tap has "been revived, but not revitalized, not yet refashioned for our times. What's needed are expert tappers, innovative choreographers, and creative individuals with conceptual and practical powers to put forth new musicals, new films,

Opposite: Fred Astaire in **Top Hat, 1935.**

*"Hoofer" refers to the dancer who does *only* footwork, the feet spelling out their music in sound. The "dancer" will add arm and body movement, turns, and leaps to give an overall visual effect.

Tap shoe.

and new forms for the presentation of tap." The Jerry Ames Tap Dance Company made its New York debut in September 1976, and continues to get rave notices: "Ames has taken a dance form popular in the 30's and made it fit the mood of the 70's.... Not only has tap found itself a vehicle, but it indeed seems due for a comeback," wrote Ann Wheelock in the *Austin Citizen*.

Bill Robinson and Shirley Temple in The Little Colonel, 1935.

Tap Classes

Tap dancing is fun, and anyone can learn the essentials. It doesn't *have* to cover as much space as other forms of dance, and the whole body does not *have* to get involved, only the feet. You can hear your own music as you tap it out. Body shape and age do not influence your ability to enjoy tap dancing. And you don't have to have a partner. This is America's true folk dance.

Tap dancing has basic rudiments such as the shuffle, ball change, brush, flap, heel drop, slap, stamp, step, and stomp, and many of the step patterns have names. Traditional steps can be combined into routines which have become the classics of tap dance: the soft shoe, the waltz clog, the military.

There are also the time steps, originally used to set the tempo ("time") for improvisational dancing. These have now been formalized and range from the single buck time step to the cramp roll*, and finally to the double wing time step.

Once these basic movements are mastered, it is a matter of practice to gain facility and a look of ease in manipulating the feet to produce sharp clear sounds.

WHAT TO WEAR

You can learn to tap in any kind of well-fitting leather-soled and leather-heeled shoe. But the beginner will soon want to hear the sounds he is producing and will want to purchase "taps," the metal plates that attach to the toes and heels. Even when the tap shoe is bought from the dancewear dealer, taps are purchased separately. There may be a choice of several shapes and sizes.

First you must consider the shoe. If you decide to use a pair of old shoes, be sure they have leather heels and that the leather sole is not an "extension" sole. The shoe should have a tie or strap so it will stay with the foot when the heel is lifted; loafers and sling pumps do not work well. If you are purchasing a standard tap shoe from a dancewear merchant, the woman's shoe may have a ribbon tie or leather strap and, depending on personal preference, either a wide one-inch heel or a higher two-inch heel. For the beginner, a lower heel is better.

When you have decided on your shoes, fit the taps to the toes. Most taps have a right and left. Buy the tap that best fits your shoe and can be attached with screws. The tap should cover the area under the toes and be at least the length of the big toe. Some taps are hollow, and some will fit flat against the shoe. Different instructors will have different preferences, which are simply a matter of personal choice. The sound produced depends primarily on how you move your feet.

*Russell Markert, choreographer for the Rockettes for many years, used the cramp roll time step as standard audition fare. Broadway choreographers will generally ask for the triple buck time step at auditions.

Heel taps should cover the whole heel. Do not be persuaded to buy "jingle" taps or to put a washer into the heel tap. This was a fad at one time, and it seems some merchants are attempting to revive it, but there is nothing more disturbing than the messy sound of jingles in what might otherwise be clean footwork.

You must take your shoes and taps to the shoe repair shop to be attached. Your dancewear merchant may be able to recommend one who specializes in such work for dancers. Have your taps attached with screws, usually no more than four in the toe tap and sometimes only three in the heel tap, depending on the placement of the holes. The toe taps should fit firmly, but you have the option of using a small screwdriver to loosen the screws in the heel tap a fraction of a turn for a fuller sound.

Before you leave the shoemaker, make sure that the screws are set inside the hole of the tap and that no sharp edges are left protruding. There is no excuse for marring and digging up a floor, or leaving ugly gouges with an improperly attached tap. Also by running your finger around the inside of the toe, check to be sure there are no small bulges on the inside of the shoe. After a half hour of dancing, your weight could cause the sharp point that made the bulge to puncture through. The shoemaker can easily correct it on the spot if care is taken to discover it.

The professional dancer will have thin rubber soles placed on the ball of the shoe behind the tap to prevent slipping, as well as heel braces on the woman's shoe. These are added expenses which are not likely to be necessary for the beginner, but you should be aware that the adjustments in the shoe can be made if needed.

WHAT TO READ

Ames, Jerry, and Siegelman, Jim. *The Book of Tap.* New York: David McKay, 1977.

Stearns, Marshall and Jean. *Jazz Dance.* New York: Macmillan, 1968.

Below: Children's tap class at The Dance Theater of Harlem School. Pages 168-69: Busby Berkeley's 42nd Street, 1933. Pages 170-71: Rockettes, Radio City Music Hall, New York.

WHERE TO STUDY

Jerry Ames
Theatre Teachers Alliance
Act 48 Studios
209 West 48 Street
New York, N.Y. 10036
(212) 541-9518

Bob Audy
Showcase Studios
950 Eighth Avenue
New York, N.Y. 10019
(212) 586-7947

Buster Brown
884 Riverside Drive
New York, N.Y. 10032
(212) 795-6213

Brenda Bufalino
"Dancing Theater"
6 North Front Street
New Paltz, N.Y. 12561

Danny Daniels' Dance America
310 Wilshire Boulevard
Santa Monica, Calif. 90401
(213) 395-7331-33

Ron Daniels
American Ballet Center
434 Avenue of the Americas
New York, N.Y. 10011
(212) 254-8520
and
New York School of Ballet
2291 Broadway
New York, N.Y. 10024
(212) 799-5445

Louis DaPron
Topanga Canyon
Los Angeles, Calif.

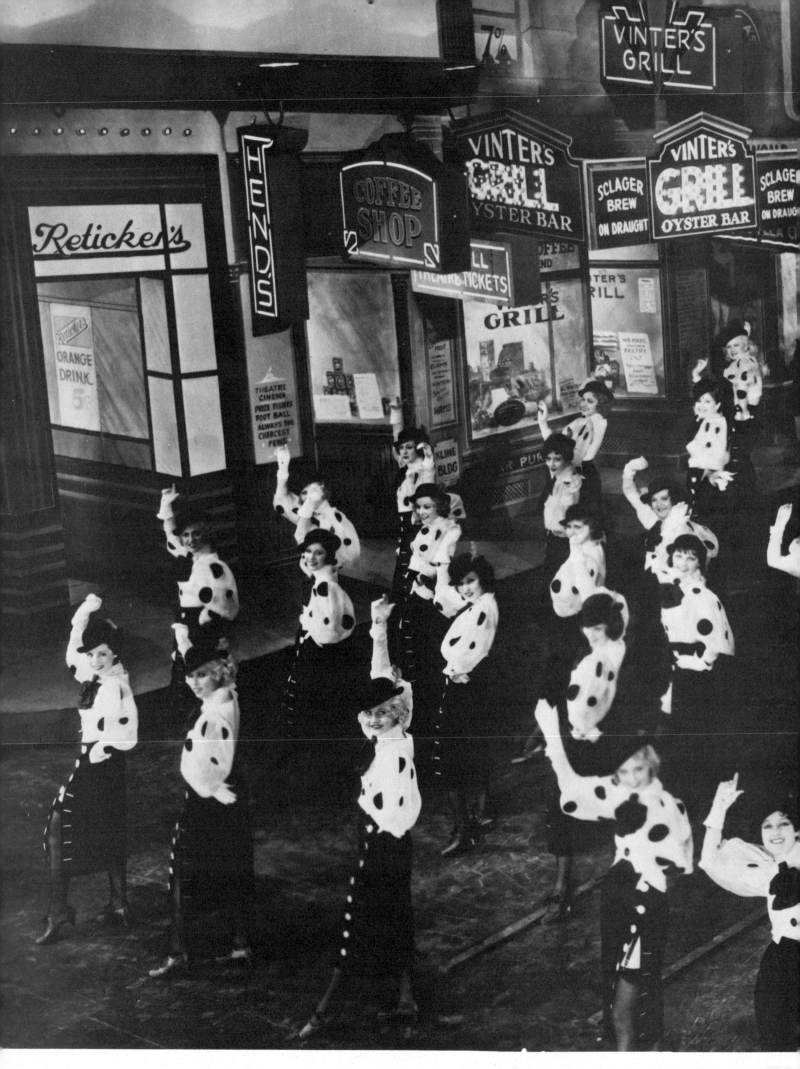

"42 ND STREET" with 14 STAR 200 GIR

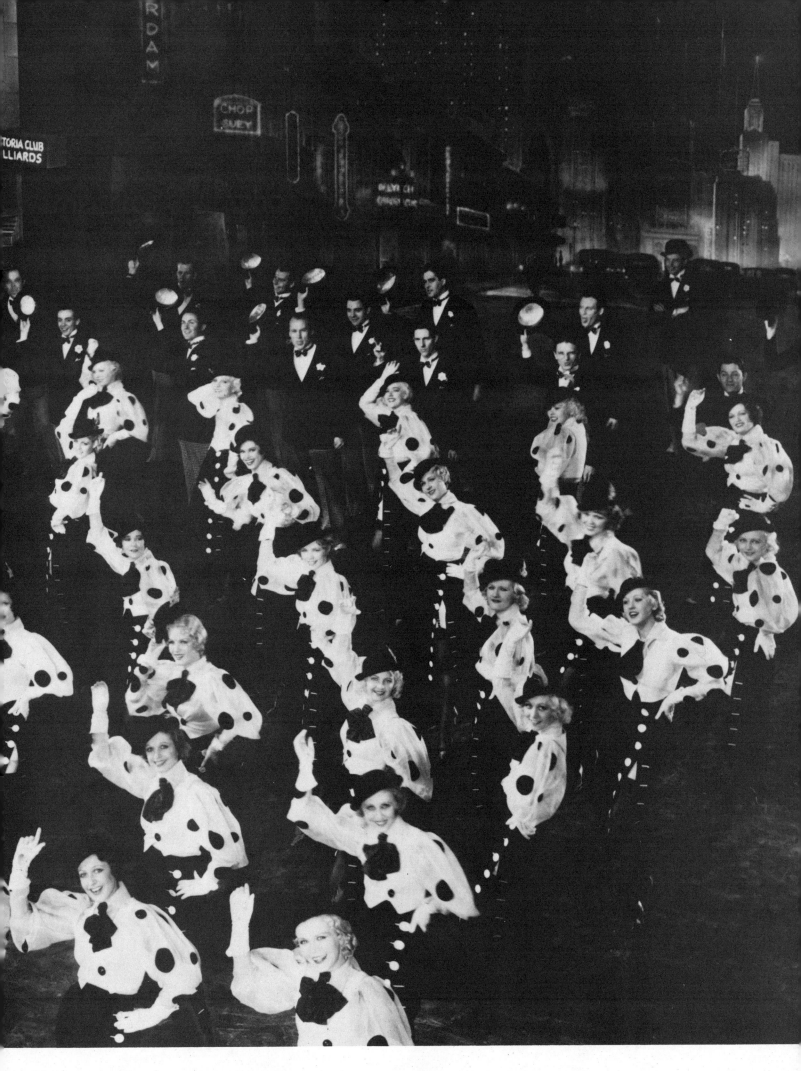

A Warner. Bros. & Vitaphone Picture ^{MADE IN U.S.A}

GYMNASTICS, MARTIAL ARTS, FENCING, YOGA, EXERCISE, MIME, FOLK DANCE, BALLROOM DANCING

By Dawn Lille Horwitz

Gymnastics

Gymnastics, one of the oldest forms of organized phyical activity, has been called the most artistic of sports. It is popular as a school sport, a competitive event (Olga Korbut and Nadia Comaneci are practically household names), and a form of pleasurable exercise.

The word *gymnastics* comes from the Greek *gymnos* meaning "naked"; the gymnasium was the public place where Greek youths exercised. Gymnastics was also practiced during the Middle Ages and down through the eighteenth century. Modern gymnastics developed as a competitive sport in Denmark, Sweden, and, since World War II, Germany. The television coverage of the 1970 Olympics, particularly the Soviet girl gymnasts, resulted in renewed interest.

There are two major areas in gymnastic training: competitive and exhibition. Both include a great deal of dance and tumbling. Exhibition gymnastics includes rolls, somersaults, cartwheels, head- and handstands, and handsprings with and without supports (the latter known as aerials).

Competitive gymnastics for women (also called artistic gymnastics) usually starts with a floor exercise one and one-half minutes long, which includes tumbling and dancing to music played on a single instrument and must cover a 40' x 40' matted area. This is followed by the following compulsory apparatus exercises:

Uneven Parallel Bars. Two free-standing bars, one 7' 6½" and one 4' 11" from the ground. The unevenness enables the performer to execute many flowing and swinging movements in constantly changing directions while circling the bars.

Vault. Used by German knights to improve their skills, this is a padded surface 5' 3" long, 15¾" wide, mounted 3' 7" from the floor, and called "the horse." Vaulting is done over the width of the horse.

Balance Beam. A slightly rounded wooden beam mounted 4' from the floor on two supports, of which the regulation size is 16' 3" long, 4" wide, and 6" thick. The exercises are a combination of dance and tumbling, requiring good balance and precision.

Competitive gymnastics for men also starts with floor work—tumbling and somersaulting—but without music, and then includes the following compulsory exercises:

Side Horse (Pummel Horse). A leather-covered horse almost trapezoidal in shape, 3' 7½" high, 5' 4" long, and 1' 1½" thick. The pummels or handles are on the center of the upper surface. The competitor grabs these and executes a continuous swinging movement.

Parallel Bar. Two bars of flexible wood 2" thick, 11' 5¾" long, 5' 7" above the floor, and approximately 1½' apart. They are oval in cross section. Circular swinging movements such as somersaults are performed on bars.

Vault (Long Horse). The vault for men is 4' 5¼" from the floor; competitors vault lengthways with a twist or turn of the body.

High Bar. A steel bar mounted on posts 8' 2½" above ground which is 7' 10½" long, 1⅛" thick and requires flow rather than strength on the part of the performer.

Still Rings. Two rings with an inside diameter of 7" hang from wire cables 8' 2½" above the floor and 1' 7¾" apart. They require great strength in the static positions and the two inverted (handstand) positions.

The Olympics involve competitive gymnastics for men and women (rhythmic gymnastics were eliminated in 1956). Now called modern gymnastics, this category consists of exercises with hand accessories such as balls, ropes, hoops, Indian clubs, scarves, and ribbons, as well as free floor routines. The trampoline, not included in the Olympics, is accepted in meets in the United States.

Judges for all gymnastic events are specially trained and selected according to the criteria established by the presenting organization. Rules for events are drawn up by the International Federations of Gymnastics (FIG) after each Olympiad. All groups use these international rules, although some may modify them at times.

Exhibition gymnastics, either performed by competitive teams or simply as entertainment, may contain some or all of the routines of competitive gymnastics, as well as those of rhythmic gymnastics. An exhibition may include walking, running, marching, skipping, and jumping in lines and formations, as well as human pyramids, tableaus, balancing acts, and comedy gymnastics. Music, costumes, and makeup are often used, and most exhibitions revolve around a theme.

The role of dance in gymnastics is tremendous. Many exhibition groups hire a dance teacher and choreographer as part of their standard coaching staff and freely use elements of ballet, folk, modern, jazz, and ballroom dance in the routines. Most books on the subject devote a considerable amount of space to dance techniques, warm-ups, and combinations. Both the beam and floor events for women are choreographed and combine dance steps with gymnastic moves. In rhythmic gymnastics, the movements are often pure dance, and many gymnasts have both ballet and modern dance in their training. It is said that the East European women's teams spend three hours a day in ballet class!

Programs in gymnastics are found in schools and colleges, Ys, recreation centers, special gymnastic schools, and in some exercise centers.

Opposite: Trampoline.

Gym shoe.

WHAT TO WEAR

Competition. Women wear a short one-piece costume or leotard. On their feet are soft gymnastic slippers or peds which have been well rubbed with rosin.

Balance beam.

Men wear long wide trousers with suspenders and white sleeveless T-shirts. On their feet are very light slippers. Younger boys usually wear gym shorts and T-shirts, and are sometimes barefoot.

Exhibition. Performers either wear the same clothing as for competitive gymnastics or special costumes related to a particular theme. Men will often wear long pants that taper at the ankle and have a stirrup going under the foot so they do not ride up.

FOR MORE INFORMATION

Amateur Athletic Union of the United States
515 Madison Avenue
New York, N.Y. 10022
(212) 371-4835

American Alliance for Health, Physical Education and Recreation
1201 16 Street NW
Washington, D.C. 20036
(202) 833-5541

International Gymnastic Federation
Rue de Bienne 22
3250 Lyss
Switzerland

United States Gymnastic Federation
P.O. Box 4699
Tucson, Ariz. 85717
(602) 795-2920
(Has programs for specific age levels. International Rule Books and Code of Points may be obtained from them.)

United States Gymnastic Safety Association
17241 Dulles International Airport
Washington, D.C. 20041
(202) 543-3403
(Developing a program to train and certify instructors.)

WHAT TO READ

Bowers, Fie, and Kjeldsen, Schmid. *Judging and Coaching Women's Gymnastics*. Palo Alto, California: National Press Books, 1972.

Drury, Blanche, and Schmid, Andrea B. *Gymnastics for Women*. Palo Alto, California: National Press Books, 1977.

Hughes, Eric. *Gymnastics for Men: A Competitive Approach for Teacher and Coach*. New York: Ronald Press, 1966.

The International Gymnast Magazine. P.O. Box 110, Santa Monica, California 90406
(Information on meets, camps, teachers, schools, and some skill analysis.)

Martial Arts

The arts of unarmed combat and the systems of physical and mental preparations used by warriors of the East are all considered martial arts. These Oriental fighting skills can be traced back to early hand and foot wrestling and stick fighting. Ancient Egypt, Crete, and Greece also developed similar types of boxing and wrestling.

Cheena-adi, the Chinese art of unarmed attack and defense, goes back to mythological times: The Chinese system, also called kempo, found its way to Korea, Japan, Java, Ceylon, Mongolia, and Okinawa (mostly through wars) and was influenced and changed by local customs.

The Japanese practiced an ancient method of combat which developed into the wrestling style now known as sumo. In the thirteenth century, jujitsu broke away from sumo and evolved into a separate technique. The Japanese believed that jujitsu was revealed to the Samurai warriors via the gods. Karate, judo, and aikido emerged as distinct forms in the twentieth century, during which time the arts also began to find their way into the West. At present the most common are:

Karate (literally, "fighting with empty hands"). What is now called karate is a mixture of Japanese jujitsu, Okinawan te, Korean chabi, ancient Chinese kempo and some modern concepts. The breathing methods are from India, the smooth round movements from China, and the low hip stance from Japan. There is also a strong spiritual tradition. The white wrap-around jacket with wide sleeves worn for karate is called the gi. The color of the belt indicates the wearer's level of skill.

Judo (the modern form of jujitsu). There are three categories: nage-waza, which is a type of wrestling for sport or exhibition, ateme waza, or self-defense using knock-out blows, and katsu, which teaches how to revive the victim after a blow. They all require balance, leverage, spring action, and momentum.

Kung fu (also known as Gung fu). An older Chinese form of karate which probably derived from an even older Indian style of hand and foot fighting. Clawing and a stabbing hand blow are often used. The soft style stresses speed and the hard style uses kicks.

Aikido is a new Japanese art, the purpose of which is to strengthen the mind, the body, and the spirit. It was introduced in the United States in the early sixties. The movements are circular rather than linear.

Tai Chi is the circle exercise form in which the whole body is involved and all bending is forward. It is a flowing style which stresses balance and rhythmic coordination; it seems to have originated as an exercise to increase the agility of kung fu practitioners in China.

There are schools teaching the different martial arts in almost every city in the country, and some classes are offered at recreation centers, children's camps, etc. Many

choreographers have used elements of these arts as themes for dance works.

FOR MORE INFORMATION

United States Judo Federation
R.R. 21, Box 519
Terre Haute, Ind. 47802
(Has several publications, many regional and local groups)

Women's Martial Arts Union
P.O. Box 879
New York, N.Y. 10025

Top: Fencing. Above: Karate. Forward punch.

WHAT TO READ

Oyama, Masutatsu. *What Is Karate?* Tokyo and San Francisco: Japan Publications Trading Co., 1974.
Bruce Tegner has written books on every form of the Eastern martial arts presently taught in the United States. They are published by the Thor Publishing Co., Ventura, California.

Fencing

In the Western world, boxing, wrestling, and fencing have been the chief forms of unarmed combat, although fencing, in which a foil is used, is considered unarmed only because it has been illegal as a form of armed combat for some time.

Fencing has a very clear relationship to dance. Some of the early ballet steps in court were modeled on the fencing positions of the feet, and many ballets contain choreographed duels.

As a form that requires agility and balance, fencing is practiced competitively by many college teams and is also of interest to many individuals as a physically and technically demanding sport. Many actors and dancers study it, particularly those interested in performing in the classics.

FOR MORE INFORMATION

Amateur Fencers League of America
601 Curtis Street
Albany, Calif. 94706

International Fencing Federation
53 Rue Vivienne
Paris, France

WHAT TO READ

American Fencing. Amateur Fencers League of America, Albany, California. A bi-monthly magazine.
Gordon, Gilbert. *Stage Fights.* New York: Theatre Arts Books, 1974.

Limbering exercises.

Yoga

Yoga is an ancient school of Hindu philosophy whose founder, Pantanjali, lived in the third century B.C. Travelers returning from the East as far back as Marco Polo's time talked about Yogi sages who were serene, in excellent physical condition, lived a long time, and possessed great healing powers. Many of these men were also gurus or teachers.

Yoga is a system of physical and mental fitness. It deals with gradual mastery of the body through physical and mental exercise and breath control. There are many forms of Yoga, but in the West most people teach and learn Hatha Yoga, the path of physical perfection. The name is derived from the Sanskrit *Ha,* which stands for the female principles and *Tha,* which stands for the male principles. This is a slow, graduated form of exercise suitable for both sexes. Forgetting the aspect of spiritual and physical purification common in the East, Hatha Yoga in the West is concerned with rhythmic breathing and basic exercises or "asanas."

The only equipment needed is loose clothing and a foam rubber mat. Classes are given in community centers, Y's, health clubs, colleges, etc. Since the individual student progresses at his own pace, the study of Yoga can begin at any age and in any physical condition.

FOR MORE INFORMATION

3 HO Foundation
1620 Pruess Road
Los Angeles, Calif. 90035
(213) 550-9043
(Operates centers all over the world and puts out several publications)

WHAT TO READ

Hittleman, Richard. *Yoga for Physical Fitness.* New York: Warner Books, 1974.
Majumbdar, S. *Introduction to Yoga Principles and Practices.* Secaucus, N.J.: University Books, 1964.

Exercise

One of the legacies of the 1960s and its awareness of self has been the proliferation of health clubs and spas in direct response to the at-home enthusiasts who had started stretching, running in place, and doing exercises from the manual of the Royal Canadian Air Force. Although jogging seems to have taken over the nation, and swimming is also popular (many dancers swim, few run), one can still find old-fashioned exercise classes. Many combine some elements of a dance warm-up with the traditional "keep fit" exercises; others have introduced the regimen of Aerobics. In the exercise room of many health clubs, there is often someone who will devise a personal program of exercise for each individual. Those who wish to dance in the water might try reading *Allegra Kent's Water Beauty Book,* which contains many exercises practiced by the author, a principal dancer with the New York City Ballet.

Most people do exercises of any sort for two reasons: to burn up calories and to increase muscle tone. The best and most lasting way to achieve firm muscles is not to tighten them into a bulge but to lengthen them into a long, firm, smooth state. (Proper dance training also accomplishes this.) Bulging muscles are not necessarily stronger, and they quickly return to a flabby condition.

WHAT TO READ

Cooper, Kenneth H., M.D. *Aerobics.* New York: M. Evans, 1968.

Craig, Marjorie. *Miss Craig's 21 Day Shape-Up Program for Men and Women.* New York: Random House, 1968.

Fixx, James F. *The Complete Book of Running.* New York: Random House, 1977. *An encyclopedia that covers every aspect of running.*

Kent, Allegra. *Allegra Kent's Water Beauty Book.* New York: St. Martin's, 1976.

Prudden, Bonnie. *Fitness from Six to Twelve.* New York: Harper and Row, 1972.

Mime

Mime is a silent form of drama in which specific events and/or emotions are indicated in gesture by the body and by facial expression. A mime "speaks" by very carefully delineating objects in space or by indicating with his body (no words) the stimuli that have produced an emotion.

Mime performances existed among the ancient Chinese, Hebrews, Egyptians, and Romans. Mime is an essential component of the Italian commedia dell 'arte but had no formal organization until the twentieth century, when the Frenchman Etienne Decroux codified it as a discipline that could be taught to others. Among his pupils were Jean-Louis Barrault and Marcel Marceau.

Mime was introduced into ballet in the nineteenth century as a means of quickly furthering the plot, and a special form of ballet mime with a recognized sign language of its own had developed by the end of the century. It may be observed in such ballets as *Sleeping Beauty* and *Swan Lake.* Marriage, for example, is indicated by pointing to the fourth finger of the left hand; a beautiful woman by tracing a circle around the face. The small Nutcracker Prince recounts his adventures by revolving his hands, waist high, around each other, as if holding them in a muff.

Mime is now taught in many studios and universities throughout the United States. (For a long time one had to go to France to study.) There are mime companies as well as solo performers (see pages 108-111).

Formal classes begin with warm-ups which usually start in a neutral or "zero" position, similar to first position in ballet, and proceed through a variety of exercises including the four basic hand positions (spatula, grapefruit, crab, and daisy). In mime training, the body is generally divided into four parts: head, torso, arms, and legs. Once the performer has learned to use all parts of the body he must learn to place them in such a way as to convey a mood, action, or object to an audience.

Mime can be studied as an art in itself or to enrich that of the dancer or actor.

WHAT TO WEAR

Leotard and tights and soft slippers on the feet are generally preferred, although any loose clothing will do.

FOR MORE INFORMATION

International Mimes and Pantomimists
The Valley Studio
Rte. 3
Spring Green, Wis. 53588
(608) 588-2514
(Founded in 1973 by the American Mime Theatre of New York City to promote mime and pantomime. It acts as an information agency and employment service for members. It also publishes a quarterly newsletter and biennial Directory.)

WHAT TO READ

Lawson, Joan. *Mime.* 1957. Paperback, New York: Dance Horizons, 1972.
Nicholl, Allardyce. *Mimes, Masks and Miracles.* London: George Harrap, 1963.

Mime. Yass Hakoshima.

Folk Dance

Folk dances—dances created by people of an essentially agricultural society for their own participatory enjoyment —also reflect the characteristics and moods of a particular time and place. Since they are passed from one generation to the next, many changes occur. In fifteenth- and sixteenth-century Europe, folk dancing was clearly distinguished from the courtly dancing of the upper classes, although it has influenced both ballroom and theater dance.

Many folk dances were originally related to religious beliefs. The Morris and Maypole dances of Great Britain date back to primitive fertility rites. In the Middle and Far East (Japan, Burma, Ceylon, Turkey), many folk dances still retain much of their religious significance.

The square dance in its infinite variety is an American folk dance. To perform it, an even number of couples is arranged in a square, in two lines, or in a circle. Other folk dances may be executed by individual couples or by groups of men or women. In truth, all American folk dance is derived from the dances of the various peoples who came here. (Two truly indigenous American dance

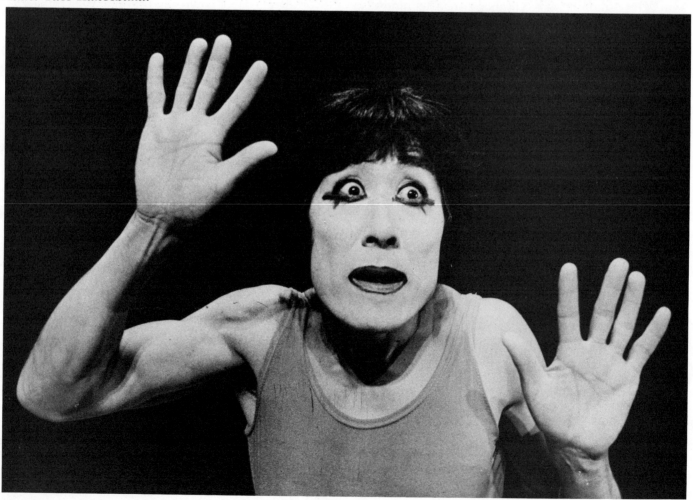

forms, jazz and tap, are discussed on pages 154-167.) Hence we do polkas, mazurkas, flings, jigs, horas, and tarantellas, all of which originated elsewhere.

In almost every city in the United States, one can find folk dance groups and leaders in Ys, churches, synagogues, schools, and colleges. There are also many groups devoted to the dances of a single country or area, such as Scotland, the Ukraine, Israel, Ireland, and Greece. There are many resort camps, weekends, and evenings organized around folk dancing for all age groups.

FOR MORE INFORMATION

Callerlab
International Association of Square Dance Callers
Pocono Pines, Pa. 18350
(Callers who call at least once a week. Purpose is to promote and perpetuate square dance. Publishes a newsletter and quarterly magazine.)

Country Dance and Song Society of America
55 Christopher Street
New York, N.Y. 10014
(212) 255-8895
(Promotes the use of English and American folk dances, songs and music. Publishes a newsletter and books.)

Folk Dance House
Box 201
Flushing, New York 11352
(212) 784-7407
(Library; costume collection; referral.)

National Council For The Traditional Arts
1346 Connecticut Avenue NW
Washington, D.C. 20036
(202) 296-0068
(Publishes a directory of U.S. and Canadian Folk Festivals and assists the National Park Service.)

Professional Square Dance Callers Association
330 Wadsworth Avenue
New York, N.Y. 10040

WHAT TO READ

Folk Dance Directory, pub. by the Folk Dance Assoc., P.O. Box 500, Midwood Station, Brooklyn, N.Y. 11230
(Lists folk, square and round dancing held on a regular basis, grouped according to regions throughout the U.S.)
Kraus, Richard. *Folk Dancing: A Guide for Schools, Colleges and Recreation Groups.* New York: Macmillan, 1962.
Nevill, Richard. *A Time to Dance: American Country Dancing from Hornpipes to Hot Hash.* New York: St. Martin's, 1977.

Ballroom Dancing

Ballroom dancing is a social activity, usually performed by couples for their own pleasure and entertainment at nightclubs, restaurants, or parties. There are also exhibition ballroom dancing and ballroom dance contests. The dances were originally performed at balls given by the aristocracy and well-to-do, hence the name.

The popularity of certain dances are a reflection of a particular time and place; thus in recent history we have had the fox-trot, waltz, lindy, peabody, rumba, cha-cha, samba, charleston, and twist. In East Europe, folk dances such as the polka, mazurka, and czardas are also performed in the ballroom.

Although we no longer observe the custom of sending young girls in patent leather shoes and white gloves and young boys in blue suits with white handkerchiefs to "Miss Dolly's Classes in Dancing and Decorum," there are still studios in most cities where those interested can take lessons in the latest social dances.

Title page of The Ball-Room Bijou *by Charles Durang, ca. 1855.*

FOR MORE INFORMATION

National Ballroom and Entertainment Association
P.O. Box 338
West Des Moines, Iowa 50265
(Owners and operators of ballrooms.)

United States Ballroom Branch
Imperial Society of Teachers of Dancing
4601 North Park Avenue
Chevy Chase, Md. 20015
(For teachers of ballroom dancing. Prepares syllabi, conducts exams, sponsors competition, and publishes a monthly newsletter.)

WHAT TO READ

Buckman, Peter. *Let's Dance.* New York: Paddington, 1978.
Franks, A. H. *Social Dance: A Short History.* London: Routledge & Kegan, 1963.

BODY CORRECTIVES
By Kayla Kazahn Zalk

In the training and performing life of the dancer, with the development of skills and technique comes the heightened awareness of body function. This also often highlights the occasional physical malfunction which most people could ignore. The student begins to seek out methods of correction (or is directed to them by the conscientious teacher).

A body of knowledge and techniques has been developing to meet these needs. The three major self-corrective techniques available today are those created by F. M. Alexander, I. Bartenieff and Dr. M. Feldenkrais.

The Alexander technique has training centers primarily in New York and London. F. Matthias Alexander, an Australian actor, developed a self-awareness and self-correcting technique to overcome his own difficulties in functioning under the stress of performance. As he taught others (which became his life's work), several centers were opened which follow his teachings and principles. As noted in the 1973 Nobel Prize lecture of N. Tinbergen, this is a body-mind holistic approach which operates through gentle touch guidance and self-monitoring to correct and adjust any habitual misuse of the self. Usually the work is one to one. The technique is in use with handicapped individuals as well as performers and laymen. There are classes for teachers and individuals at the American Center for the Alexander Technique, 142 West End Avenue, N.Y. 10023 (212/799-0468).

The fundamentals and correctives technique taught by Irmgard Bartenieff and her followers is somewhat differently based. Bartenieff was a Laban-trained teacher in Germany in the 1920s. Her movement observation, and her notation and teaching and dance performing background, together with her many years as a physiotherapist in New York, led to a new unification of these disciplines. The methodology of the fundamentals and correctives work is experiential, in a group or class. As the name suggests, the attempt is to go back to the most elementary movements such as rolling over, sitting up, standing, and walking, to make basic corrections and carry them into everyday life. Courses are taught at a number of centers, including the new Laban Institute of Movement Studies, founded by Bartenieff, 151 West 19 Street, New York, N.Y. 10011 (212/255-6800).

"Loving your body through awareness movement" has been used as the title for workshops in the techniques of Dr. Moshe Feldenkrais, an Israel-based teacher whose courses are offered (in addition to those in Tel Aviv) in Esalen, California, and New York City. The pleasuring aspects of learning are achieved through the acknowledgment and appreciation of one's body and thereby oneself. Changes are accomplished by gentling, sensing oneself,

Irmgard Bartenieff and student working on body connections from an upright position at the Laban Institute of Movement Studies, New York.

and facilitating "greenhouse conditions" to promote personal individual change. Feldenkrais teachers work primarily in growth centers (i.e., Ruth Alon, New England Center for Personal and Organizational Development, Leverett, Mass. (413/549-0886), and some course work is now available on cassettes through Hot Springs Lodge, Big Sur, Calif. 93920. Recent training courses on the East and West coasts have produced teachers who can be contacted through the centers mentioned above.

All of these methods depend on the holistic approach and embody some acknowledgment of the body as partner of the mind.

WHAT TO READ

Barker, Sarah. *The Alexander Technique: The Revolutionary Way to Use Your Body for Total Energy.* New York: Bantam, 1978.
An illustrated guide (including history and photographs) to attempting the technique as a home-study project.

Bartenieff, Irmgard. *Notes on a Course in Correctives.* New York: Dance Notation Bureau, 1970.
Currently only available as text to those enrolled in the course, but included in a book now in preparation.

Dell, Cecily. *A Primer for Movement Description: Using Effort-Shape & Supplementary Concepts.* New York: Dance Notation Bureau, 1970.
An extensive presentation of the system of movement analysis and observation first developed by Rudolf Laban.

Feldenkrais, Moshe. *Awareness through Movement.* New York: Harper & Row, 1972.
An outline of his theory and practical lessons in posture, breathing, improvement of self-image.

III.
Dance
& the
Liberal Arts:
Dance
Education in
Colleges,
Universities,
&
Conservatories

History of Dance Education in the United States
By Henley Haslam

ome form of dance education has been advocated for thousands of years for its benefits to health and physical development, but Puritanism and the strong work ethic in early America slowed the acceptance of dance as a subject suited for general education. A few private dancing schools existed in colonial times, but there was very little theatrical dancing and no great demand for the study of dance as an art.

In the nineteenth century, dance gained some acceptance in private seminaries and colleges for women as a means of acquiring poise and for its physical benefits. Simple exercises and movements done to music were taught at Mt. Holyoke College in the 1850s. About that time, François Delsarte, a French drama teacher, developed a popular system of expressive movement and gesture which included many dance movements and was influential in helping to bring about the acceptance of dance in education.

By the early twentieth century, dance had become widely adopted in schools and colleges as a form of physical education. It was usually divided into "aesthetic dance" for women, a combination of some ballet and ballroom movements influenced by Isadora Duncan's "expressive dance," and a system of simple, coordinated strenuous movements called "gymnastic dance" for men.

In New York City, at Teachers College, Columbia University, Gertrude Colby taught a system of physical education based on natural movement. At Barnard College, Bird Larsen developed a technique using principles of anatomy and kinesiology. The experimental work of Colby and Larsen, and the musically oriented work of Alys Bentley, were studied by Margaret H'Doubler, a key figure in dance education. She developed a system of movement which used the body as an instrument of expression; its movements were based on a knowledge of anatomy and kinesiology. In 1918, she was instrumental in founding Orchesis, a student dance performing club; similar groups can now be found throughout the country. In 1926, she succeeded in establishing the first major in dance at the University of Wisconsin, thus gaining recognition for dance in college and university education.

The influence of the performances in the 1920s and 1930s of such professional dancers as Martha Graham, Doris Humphrey, and Charles Weidman was felt in dance education, and brought a greater emphasis to the study of technique and the artistic potential of modern dance. By 1940, modern dance was an integral part of many college and university programs, accepted as an educational experience that was physical, intellectual, and creative. Modern dance, more accessible than ballet to the older student, continues to be more widely taught than ballet in institutions of higher education.

Since the end of World War II, there has been a tremendous expansion of dance in the colleges and universities at both undergraduate and graduate levels. Acceptance of modern dance as an art form along with an interest in the creative growth and self-fulfillment of individuals has increased the number of students wanting to study dance. There has been a tendency to move dance from physical education departments, where it was formerly relegated, into separate departments of dance, or to combine it with drama, fine arts, or theater. This has increased the number and variety of courses taught, as well as the types of degrees being offered. There has also been an expansion of summer programs and workshops since the first summer program established in 1934 at Bennington College, Vermont, by Martha Hill and Mary Josephine Shelley.

A college or university dance program in a liberal arts setting will offer not only dance technique courses but a strong liberal arts foundation of work in music, theater, languages, philosophy, history, mathematics, science, and fine arts. A dance program in a conservatory or school of music will stress technique courses with a performing emphasis and dance-related courses, supplanted by a smaller selection of courses in such areas as music, drama, languages, history, English, and the humanities. The aim of most undergraduate programs is to produce dancers, choreographers, teachers, or specialists in history and criticism. On the graduate level, there is less emphasis on technique and performing, and more on theoretical, philosophical, or historical studies.

The degrees usually offered today are:

A.A.—usually a two-year program with performing emphasis offered by a conservatory.

B.A., B.F.A.—performing emphasis.

B.A., B.S.—dance education emphasis.

M.A., M.F.A.—concentration in performing arts.

M. Ed., M.S.—concentration in dance education.

Ph.D., Ed. D.—usually interdepartmental with dance emphasis.

Dance in higher education has come a long way from the first dance major in 1926 to the over-200 undergraduate and graduate programs offered today.

WHAT TO READ

Krause, Richard. *History of the Dance in Art and Education.* Englewood, N.J.: Prentice-Hall, 1969.

Opposite: Kazuko Hirabayashi teaching modern dance. Overleaf: Hanya Holm teaching advanced students techniques of performance at The Juilliard School.

III. Dance & the Liberal Arts:

Courses Offered in Colleges and Universities

Some colleges and universities offer a wide range of dance courses and some offer only a few for physical education majors or service courses for the entire student body. Departments are dependent on individuals for special strengths, and when individuals leave, the nature of their courses often changes. There are unique courses such as "Dance Lecture-Demonstrations" at the University of Utah and "Development of Stage Presence" at North Carolina School of the Arts. The list below gives examples of the variety of courses with a general description of their content. (Course titles and exact content vary with each school.) Schools that are particularly strong in certain areas are mentioned after the course description.

Anna Sokolow rehearsing students for performance of **The Night of the Mayas** *at The Juilliard School.*

Anatomy and Kinesiology. Study of the human body's structure and major organ systems, major joints, muscle location, and principles of muscle action and relationship to movement.
Hunter College, CUNY, New York, N.Y.

Biomechanics. A more advanced course on a graduate level in the above area. "Gross anatomy and function of human skeletal and muscular systems, mechanics of human movement, and analysis of skills in dance and physical education."
Teachers College, Columbia University, New York, N.Y.
University of Waterloo, Waterloo, Canada

Character Dance. Study of theatrical dance based on the national or ethnic dances, such as the mazurka and czardas, of Middle and Eastern European nations.
Jordan College of Music, Butler University, Indianapolis, Ind.
Duquesne University, Pittsburgh, Pa.

Composition Fundamentals. Elements of form and structure in dance composition; theories of space, design, time, and rhythm and their application to dance studies; development and use of movement themes.
University of Illinois, Urbana-Champaign, Ill.
School of the Arts, New York University, New York, N.Y.

Dance History. Development of dance as an art form from primitive to contemporary times; trends, philosophies, events, and dance personalities are examined and related to other art forms (see pages 230-241).
University of California/Riverside, Riverside, Calif.
University of Rochester, Rochester, N.Y. (major use of films)
York University, Toronto, Ontario, Canada

Dance Notation. Comparative study of the main systems of contemporary dance notation, usually with work in the analysis, recording, and reconstruction of movement through Labanotation (see pages 194-203).
Ohio State University, Columbus, Ohio
Sarah Lawrence College, Bronxville, N.Y.

Dance Therapy. Therapeutic use of movement, its theory, methods, and areas of application, with a focus on body awareness and movement observation (see pages 204-205). (Undergraduate courses are usually introductory, degrees are on the graduate level.)
Marygrove College, Detroit, Mich.
Southern Methodist University, Dallas, Tex.
Hahneman Medical College, Philadelphia, Pa.

Ethnic Dance. Study of indigenous dance arts such as African, American and East Indian, Caribbean, Ceylonese, Chinese, Hawaiian, Japanese, Javanese (see pages 146-153).
American University, Washington, D.C.
University of California/Los Angeles, Los Angeles, Calif. (with a particularly strong emphasis on ethnomusicology)
University of Hawaii at Manoa, Honolulu, Hawaii
San Francisco State University, San Francisco, Calif. (with a particular emphasis on Asian Arts)

Folk Dance. The basic steps and formations of folk dance; traditional dances done for pleasure (see pages 178-179).
Berea College, Berea, Ky. (particularly American)
Duquesne University, Pittsburgh, Pa.

Historical Dance. The movement patterns and techniques of the authentic pre-classic dance forms of Europe, such as the Baroque minuet.
Ohio University, Athens, Ohio
Stanford University, Stanford, Calif.

Improvisation. Spontaneous dance and movement exercises used to examine the principles of elementary

composition and to develop creativity in dance.
University of Illinois, Urbana-Champaign, Ill.

Introduction to Dance. Historical study of dance forms, personalities, contemporary trends, and criteria for appreciative viewing of dance. This course is often found in schools of continuing education.
New York University, New York, N.Y. (School of Continuing Education)

Music for Dancers. Fundamentals of music as they relate to dance: rhythm, phrasing, form.
The Juilliard School, New York, N.Y.
Indiana University, Bloomington, Ind.

Pedagogy. Concepts, aims, methods, and materials for teaching dance, usually with practice, discussion, and evaluation; analysis and breakdown of technique into individual steps and positions.
Modern:
New York University, School of Education, New York, N.Y.
Ohio State University, Columbus, Ohio
Teachers College, Columbia University, New York, N.Y.
University of California/Los Angeles, Los Angeles, Calif.
Wayne State University, Detroit, Mich. (particularly elementary & secondary levels)
Ballet
Texas Christian University, Fort Worth, Tex.
University of Utah, Salt Lake City, Utah
Virginia Intermont College, Bristol, Va.
Jordan College of Music, Butler University, Bloomington, Ind.

Philosophy, Aesthetics, and Criticism. Critical analysis of dance as a creative experience and the role of professional and educational dance in our society; analysis of aesthetic theories applied to dance; function of criticism in dance (see pages 234-241).
Barnard College, New York, N.Y.
Sarah Lawrence College, Bronxville, N.Y.
York University, Toronto, Ontario, Canada

Production and Stagecraft. Theory and practice of staging dance productions; lighting, costume, and set design (see pages 206-221).
University of California/Los Angeles, Los Angeles, Calif.

Technique, Ballet. The principles, theory, and practice of ballet; can also include partnering, pointe, and men's classes (see pages 118-129).
Indiana University, Bloomington, Ind.
University of Akron, Akron, Ohio
University of Iowa, Iowa City, Iowa
University of Oklahoma, Norman, Okla.

Technique, Modern. The principles, theory, and practice of modern dance (see pages 136-145).
Most colleges with a dance emphasis offer a major in modern dance.

Theater Dance. Dance styles and forms of the musical theater; can include tap and jazz, or these can be taught as separate classes (see pages 154-167).
Point Park College, Pittsburgh, Pa.
United States International University, San Diego, Calif.
University of Utah, Salt Lake City, Utah

In addition to the above schools, the following colleges and universities have produced excellent performers. They provide exceptional performing opportunities for qualified students and generally have fine performing companies connected with the schools.
College-Conservatory of Music, University of Cincinnati, Cincinnati, Ohio
New York University, School of the Arts, New York, N.Y.
North Carolina School of the Arts, Winston-Salem, N.C.
Ohio State University, Columbus, Ohio
State University of New York/Purchase, Purchase, N.Y.
The Juilliard School, New York, N.Y.
University of Utah, Salt Lake City, Utah

Colleges and Universities that are outstanding for the general strength of their departments or divisions of dance:
Mills College, Oakland, Calif.
Ohio State University, Columbus, Ohio
Texas Christian University, Fort Worth, Tex.
Wayne State University, Detroit, Mich.
University of California/Irvine, Irvine, Calif.
University of California/Los Angeles, Los Angeles, Calif.
University of California/Riverside, Riverside, Calif.
University of Florida, Tallahassee, Fla.
University of Michigan, Ann Arbor, Mich.

FOR LISTINGS OF DANCE PROGRAMS IN COLLEGES AND UNIVERSITIES

Dance Magazine College Guide (1978 Edition)
10 Columbus Circle
New York, New York 10019

Dance Directory: Programs of Professional Preparation in American Colleges and Universities. 9th ed. 1976.
Comp. Betty Toman.
American Alliance for Health, Physical Education and Recreation
1201 16 Street, N.W.
Washington, D.C. 20036

College Preparatory Schools

Across the United States there are a growing number of college preparatory schools with dance programs for students in the ninth-twelfth grades, some even starting as early as the seventh grade. These schools usually offer academic courses in the sciences, mathematics, foreign languages, English, and social studies in addition to intensive work with a performing emphasis in either

dance, drama, or music. The dance curriculum can include basic technique courses (ballet and modern), character, dance history, jazz, music appreciation, partnering, pedagogy, pointe, and variations. Auditions are usually required for admission. The schools range from the High School of Performing Arts in New York City, established in 1947 as part of the public school system, to private boarding schools. Several of these schools are given below:

Alabama School of Fine Arts
820 North 18 Street
Birmingham, Ala. 35203
(205) 252-9241

High School for the Performing and Visual Arts
Houston Independent School District
3517 Austin
Houston, Tex. 77004
(713) 522-7811

High School of Performing Arts
120 West 46 Street
New York, N.Y. 10036
(212) 582-4197

Interlochen Arts Academy
Interlochen, Mich. 49643
(616) 276-9221

North Carolina School of the Arts
P.O. Box 12189
Winston-Salem, N.C. 27107
(919) 784-7170

Walnut Hill School
12 Highland Street
Natick, Mass. 01760
(617) 653-4312

Summer Programs

There has been a tremendous increase in the number of colleges and universities offering summer programs or workshops in dance, either for college credit or not. The April and May issues of *Dance Magazine* contain many ads for these courses. There is also a listing, "Summer Study Programs," in the *Dance Magazine Annual* which is available in libraries or can be obtained from: Dance Magazine, 10 Columbus Circle, New York, New York 10019.

Some of the special summer programs are listed below with a summary of what is offered.

American Dance Festival
P.O. Box 6097 College Station
Duke University
Durham, N.C. 27708
(919) 684-6402

Opposite: Daniel Lewis teaching modern dance class at The Juilliard School.

(performances, companies in residence, classes in modern and ethnic, dance therapy workshop, dance educators workshop)

Special events at the American Dance Festival are: Critics Conference for working professional journalists. Dance Television Workshop for TV directors.

Craft of Choreography Conferences
National Association for Regional Ballet
1860 Broadway
New York, N.Y. 10023
(212) 757-8460
(conferences in different locations each summer; sessions in choreography, technique, music, costuming, lighting, decor)

Dance at Chautauqua
Chautauqua Schools Office
Box 1095, Dept. DD
Chautauqua, N.Y. 14722
(ballet, modern, ethnic)

Harvard Summer Dance Center
1350 Massachusetts Avenue
Cambridge, Mass. 02138
(617) 495-2921
(comprehensive dance program, workshop performances, guest lecture series, dance film and concert series, course in writing for dance)

Jacob's Pillow Dance Festival
Box 287
Lee, Mass. 02138
(413) 243-0745
(performances, ballet, modern, ethnic, jazz, repertory, composition, improvisation)

FOR MORE INFORMATION

American Dance Guild
152 West 42 Street
New York, N.Y. 10036
(212) 997-0183
Founded as an organization serving dance teachers and dance educators (primary and secondary school, college and university), ADG has expanded its services to cover others in the dance field. Sponsors workshops, annual conference; publishes newsletter, Dance Scope.

National Dance Association
A Division of American Association for Health, Physical Education, and Recreation
1201 16 Street, NW
Washington, D.C. 20036
(202) 833-5557
Sponsors conventions; publishes Update, Focus.

IV.
New
&
Alternate
Careers
in
Dance

RECORDING THE DANCE

By Linda Grandey and Nancy Reynolds

ance is often called, with justification, the most ephemeral of the arts. When the dancers stop, the dance is finished, and that particular performance is over forever. There is much about the dance of other centuries that we will never know, because dances of the past cannot be recalled and replayed before us. Unlike a book, a work of art (either the real thing or in reproduction), or a piece of music (either in score or on records or tapes), until recently a dance could not be studied before its actual performance, or viewed again later, or referred to before or after the fact in any way. It had to be experienced at the moment of performance only; afterward, it "existed" only in the imperfect memory of the spectator or participant.

In the twentieth century, however, this situation has begun to change significantly. While nothing will ever replace live performance, dance is now being preserved in permanent form in two ways: in a special notation or script (analogous to music notation), and on film and tape, which capture the moving image.

The reasons for wanting to record a dance are obvious: to preserve masterworks for future generations; to increase the availability of the work beyond its immediate performance; to provide accurate tools for stylistic and structural analysis by the historian, critic, and researcher (see pp. 230-241); to furnish students and fledgling choreographers with material for study. Anthropologists, ethnologists, and sociologists look at recorded movement for clues to the work habits and folk dances of other cultures. A knowledge of notation aids teachers: it develops their powers of observation and their abilities to analyze movement correctly and to perceive its subtleties; it also enables them to jot down the essence of a movement quickly for use in their classes and their own choreography.

Choreographers of this century whose works have been notated include Doris Humphrey, Charles Weidman, Sophie Maslow, Anna Sokolow, Norman Walker, Lester Horton, Léonide Massine, Antony Tudor, Paul Taylor, George Balanchine, Alvin Ailey, and many others. Segments of Broadway shows have also been notated. Kurt Jooss has said that without the aid of notation, his impassioned outcry against war, *The Green Table,* which he created in 1932, could not be reconstructed and performed by both modern and ballet companies in various parts of the world, as it is today.

NOTATION

History of Notation

The two notation systems currently in most widespread use are Labanotation and Choreology (also called Benesh notation). In Labanotation, the length of the symbol indicates the duration of the movement. The vertical Laban staff representing the body, with columns for the

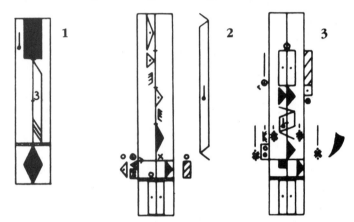

Labanotation. Triple pirouette; cartwheel (Figures 2 and 3).

arms and legs, is read from the bottom to the top of the page. Modifications and amplifications of the basic movements are written in the columns themselves or in the right and left margins. A floor plan, showing the patterns made by groups of dancers, accompanies the full Labanotation score.

Benesh Notation. Above: A sequence of classical ballet steps, printed with the music.

Benesh notation uses a five-line horizontal staff, printed in conjunction with the musical staff. The bottom line represents the floor, and other lines are for knees,

Opposite: The Green Table (Kurt Jooss), 1932.

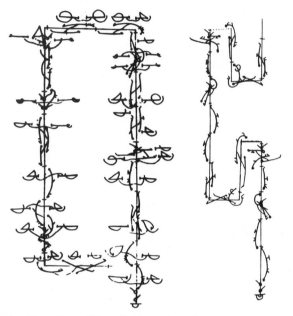

Feuillet Notation ("track drawing").

waist, shoulders, and head. Symbols for the movements are written on the appropriate lines.

Although these two systems are the only ones considered sufficiently comprehensive and well documented, as well as theoretically sound enough to be deciphered in the distant future, attempts to notate dance go back to the fifteenth century. As early as 1450, words and abbreviations were written opposite the corresponding musical notes as a form of notation. This system flourished for about 200 years and is credited to Thoinot Arbeau, who described it in his book *Orchesography* (1588). By 1700, *L'art de décrire la danse* had appeared, which outlined a system, invented by Beauchamps and perfected and credited to Raoul Feuillet, known as "track drawing" because it recorded footwork along the line of the floor pattern. This notation was an attempt to record the steps which formed the basis of classical ballet, but it lacked a clear indication of rhythm. Next to appear were stick figure drawings, mainly of arms and legs, placed under the musical staff as a means of showing body positions. They were introduced in 1852 in Saint-Léon's *Sténochorégraphie* and perfected in 1877 in Friedrich Albert Zorn's *Grammatik der Tanz Kunst* ("Grammar of the Art of Dancing"), intended for use as a textbook in

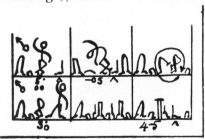

Sténochorégraphie.

dance academies. Timing was general, positions rather than movements were recorded, and the definition of space was unclear. Because of the importance of indicating accurate rhythm, systems based on music notation emerged.

In 1892, Stepanov's *Alphabet des Mouvements du Corps Humain* used the principles of music notation to record movements of the whole body in anatomical terms. The author died young, however, and his system was not developed. The Russian classics *(Swan Lake, Sleeping Beauty, The Nutcracker,* etc.) were all notated in Stepanov, and made accessible to the West when Nicholas Sergeyev fled the Revolution taking the notation notebooks with him.

In the twentieth century, many types of dance script were attempted, including those created by Eugene Loring, Letitia Jay, and Alwin Nikolais. None was successful enough to be embraced on a wide scale. The primary reason for the slow development of a comprehensive dance notation is that dance exists in time and space; formulating a system that can be written and read as a complete description of movement in time and space poses numerous problems and is extremely challenging.

Stepanov Notation.

The basic system must also accommodate changes in movement style (which have been so prevalent in this century). A system of notation must either have enough flexibility to adapt to changing dance styles or be doomed to extinction along with the dances it records.

Laban's system, published in 1928 (called *Shrifttanz* or "written dance") and extensively developed both in the United States and Europe, is now widely used by many ballet and modern choreographers. As an additional tool for movement analysis and recording the dynamics of movement, Laban's system of Effort is also used by dancers, teachers, choreographers, dance therapists, and behavioral scientists.

Created in England in the 1950s, the Benesh system has been employed by the Royal Ballet (many Ashton and Cranko works have been notated), by Balanchine, Joffrey, and the National Ballet of Canada.

Sutton Movement Shorthand was developed in 1970 by Valerie Sutton to record the Bournonville ballet schools

(see p. 121, Ballet). Used by the Royal Danish Ballet, this system records dance forms, sports, and the sign-language of the deaf. Essentially it is a symbolic script below stick figures written on the musical staff.

Eshkol and Wachmann developed a script in 1946-56 in Israel, where it is mainly used today. The system, a mathematical description of movement, employs a horizontal column divided into seventeen parts, with numerals indicating degrees of change in vertical, horizontal, and rotary motion. Works of the Bat Dor Company of Israel and the exercises of Dr. Moshe Feldenkrais are notated in Eshkol (see p. 181).

Careers in Notation. Notation is unique in that it deals with the past, present, and future of dance at the same time. Past and present dances are notated either when created or when restaged. (Notators need the benefit of the slow, careful rehearsals which the creation of new works or their restaging requires; it is not possible to write fast enough to notate a dance at a single "run-through" rehearsal.) The systems, flexibility in accommodating current dance trends and future styles not yet imagined is imperative; notators can record the evolution of dance. Thus, careers in the field are endlessly interesting, personally rewarding, and culturally important.

Notator

The principal work of a notator is to notate particular dance works while they are being created or restaged. A notator attends rehearsals and performances and consults with the choreographer and dancers. He then spends additional time organizing and recopying all his working notes into the final, precise score. In the United States, most notators secure work through the Dance Notation Bureau in New York (see below). Others work independently, and a few dance companies employ a staff notator. (A twenty-minute score takes one to three months to complete, depending on its complexity.)

A notator should possess the following characteristics: ability to understand and analyze the motivation of

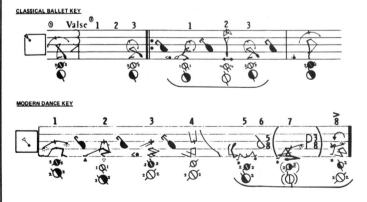

Sutton Movement Shorthand. Classical ballet key and modern dance key.

movement and describe it clearly and efficiently; musical astuteness; curiosity about all parts of the body in movement and how the individual parts contribute to the whole movement. An additional aid is the theoretical knowledge gained from years of dance training, which notators have invariably undergone.

The *Dance Magazine Annual* has a lengthy list of professional notators.

Teacher

A notation teacher may be a specialist, or perhaps combines notation with the teaching of studio technique, composition, and/or improvisation. Teaching notation is a growing field. In the United States, ninety-six colleges and universities now include notation as an integral part of their dance curriculum. Positions can be full-time or part-time, depending on the scope of the program and the versatility of the teacher. Notation is also taught at dance studios, Y's, and community centers for children and adults.

Reconstructor

The restaging of a dance from the notation score is the work of a reconstructor, who often travels a great deal, spending from three days (to polish and clean a dance already learned from score—a teacher fluent in notation can reconstruct the bulk of a dance from a score with students; a reconstructor can then check it for performance) to three weeks or more (to restage an entire dance for a company) on a single job. Restaging-reconstruction projects are often federally funded through the Dance Notation Bureau in New York or budgeted as a company expense.

Autographer

An autographer makes the final copy of a dance score for publication and/or printing. In most notations, the final copy is done in ink, by hand, with scrupulous exactitude. An autographer must be exceedingly careful, precise, patient, interested in detail, and possess good, sharp eyes and a steady hand. A complete guide on orthography (drawing of symbols for finished scores) is available at the Dance Notation Bureau.

An extension of the autographer, the IBM Selectric/ Labanotation element typewriter, which appeared in 1973, took many years to develop because of the mechanical difficulty of producing identical symbols of different lengths. Typing dance scores in their final version is a great timesaver over the "by hand" method exclusively used until recently, and the final version has great clarity and precision.

A computer-notator system, still under development, will not replace the notator, but will enable him to work at a faster pace to produce scores. It has been designed to allow notators to write, edit, alter, replace, index and/or categorize any part of a notated score within minutes. The computer can also store in memory one page or an entire score and produce a print-out by an attached copy machine on command.

When the computer is linked to the IBM Selectric typewriter (with Labanotation element), it will print out a finished version of the score in a fraction of the time it would take an autographer. Although at present this has been attempted only in Labanotation, it is conceivable that other systems will develop automated processes.

Courses of Instruction in Labanotation

For the training of notator, teacher, reconstructor, and autographer (now combined with computer training), the Dance Notation Bureau offers the following courses (among many others):

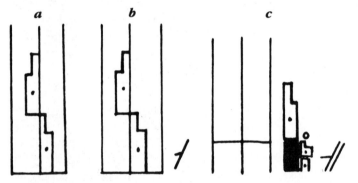

Effort/Shape. a. Simple forward walk. b. Same movement performed with a light, direct ("glide") quality. c. Slow forward arm gesture performed with a strong, direct ("press") quality. Drawings by Linda Grandey.

Elementary Labanotation. Fundamentals of writing and reading steps, gestures, turns, jumps, circling, and floor plans.

Intermediate Labanotation. More advanced reading and writing of limb movements, touch, brush, slide, torso rotation, lying, sitting, kneeling.

Advanced Labanotation. Includes center of weight, shifting weight, acrobatics, pelvic movements, partial support, handling of props, partner work, group work, hand movements.

Effort/Shape. The American development of the analysis of movement quality originated by Laban. Some examples of movement quality are: "He's coming on *strong*"; "She has a *light* touch." Effort/Shape is a system for analyzing, observing, and notating the affect or human qualities or texture of movement.*

---

*Complete Effort/Shape Certification training, as developed by Irmgard Bartenieff at the Dance Notation Bureau in 1965, is available at the Laban Institute for Movement Study, 151 West 19 Street, New York, N.Y. 10011; 212/255-6800.

Labananalysis. An introductory course presenting Effort/Shape and Labanotation for movement-oriented students interested in the perception, analysis, and recording of various dance styles and movement behavior patterns. Also includes a study of anatomy and kinesiology, fundamentals of movements, rhythmic patterns, and other notation systems.

Ballet Director's Program. Concentrates on reading classical ballet vocabulary to reconstruct and stage ballets from score.

Courses of Instruction in Benesh

A Benesh notator is called a choreologist. The three-year full-time program includes courses in notation, technique in ballet, modern dance, Indian, historical, and folk dance; music, art, kinesiology, anatomy, physiology, drama. One semester is spent as an apprentice to a resident choreologist of a dance company, attending rehearsals, checking scores, and, finally, completing a score. This comprehensive training in Benesh notation is taught only at the Institute in Sussex, England (see below).

FOR MORE INFORMATION

Dance Notation Bureau
19 Union Square West
New York, N.Y. 10003
(212) 989-5535

(Provides total training, teaches Labanotation, Benesh notation, and numerous related courses; certification program)

The Bureau is actively involved in research, publication, and education in the field, and dedicated to the preservation and advancement of movement analysis and notation. A library of scores (published and unpublished) is maintained; some of the scores circulate. Reconstruction of a dance is generally arranged through the Bureau, which often provides the reconstructor and the score, and contacts the choreographer for permission to stage his work. The Bureau also provides certified notators to those who wish their dances notated, either in Labanotation or Benesh. The Bureau also undertakes to notate scores with its own and outside funds (generally from the government) at no cost to the choreographer (who retains the copyright).

ICKL (International Council of Kinetography Laban). Laban's system of notation is known as Kinetography Laban in Europe. This association of specialists from both sides of the Atlantic meets every other year to discuss ongoing research in the area of

notation theory and the adoption of new symbols. Contact the Dance Notation Bureau.

Dance Notation Bureau Extension
Ohio State University
1813 North High Street
Columbus, Ohio 43210
(614) 422-6446
(Provides one-half to three-quarters of training necessary for professional career in Labanotation)

Institute of Choreology
Highdown Tower
Littlehampton Road
Worthing, Sussex BN126PF
England
(Total training in Benesh notation; nothing comparable in the United States)

The Movement Shorthand Society (Sutton Movement Shorthand)
P.O. Box 4949
Irvine, Calif. 92716
(714) 644-8342

WHAT TO READ

Arbeau, Thoinot. *Orchesography.* 1588. With examples in Labanotation, New York: Dover, 1967.

Benesh, Joan and Rudolph. *An Introduction to Benesh Dance Notation.* London: A. and C. Black, 1956. Basic text.

Causely, Marguerite. *An Introduction to Benesh Movement Notation.* London, 1967.

Cook, Ray. *The Dance Director.* New York: Dance Notation Bureau, 1977. Reconstructor's guide.

Dell, Cecily. *Primer for Movement Description.* New York: Dance Notation Bureau, 1970. Basic Effort/Shape text.

Eshkol, Noa, and Wachmann, Abraham. *Movement Notation.* London: Weidenfeld and Nicholson, 1958. Basic text.

Hutchinson, Ann. *Labanotation.* New York: Theatre Arts Books, 1977. Basic text.

Stepanov, V. I. *Alphabets of Movements of the Human Body.* 1892. Trans. Lister, 1958. Reprint, New York: Dance Horizons, 1969.

Sutton, Valerie. *Sutton Movement Shorthand: Book One, The Classical Ballet Key* and *The Notation Supplement to Book One.* Available from the author (see above).

FILM AND TAPE

Archival films and videotapes (that is, documentary records, not necessarily "artistic" or creative uses of the medium) have grown greatly in popularity over the past twenty years as a means of preserving dances. Their acceptance was slow in coming, but now, often with aid of government grants, the field is bustling with activity.

Loie Fuller's famous *Fire Dance* was filmed in 1906, and we have various filmed snippets of Pavlova. But, so far as we know, no films were ever made of Nijinsky and probably none of Isadora Duncan. Closer to our own day, we have almost no filmed record of Martha Graham in her prime. There are those who would argue that the rudimentary film technology of the early twentieth century, the poor lighting and jerky camera action, cannot possibly have done justice to such an artist as Pavlova, and indeed, one discovers many flaws, artistic and technical,

Sound mix facility.

in the films of her. But one could as well argue against the earliest Caruso recordings, off-key though they may sound today. For phrasing and interpretation they are priceless. What would we not give for a glimpse, however distorted, of the original *Rite of Spring* (1913) as performed by Diaghilev's Ballets Russes?

For a "complete" record of a dance, it would be desirable to have a notated score, a film or tape, many color photographs, and an interview with the choreographer (plus, in the best of all possible worlds, the composer and designer, as well as principal dancers talking about their interpretations, the coaching given them by the choreographers, etc.). "Complete" is, of course, a relative term: no two performances are exactly alike, and no performance is ever "definitive." In any case, such extensive documentation is virtually never possible. If one must choose between film and notation, each has its good points.

Some advantages of film and video over notation are obvious: the images have a visual immediacy and an instant legibility lacking in the abstract markings of a notated score; they are accessible without years of training. Costumes, lighting, the "look" of the work, stylistic essences, and movement flow are apparent in a way not possible in notation. Group patterns, especially if shot from above, are sometimes more easily grasped than in the line drawings of floor patterns accompanying notation. And a film or tape can capture a memorable performance. Who among us, for example, would ever have seen Ulanova dance the Swan Queen if the Soviets had not made a film of her?

The machinery, particularly the video camera, is fairly easy to operate, and video equipment is relatively inexpensive. The video image can be played back right away. Both film and video can be analyzed frame by frame. Film can also be slowed down, so that complicated passages can be studied in slow motion.

There are also drawbacks: video, and more particularly filming, require special rehearsals (extra payment) with special lighting (more sensitive in the case of film than in video); dancers may be asked to put on performance makeup and costumes, also an extra expense by union rulings; and an orchestra call may be necessary (many archival tapes are done to piano accompaniment, however, for purposes of restaging only; the general public will not see the films). The notator, by contrast, works unobtrusively during rehearsals that are already scheduled (notators may take individual dancers aside during breaks and ask them to demonstrate particular passages, but this does not take anyone else's time or require additional "union time").

Furthermore, when film or video are shot from straight front, which is usually the case (otherwise, more than one camera is required), formations, particularly the arrangement of people in the back of the group, may be obscured (unless shot from above, in the manner of Busby Berkeley movies, and then the front view is missing), as can details of partnering.* Rhythmic exactitude cannot be as precisely indicated as in a notated score. There is an additional practical point. Most films are shot from the front, to make a record of what the dance looks like from the audience (for whom it is intended); but, to reconstruct the dances, a dancer must reverse all the movements. The notator, by contrast, stands behind the dancers while working, and so takes everything down from the dancer's point of view; the notated right corresponds to the dancer's right.

Another major consideration in the case of video is that no one yet knows how long videotapes last; tapes should not be considered a *permanent* record. After five years or so, even with careful storage, bits of the image have been known to flake off the tape.

For more information on the care of both tape and film,

consult *Preserving the Moving Image* by Ralph N. Sargent, available from the Corporation for Public Broadcasting (475 L'Enfant Plaza West, Washington, D.C. 20024).

The expense of recording a dance—by one method or another—can be quite staggering. Government grants are sometimes available for "worthy" or experimental causes. In many colleges and universities, the communications, film, or audio-visual departments (depending on the school) can help merely for the price of materials.

The real financial crunch comes when you are dealing with professional companies and unions are involved. If the dancers are not paid for the filming, the "audience" is restricted to the point where only people associated with the company—primarily the rehearsal master, or occasionally those staging a ballet for another company—can view the results. If the dancers are paid a union wage for the filming time, costs are prohibitive. A case in point is the New York City Ballet. A number of the greatest Balanchine and Robbins works have been filmed, but, because of union restrictions, no one but company personnel (not even accredited scholars and researchers) may view the results. In some instances, the dancers are not permitted to look at films of themselves.

The single most important name in the field of dance films and tapes is that of John Mueller (University of Rochester, Rochester, N.Y. 14627). He maintains a film archive, seems to know about everything that is around (both under and above ground), writes a monthly column for *Dance Magazine* assessing new dance films, which includes information on where to rent or purchase them (sometimes, for one reason or another, they are not available commercially in any form), and has written an invaluable book on the subject, *Dance Film Directory: An Annotated and Evaluative Guide to Films on Ballet and Modern Dance* (Princeton Book Co., 1978). Other sourcebooks include *The Guide to Dance in Films,* ed. David L. Parker and Esther Siegel (Detroit: Gale, 1977) and *Catalog of Dance Films,* published by Dance Films Association, Inc. (250 West 57 Street, New York, N.Y. 10019). A mine of information in this area, as in many others, is the *Dictionary Catalog of the Dance Collection,* owned by many libraries.

For filming or taping your own dance (*not* in a theater during a performance—this will get you tossed out of the place), consult the magazine *Access,* which gives sources of equipment throughout the country (write to American Film Institute, John Fitzgerald Kennedy Center for the Performing Arts, Washington, D.C. 20566).

The *Poor Dancer's Almanac* lists equipment sources in New York (Association of American Dance Companies, 152 West 56 Street, New York, N.Y. 10019); the *Survey of Dance* by Joanne Kelly (Bay Area Dance Coalition, 1412

---

*The Dance Notation Bureau's video system, to be used in conjunction with the notated score, has five synchronized cameras filming a single performance from different angles. The tapes are then viewed separately.

Opposite, top: Editing bench. Bottom: Sound mixing console.

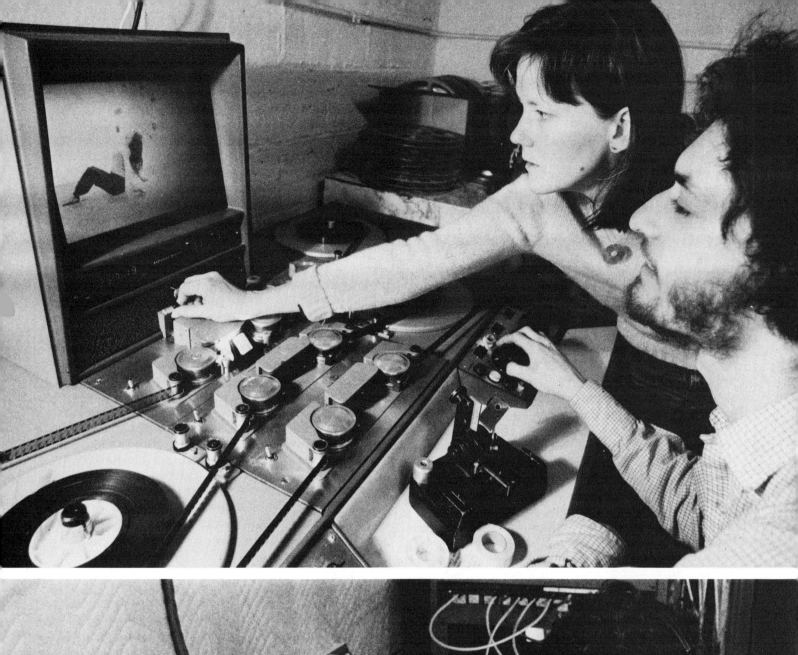

Van Ness Street, San Francisco, Calif. 94109) gives California sources. (Both of these magazines are at least two years old and may be available only at libraries.) Media Equipment Resource Center, 4 Rivington Street, New York, N.Y. 10002, (212) 673-9363, a division of Young Filmakers/Video Arts. offers low-cost film and video services to artists and organizations, including equipment loans, editing facilities, a video studio, technical assistance, and a variety of workshops. Organizations can apply for subsidy toward film rental and film speakers' fees. YF/VA can also be commissioned to produce films or videotapes for organizations. At The Kitchen Center for Video and Music (59 Wooster Street, New York, N.Y. 10012, (212) 925-3615) people can view their own tapes or tapes of performances that have taken place on the premises (Trisha Brown, Steve Paxton, Laura Dean, et al.); it also offers expert technical advice on producing new works, and on programming development for radio and television broadcasts.

If you want to show your videotape on cable TV, two outlets are Manhattan Cable Television, 120 East 23 Street, New York, N.Y. 10010, (212) 477-8733 (rental of equipment, plus reservations on Channel C or D) and Viacom Cable, Channel 8, 1175 Potrero, San Francisco, Calif. 94110, (415) 285-0776. The *Dance Magazine Annual* carries a lengthy list of filmmakers and videotape specialists, if you need advice.

Archives of Dance Films

Local libraries often lend or rent dance films to area residents for a small fee. Check yours. Many statewide library systems make dance films available free or for very low rentals to residents of the state. Money for acquisitions is furnished by state arts councils. Some states active in this area are:

Connecticut
June Kennedy
Connecticut Commission on the Arts
340 Capital Avenue
Hartford, Conn. 06106
(203) 566-4770
(information)

Center for Instructional Media and Technology
University of Connecticut
Storrs, Conn. 06268
(203) 486-2000
($3.50 service charge)

New Jersey
New Jersey State Museum
Film Loan Service
West State Street
Trenton, N.J. 08625
(609) 292-6313
($1.50 service charge plus postage)

Tennessee
Tennessee State Museum Extension Services
War Memorial Building
Nashville, Tenn. 37219
(615) 741-2692
(postage only)

Indiana
Arts in Education Center
4200 Northwestern Avenue
Indianapolis, Ind. 46208
(317) 925-9074

Other important archives, which may or may not circulate films, include:

Dance Collection
Library and Museum for the Performing Arts
Lincoln Center
New York, N.Y. 10023
(212) 799-2200
(advance appointment necessary; written permission of choreographer sometimes required)

New York Public Library, Donnell Branch, Film Library
20 West 53 Street
New York, N.Y. 10019
(212) 790-6418

Audiovisual Archives Division of the National Archives and Records Service
Washington, D.C. 20408
(202) 655-4000

In addition, many universities have active, circulating film archive/rental services, frequently through the institute's Audio-Visual department. A few include:

Educational Resources
University of South Florida
Tampa, Fla. 33620
(813) 974-2874

Visual Aids Service
University of Illinois
Champaign, Ill. 61820
(217) 333-1000

Extension Media Center
University of California
Berkeley, Calif. 94720
(415) 642-4111

Television

Although television has long been considered an "uncongenial" medium for dance, there has, in fact, been a great deal of dance on television. Excluding incidental divertisements, which would be almost impossible to find (Andre Eglevsky once said that during the 1950s, Balanchine choreographed a "little something" for him

every week on the Kate Smith Show), over the years *Omnibus, Bell Telephone Hour, Camera Three, Dance in America, Live from Lincoln Center,* and *In Performance at Wolf Trap,* among others, have devoted extensive footage to dance. Many of these shows are available in video cassette. Educational institutions in New York State can obtain them merely by sending the proper amount of blank tape, and others by sending tape and about $40, to: PACT, Media Duplication and Distribution Service, 55 Elk Street, Albany, N.Y. 12224.

Copyright

In 1958, in a volume of her commanding autobiography, *And Promenade Home,* Agnes de Mille lamented the lack of copyright protection for her hit dances from *Oklahoma!* and, later, for those from *Carousel.* Although she was receiving modest royalties for performances of *Oklahoma!* by national companies, she suspected that dozens of summer stock companies were producing some version of her work without her approval and without any

recompense to her. At the time, she had no established legal recourse.

Fortunately, that situation no longer pertains. Choreographic compositions can now be copyrighted through the Library of Congress, like a book or a song. The holder of copyright has the exclusive right to distribute copies of the registered work and the exclusive right to perform it or grant performance permission to others.

Effective January 1, 1978, the copyright law has a category for choreography (under Performing Arts). The new law also states that "the author" (this includes the choreographer as well) retains the rights to the work for life plus 50 years. This protection covers published and unpublished works. For further information, write for "Highlights of the New Copyright Law," Circular R99, Public Law 94-533, Copyright Office, Library of Congress, Washington, D.C. 20559. For dance, the person to contact is Gail T. Harris at the Copyright Office. Notated scores, films, or tapes of dance works will all be accepted for copyright.

Dance Theater of Harlem's Dougla *being televised for "Dance in America."*

DANCE THERAPY:
THE OLDEST FORM OF HEALING
AND A NEW PROFESSION
By Kayla Kazahn Zalk

Dance may well be the oldest healing art. The Encyclopaedia Britannica cites cave wall drawings of the Stone Age which depict shamans in dancing attitudes and date from around 4000 B.C. The concept of the dancer as healer with magical powers is an ancient one.

Dance therapy is a relatively young profession, originating in the 1940s, and usually defined as the use of dance or movement as the modality for working with the emotionally or physically handicapped. Current research in right and left brain function and in body-mind relationships seems to build the case for dance therapy as a primary tool in therapeutic encounters and development. Usually used as an adjunctive therapy in institutions, this new and vital field has become a strong element in therapeutic practice, particularly in America and also in other parts of the world.

A dance therapy session could include any one of the following scenarios:

1) an adult cradling the curled-up form of a blind child with her body and gently leading the child into explorations of space;

2) a circle of patients in a mental hospital holding hands and being led in rocking side to side by the participating therapist;

3) a partner dance led by a patient or client and mirrored by the therapist;

4) a group of aged men and women sitting in chairs and reaching with alternate arms for the ceiling and the side walls;

5) a group of people of varied ages exploring the space of a large loft in many ways, following the initiating image of the observing and guiding therapist;

6) A group of people moving around a room, encountering each other and responding to cue words called out by the participants and the therapist.

The development of dance therapy as a treatment modality grew out of the changing needs of mental health treatment following World War II. In 1942, Marian Chace, a dance teacher who stressed individuality and improvisation, began working at St. Elizabeth's Hospital in Washington, D.C. as a member of the treatment team. She had made her own dance students (children and adults) conscious of their emotional as well as physical growth, which aroused the interest of some psychotherapists in the area. When staff psychiatrists at St. Elizabeth's invited Marian Chace to explore new avenues in group work to deal with the needs of the large numbers of returning veterans, the beginnings of twentieth-century dance therapy were established. On the West Coast, Trudi Schoop and Mary Whitehouse were developing similar yet distinctly individual uses of dance as therapy.

The discovery of tranquilizers during the 1950s and changing attitudes toward institutionalized patients allowed dance therapists to work with people who had previously been physically and emotionally isolated. The human potential movement of the 1960s and the growing research in non-verbal communication were fertilizer for the further growth of dance therapy as a modality.

The growth of the profession is obvious in the following facts. Seventy-three charter members founded the American Dance Therapy Association in 1966. The current membership includes more than one thousand people, located in forty-one states and twelve countries. However, the relationship with older therapies is various and complicated. Dance therapy is perceived by some as a "new" and unproven adjunctive tool, and by others as a clearly valuable primary treatment mode.

Dance therapy is applicable to many groups in a variety of settings. From its beginnings in mental institutions (or in the earliest ritual healing ceremonies), it has developed and adapted to serve daycare centers, family treatment centers, correctional facilities, drug addiction centers, halfway houses, out-patient clinics, special schools and camps for exceptional children, special education programs, nursing homes, geriatric centers, residential and community mental health programs. Patients or clients range from the very young to the very old, from the "normal neurotic" to the deeply psychotic or severely impaired. The approaches reflect all the psychological, psychiatric, and psychoanalytic influences from Jung and Freud to meditation and structured systems of analysis. In addition to their work in agencies and centers, dance therapists have become private practitioners, and contributors and investigators in research.

Training to become a dance therapist begins with dance—all kinds and all aspects and preferably three or more years of professional work in the field. The road then diverges, according to level of profiency, age, and experience. Listed in the current American Dance Therapy Association educational bulletin are nine graduate degree programs (M.S., M.A., or M.Ed.) and eight undergraduate degree programs with specialization in dance therapy. There are additional courses and workshops in colleges, universities, and training centers in arts and growth as well as dance studios. There are numerous courses and workshops of the introductory, intensive, or on-going variety. All of these classes are led or coordinated by a registered dance therapist (D.T.R.). Training courses leading to a degree (either undergraduate or graduate) include a minimum two-year commitment to concentrated course work in theory and practice, anatomy, kinesiology, psychology, and diagnostic, therapeutic, and intervention techniques. Some programs include other arts and intermodal therapies. All include

field work and supervised internship and some require a thesis. After practice in the field and review, Dance Therapy Registry (D.T.R.) certification is available through the ADTA, but not essential in order to practice.

FOR MORE INFORMATION

American Dance Guild
152 West 42 Street
New York, N.Y. 10036
(Careers information sheet with several sources listed.)

American Dance Therapy Association
2000 Century Plaza
Columbia, Md. 21044
(Membership information, publications, etc.)

AIM (Adventures in Movement for the Handicapped)
945 Danbury Rd.
Dayton, Ohio 45420
(Information on volunteer training and placement)

The Dance Magazine Annual contains a listing of many types of dance therapist. These include physiotherapists, licensed medical masseurs, kinesiotherapists, osteopathic and orthopedic physicians, and chiropractors, in addition to the usually understood dance therapist designation.

ADTA defines dance therapy as "the psychotherapeutic use of movement as a process which furthers the emotional and physical integration of the individual." Those who may benefit are "individuals who require special services because of behavioral, learning, perceptual and/or physical disorders; and rehabilitation of emotionally disturbed, physically handicapped, neurologically impaired and the socially deprived of all ages, in groups and individually."

AIM is a "national, non-profit organization which trains volunteers to teach movement to blind, deaf, retarded, crippled and emotionally disturbed children." After a brief training period, AIM teachers work in schools for the handicapped in weekly sessions on a volunteer basis.

As a new career for dancers, dance therapy has grown enormously. It seems to promise further growth and development both as individual treatment modality and as an adjunct. In addition, it seems to be reappearing as a preventive as well as a healing therapeutic agent. The power of dance for integration as well as recreation is re-emerging, and it is hoped by many that science and art will merge and flower in this field.

WHAT TO READ

American Dance Therapy Association (see address above). Conference proceedings and monographs available. Selected articles concerned with dance therapy practices, procedures, theory, and philosophy.

Bernstein, Penny L. *Theory and Methods in Dance Movement Therapy.* Dubuque, Iowa: Kendall/Hunt, 1972. A presentation of a wide range of dance therapy techniques. Illustrated.

Canner, Norma. *And a time to dance.* Boston: Beacon, 1968. A pictorial essay on movement therapy with retarded children.

Chace, Marian. *Her Papers.* ADTA, 1975. A collection of the writings of one of the foremost pioneers.

Davis, Martha A. *Understanding Body Movement: An Annotated Bibliography.* New York: Arno, 1972. An extensive, detailed bibliography of writings on non-verbal communication.

Dance therapy with handicapped children.

Mason, Kathleen C., ed. *Dance Therapy: Focus on Dance VII.* AAHPER, 1201 16 Street NW, Washington, D.C. 20036. A collection of articles by practitioners from a wide variety of viewpoints. Includes bibliography.

Schoop, Trudi. *Won't You Join the Dance; A Dancer's Essay into the Treatment of Psychosis.* Palo Alto: National Press, 1974. A personal account of the successes and failures of a pioneer dance therapist.

Wethered, Audrey G. *Movement and Drama in Therapy.* Boston: Plays, Inc., 1973. A general statement of dance and drama techniques, based on Laban's theories, which are helpful with patients and normal groups.

PRODUCTION
By Mary Pat Robertson

The logistics involved in transforming a few dances into a full-scale performance can be staggering. Where to perform, with what music, costumes, lights, makeup? But participating in this process can also be tremendously rewarding, either for the amateur assistant or the dancer-choreographer who wishes to have a hand in the total production. Few are as multiply-gifted as Martha Graham, who has costumed her own dances with such imagination, or Alwin Nikolais, who handles all aspects of his dance-theater pieces, but the more acquaintance one has with production skills, the more rewarding collaborations with designers can become.

There are several non-profit organizations which serve as advisors for non-professional as well as professional performing groups. Many of these, such as Opportunity Resources, Technical Assistance Group, Dance Theatre Workshop, and The Costume Collection, are discussed elsewhere in this book (see pp. 249-251).

FOR MORE INFORMATION

US Institute for Theatre Technology
1501 Broadway, Room 1408
New York, N.Y. 10036
(212) 354-5360

Theatre Communications Group, Inc.
355 Lexington Avenue
New York, N.Y. 10017
(212) 697-5230

Technical Design-Management Services
4772 S. Ichabod Place
Salt Lake City, Utah 84117
(801) 466-8607

WHAT TO READ

Ellfeldt, Lois, and Carnes, Edwin. *Dance Production Handbook, or Later is Too Late.* Palo Alto: National Press, 1971.
Impulse—The Annual of Contemporary Dance. San Francisco: Impulse Publications.
    1952—Production Issue
    1967—The Dancer's Environment
Melcer, Fannie Helen. *Staging the Dance.* Dubuque, Iowa: Brown, 1955.
Schlaich, Joan and DuPont, Betty, eds. *Dance; The Art of Production.* St. Louis: Mosby, 1977.

FOR MORE INFORMATION

Two basic tools to help you organize production aspects are the *Dance Magazine Annual* and *Simon's Directory.* The *Annual* concentrates more on people—designers, stage managers—while *Simon's* is mainly a listing of businesses—scenery shops, lighting and sound sales outlets. Each has a broad geographical spread, and will be referred to in these pages for additional listings.
Dance Magazine Annual, Catalogue of Dance Attractions, Resources, and Services. Published yearly by Danad Publishing Company, Inc., New York.
Simon's Directory of Theater Materials, Services, and Information. Package Publicity Services, Inc. New York.

Another publication which is very useful, but might be hard to find, is the *Poor Dancer's Almanac.* This is a production and management guide dealing mainly with the Manhattan dance scene, but much of the information could be useful wherever one lives.

Poor Dancer's Almanac: A Guide to Living and Dancing in New York. Association of American Dance Companies, New York, 1976.

WHERE TO BUY

The *Audio Visual Source Directory* has listings about all aspects of theatrical sound systems, recordings of music and sound effects, and also lighting equipment.

Audio Visual Source Directory. Motion Picture Enterprises, Tarrytown, New York.

There are also several theatrical "department stores" where one can find anything from wigs to curtains. Like all of the following lists, this one does not claim to be comprehensive—for many more outlets, consult Simon's.

Alcone/Paramount 32 West 20 Street New York, N.Y. 10010	*Lighting, makeup, paints, fabrics, hardware*
Associated Theatrical Contractors 307 West 80 Street Kansas City, Mo. 64114	*Lights, scenery, makeup, costumes, curtains, rigging*
Tom Field Associates 601 West 26 Street New York, N.Y. 10001	*Lighting, sound, floors, sets, makeup, portable stages*
Knoxville Scenic Studios, Inc. 1616 Maryville Pike SW Knoxville, Tenn. 37920	*Complete theatrical supplies*
Northwestern Costume House (Norcostco) 3203 N. Highway 100 Minneapolis, Minn. 55422	*Makeup, lighting, scenery, draperies, costumes*
Oleson 1535 Ivar Avenue Hollywood, Calif. 90028	*Lighting, makeup, curtains, scenery*

Stage Engineering and Supply, Inc. P.O. Box 2002 Colorado Springs, Colo. 80901	*Lighting, sound, rigging, sets*
Stagecraft Industries 1302 NW Kearny Street Portland, Ore. 97005	*Lighting, makeup, curtains, rigging, sets*
10237 Main Street Bellevue, Wash. 98004	
913 Tanklage Road San Carlos, Calif. 94070	
Stagecraft Studios 1854 Alcatraz Avenue Berkeley, Calif. 94703	*Scenic supplies, lights, costumes, makeup*
Teener's Theatrical Department Store 729 Hennepin Avenue Minneapolis, Minn. 55403	*Costumes, makeup, props, lighting, special fabrics*
Theater Production Service, Inc. 26 S. Highland Avenue Ossining, N.Y. 10562	*Makeup, special effects, scenery*
Tobin's Lake Studios 2650 Seven Mile Road South Lyon, Mich. 48178	*Complete theatrical*

Below: **Afternoon of a Faun** *(Jerome Robbins), 1953. Three "walls" of the ballet studio are constructed of lightly billowing white silk; the fourth wall—the mirror—is the audience. Decor and lighting by Jean Rosenthal.*

The Performing Space

The prelude to any production planning has to be the choice of a performance space. The definition of a performing space has broadened dramatically in the last twenty years. Dance is getting back to its origins and away from the proscenium stage. Small groups have always performed in high-school gyms, but until recently the emphasis in production books was on how to make that space look more like a proscenium space, with elaborate curtains and wings set up in the middle of the floor. In 1964, Merce Cunningham and Dance Company started presenting "events" in museums in Austria and Sweden, utilizing the space as it was instead of trying to disguise it. From museums the idea spread to gymnasiums, where the audience feels closer to the performance as it watches the dancers standing on the sidelines, waiting to rejoin the dance. Without the elaborate production aspects inherent in a large theater with orchestra pit, curtains, and scenery, dancing can stand more on its own merits.

Another space opening up in the 1960s was the church. Judson Church, in Greenwich Village, was the home base for many of the most original performers of the time, from Yvonne Rainer to James Waring. Many outdoor areas are also now being used for dance. Cunningham performed in the Piazza San Marco in Venice, and Viola Farber and her company danced in a sunken plaza in midtown Manhattan.

Unless one is willing to dance in sneakers, however, a good floor is still essential. Even traditional stages can pose problems. Is it smooth enough to turn on in bare feet? Is it non-skid enough to run on in pointe shoes? For ballet shoes or bare feet, a smooth, washed floor is much better than a waxed one. The shod dancer will slip on wax, while the barefoot dancer's feet will stick to it like glue on turns. Problems arise when bare feet and shoes share the stage in one evening, because the rosin used to secure the footing in shoes is very hard on bare toes.

The most difficult problem to solve is that of a concrete-based floor. For an evening or two, dancing on a wooden or linoleum floor laid over concrete won't kill you, but beware of dancing regularly in a studio without a "sprung" floor—a wooden floor laid on top of braces, or "sleepers," which lift it several inches above the real floor to absorb the impact of jumps.

To deal with the problems of floors that are less than perfect because of stickiness, splinters, unevenness, or a multitude of ills, we are lucky to be living in the era of portable dance floors. These come in a variety of weights and makes, suited to the different purposes of dancers. Most are of vinyl or battleship linoleum, and are sold in flexible strips which can be unrolled and taped down when you arrive at your performing space. Some have foam backing, to help out on those unavoidable concrete floors and to muffle the noise of sixteen pairs of pointe shoes. Others try to preserve the noise, to help tap come through clearly. Many are available in different colors, some are reversible. Major outlets for Marley floors (made in England) and other flooring are listed below.

WHERE TO BUY

Associated Theatrical Contractors
(see p. 206)

Brett Theatrical
91 Beach Road
Bristol, R.I. 02809

Design Concepts Scenic Studios
3049 Rigel Avenue
Las Vegas, Nev. 89103

F. Randolph Associates
1300 Arch Street
Philadelphia, Pa. 19107
Their publication, Footnotes*, *is a mail-order catalogue for books, records, and other dance supplies.*

Theatre Technology
37 West 20 Street
New York, N.Y. 10011

Simon's also has a list of outlets for portable floors.

Portable barres are also available to suit a variety of spaces. These are great for taking class while touring, since very few theaters have much to hold onto other than light poles (an ill-advised practice). Retail outlets include:

Ballet Barres
P.O. Box 717
Sarasota, Fla. 33578

F. Randolph Associates
(see above)

Lot Piece/Lawn *(Rudy Perez), 1972.*

Opposite: Viola Farber and Company in Sneakers, *1976, danced in a sunken urban plaza.*

Props and Scenery

Once a space has been found in which the dancers can move, and danger to limbs has been removed by arranging for a floor, attention can focus on how to heighten the performance experience for the audience.

Christmas Tree from **The Nutcracker** *(George Balanchine), New York City Ballet (1964 version).*

How traditional is this performance going to be? Dance props can range from the starkly symbolic sculpture of Noguchi to live wolfhounds parading across the stage in *Giselle.* The decorative baskets of grapes Giselle's friends carry are one kind of stage property, while the necklace which the princess gives to Giselle is another, a functional prop. Martha Graham's great psychological dramas are rich in symbolic props, like the chess piece which the protagonist moves at the climax of *Deaths and Entrances,* or the stylized laurel branches of *Night Journey.*

One of the ways Diaghilev entranced Paris in the early twentieth century was with his stunning use of the designs of brilliant young artists such as Rouault, Derain, and Bakst. This era of design reached a peak with the Picasso set and costumes for Massine's *Parade,* which included two Cubist costumes. These were so unwieldy that the dancers' movements were reduced to elaborate walking, a throwback to the costume problems of the seventeenth-century court ballets.

Economics affect many of these decisions—Balanchine turned necessity into a virtue when he abandoned the drops of the Diaghilev era for a plain blue backdrop, setting off his dancers like jewels against velvet. Merce Cunningham has used the work of such modern artists as Frank Stella, Jasper Johns, and Andy Warhol. During one European tour, stage manager and designer Robert Rauschenberg would re-invent the decor for *Story* every night, using whatever he could find. Once he and assistant Alex Hay ironed their shirts behind the dancers as a living backdrop.

Whatever the choice, from elaborate to minimal, props and scenery must be well-made to withstand being danced with and on. Good tips on constructing basic props and flats can be found in the production books mentioned in the introduction, as well as in many others for drama. If you have a sizable budget, the *Dance Magazine Annual* has an extensive list of scenic designers. Or you could consult local drama groups to find someone who might be looking for the experience of designing for the dance.

WHAT TO READ

Clarke, Mary and Crisp, Clement. *Design for Ballet.* New York: Hawthorn, 1978. History.
Making a Ballet. New York: Macmillan, 1974. Good chapter on design for dance.
Hake, Herbert V. *Here's How! A Basic Stagecraft Book.* New York: Samuel French, 1958. Covers construction, painting, lighting, and curtains.
Payne, Darwin Reid. *Design for the Stage: First Steps.* Carbondale and Edwardsville: Southern Illinois University, 1974. Good discussions of stage space.
Southern, Richard. *Stage-setting for Amateurs and Professionals.* New York: Theatre Arts, 1964. Explanations of basic skills, hanging curtains.
Stoddard, Richard, ed. *Stage Scenery, Machinery and Lighting: A Guide to Information Sources.* Vol. 2 of Performing Arts Information Guide Series. Detroit: Gale Research, 1977.
Warre, Michael. *Designing and Making Stage Scenery.* London: Reinhold, 1966. A good historical overview.

WHERE TO BUY

Alcone/Paramount
 Theatrical Supplies
see p. 206

Associated Theatrical Contractors
see p. 206

Crawford Studios
428 East 10 Street
New York, N.Y. 10009

Design Concepts Scenic Studios
see p. 209

J.C. Hansen Theatrical Goods
423 West 43 Street
New York, N.Y. 10036

Hart Scenic Studio
35-41 Dempsey Avenue
Edgewater, N.J. 07020

Kentucky Scenic Studios
6405 Mayfair Avenue
Prospect, Ky. 40059

Knoxville Scenic Studios
see p. 206

Messmore and Damon
530 West 28 Street
New York, N.Y. 10001

Nolan Scenery Studios
1163 Atlantic Avenue
Brooklyn, N.Y. 11216

Northwestern Costume House
see p. 206

Novelty Scenic Studios, Inc.
40 Sea Cliff Avenue
Glen Cove, N.Y. 11542

Oleson
see p. 206

Stagecraft Industries, Inc.
see p. 207

Stagecraft Studios
see p. 207

Stage Decoration and Supplies, Inc.
1204 Oakland Avenue
P.O. Box 5007
Greensboro, N.C. 27403

Stage Engineering and Supply, Inc.
see p. 207

Charles H. Stewart Co.
6-8 Clarendon Avenue
P.O. Box 187
Somerville, Mass. 02144

Texas Scenic Co., Inc.
5423 Jackwood
San Antonio, Tex. 78228

Theatre Production Service
see p. 207

Tobin's Lake Studios
see p. 207

Variety Scenic Studio
25-19 Borden Avenue
Long Island City, N.Y. 11101

PROPERTIES

Encore Studio
410 West 47 Street
New York, N.Y. 10036

Kenmore Furniture Co.
156 East 33 Street
New York, N.Y. 10016

Props and Practicals
150 West 52 Street, 5th Floor
New York, N.Y. 10019

Teener's Theatrical Department Store
see p. 207
Consult *Simon's* for more.

Above: Horace Armistead design for Act II, The Nutcracker, New York City Ballet (1954 version). Pages 212-13: Robert Rauschenberg backdrop for Merce Cunningham's Summerspace (silhouette of Cunningham in practice and the clothes rack are not part of the dance). Pages 214-15: Picasso's Cubist designs for Léonide Massine's Parade, 1917. Right: The French Manager; left: Horse.

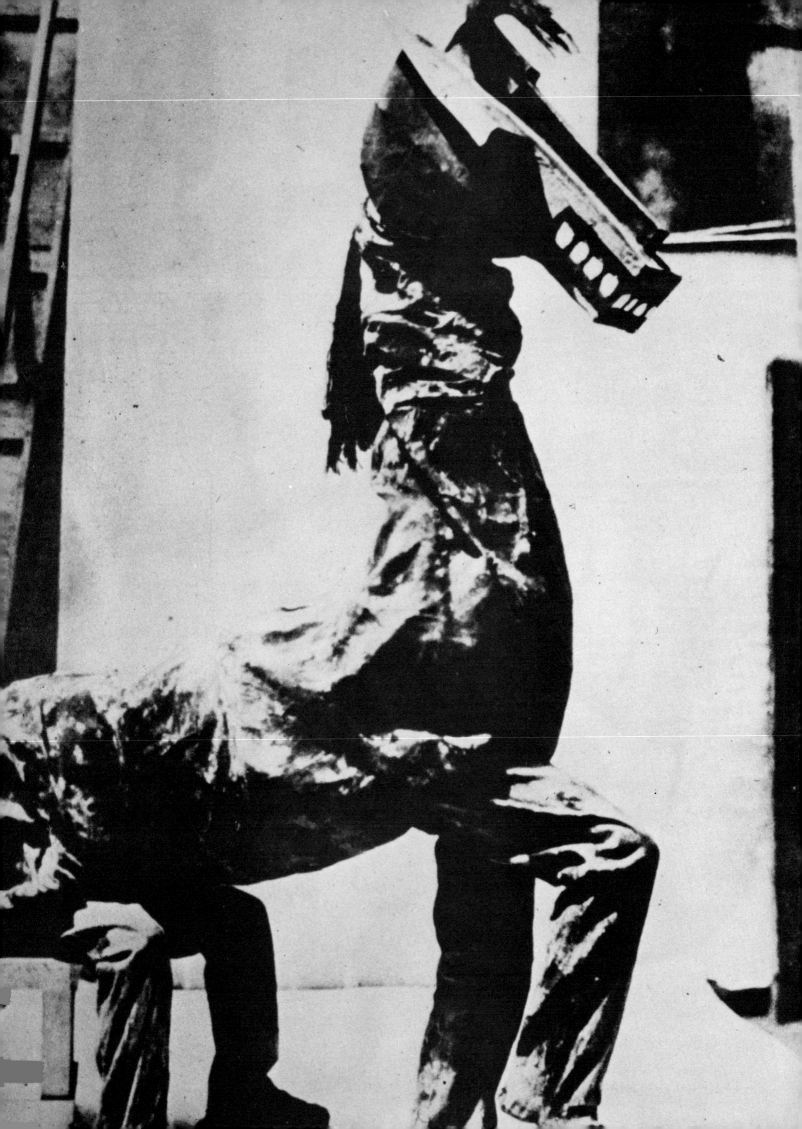

Lighting

Lighting the stage has always been a difficult, and sometimes a dangerous task. In the era of candlelight, the great question was how to light and extinguish a great number of candles quickly. Gas light was one of the contributing factors in the advent of the Romantic ballet, because of all the ghostly effects that could be achieved. The great drawback, however, was that the tulle of a ballerina's costume was highly flammable, and several dancers died when their costumes caught fire.

Backstage.

One of the pioneers of special dance lighting as we know it was Jean Rosenthal. In the first part of this century, dance had been lit from the front, mainly with footlights, which tend to make the dancers look flat. Rosenthal opened up the entire performing space, bathing it in pools of light from above and from the wings. She had the unique experience of lighting for Martha Graham, the New York City Ballet, and American Ballet Theater when all of these companies were just beginning.

The sixties brought the idea of the "light show" to dance. Alwin Nikolais is the master here, relying heavily in his dances on special effects, such as projections of either realistic photography or abstract patterns; black light,

which makes fluorescent objects seem to float; and strobe lighting, which distorts the image and flow of movement with irregular flickering. The Joffrey Ballet's rock ballet *Astarte* also made use of films projected onto the backcloth.

In a traditional theater, lights are hung from horizontal poles above the stage and from vertical poles in the wings. Additional lighting may be supplied by lights attached to the balcony, by footlights, or by a "followspot" at the back of the house. Lights are covered with a "gel," a thin sheet of colored gelatin or glass designed to help soften the light and thus create a mood for the scene. "Romantic" ballets, such as *Les Sylphides* and *Serenade,* are bathed in blue light which resembles moonlight, while most musical comedies are lit very brightly to prepare the audience for humor. Gels have to be selected while looking at the dancers in makeup and costume, because colored light can radically alter both—red lipstick can turn black, and lovely costumes can fade from view in the wrong light.

The best lighting should create a sense of place if there is no scenery, enhance what scenery there may be, and flatter the dancers and the costumes without calling attention to itself. This is a big bill to fill, and always takes much longer to arrange than you think it will, if it can be made to happen at all. Planning for lighting should start early, with the lighting designer familiarizing himself with the dance until he can recreate its mood, and then attempting to mesh his conception with that of the choreographer and the costume designer. Try to find someone who knows his business and respects yours, and let the attitude be mutual. Technical rehearsals are trying at best, and the more each participant acknowledges his ignorance and lets the expert do his work, the more painless the evening will be.

Designers can be found through the *Dance Magazine Annual* as well as through nearby colleges and drama clubs. Some of the non-profit groups listed at the beginning of this chapter have personnel files which could help you find a lighting designer in your community. In order to gain a knowledge of their field, these books would be helpful:

Bongar, Emmet W. *Practical Stage Lighting.* Theatre Student Series. New York: Richard Rosen, 1971.
Hake, Herbert. *Here's How!* See above, under Sets.
McCandless, Stanley. *A Method of Lighting the Stage.* Fourth ed., New York: Theatre Arts, 1958.
Pilbrow, Richard. *Stage Lighting.* New York: Van Nostrand, 1971.
Rosenthal, Jean and Wertenbaker, Lael. *The Magic of Light: The Craft and Career of Jean Rosenthal, Pioneer in Lighting for the Modern Stage.* New York: Little, Brown Theatre Arts Books, 1972.
Stoddard, ed. *Stage Scenery, Machinery and Lighting.* See above, under Sets.

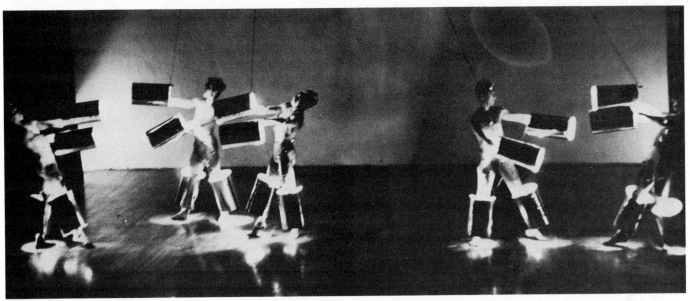

Vaudeville of the Elements *(Alwin Nikolais), 1965.*

SALES AND RENTALS OF LIGHTING EQUIPMENT

Alcone/Paramount
(see p. 206)

American Stage Lighting Co., Inc.
1331c North Avenue
New Rochelle, N.Y. 10804

Altman Rentals
57 Alexander Street
Yonkers, N.Y. 10701

Associated Theatrical Contractors
(see p. 206)

Bash Theatrical Lighting
2012 86 Street
North Bergen, N.J. 07047

Capitol Stage Lighting Co., Inc.
509 West 56 Street
New York, N.Y. 10019

Capron Lighting and Sound
278 West Street
Needham Heights, Mass. 02194

Century Strand, Inc.
5432 West 102 Street
Los Angeles, Calif. 90045

Decor Electronics
4711 East 5 Street
Austin, Tex. 78702

Four Star Stage Lighting
585 Gerard Avenue
Bronx, N.Y. 10451

Hub Electric Co., Inc.
940 Industrial Drive
Elmhurst, Ill. 60126

Kentucky Scenic Studios
(see p. 211)

Kliegl Brothers
2333 North Valley
Burbank, Calif. 91504

32-32 48th Avenue
Long Island City, N.Y. 11101

Little Stage Lighting Co.
P.O. Box 20211
10507 Harry Hines Boulevard
Dallas, Tex. 75220

Naren Industries, Inc.
1214-22 W. Madison Street
Chicago, Ill. 60607

Northwestern Costume House
(see p. 206)

Oleson
(see p. 206)

Production Arts Lighting
428 East 10 Street
New York, N.Y. 10009

Rosco Laboratories, Inc.
214 Harrison Avenue
Harrison, N.Y. 10528

36 Bush Avenue
Port Chester, N.Y. 10573

11420 Ventura Boulevard
Studio City, Calif. 91604

Spradlin Brothers Stage Lighting
5700 Mallory Road
Red Oak, Ga. 30272

Stagecraft Industries
(see p. 207)

Stagecraft Studios
(see p. 207)

Stage Engineering and Supply
(see p. 207)

Charles H. Stewart
(see p. 211)

Teener's Theatrical Department Store
(see p. 207)

Theater Production Service
(see p. 207)

Times Square Stage Lighting Co.
318 West 47 Street
New York, N.Y. 10036

Consult *Simon's* for more.

Audio

Sound has always been thought of as concurrent with or inspiration for the choreography. A choreographer with the musical intelligence of Balanchine can create *Concerto Barocco,* echoing and fulfilling the music of Bach. Graham usually commissions her scores, using the music of such contemporaries as Copland, dello Joio, and Louis Horst. When Cunningham decided to free modern dance from its extraneous trappings, dependence on music went right along with the story line. He likes to use music, particularly that of composer John Cage, but he doesn't set the dance to the music. Often the dancers hear the music for the first time as they perform the work. Audiences who enjoyed the lyric quartet in Twyla Tharp's *Bix Pieces,* set to Haydn's "Emperor Quartet," were surprised to learn that the dance had not been set to that music at all, but to something entirely different—in performance, dance and music just coexisted, and our eyes and ears inferred a relationship.

A favorite accompaniment is the tape collage. Part of the dance can be set to pre-existing music, then continue in silence for a while, then go on to the sound of a faucet dripping, or the songs of the hump-backed whale. Maurice Béjart used a tape collage in his work, *Nijinsky, Clown of God,* which was set to a combination of *musique concrète* by Pierre Henry, Tchaikovsky's "Symphonie Pathetique," and readings from Nijinsky's diary.

Another valid possibility is "internal accompaniment" —the sound of feet slapping against the floor in rhythm, breathing, counting. Jerome Robbins used this alternative brilliantly in the ballet *Moves,* danced to no music at all.

The greatest luxury is to have live music, such as a string quartet or a jazz clarinetist improvising as you dance. Live music can range from a single piano, used by Robbins for ballets from *The Concert* to *The Goldberg Variations,* all the way up to an orchestra plus singers with no less than four pianos, as in his production of *Les Noces.*

If you have the funds to hire a composer or musicians to play standard repertory, local music teachers might have students to recommend. Community groups are often interested in sharing costs for a program, but this can lead to problems about dividing the stage space, since the musicians will not really want to hide in the pit.

Schools and some sound stores can often help in making tapes. Organizations such as Media Equipment Resources Center (see p. 218) have sound studios and equipment that can be rented to non-profit organizations. An excellent discussion of music for choreography can be found in *Making a Ballet* by Mary Clarke and Clement Crisp (New York: Macmillan, 1975). Places to consult for rental or purchase of sound equipment are:

Ace Sound
461 Park Avenue South
New York, N.Y. 10016

Capron Lighting and Sound
(see p. 217)

Gary and Timmy Harris Sound for Dance
236 West 55 Street
New York, N.Y. 10019

Masque Sound and Recording Corporation
331 West 51 Street
New York, N.Y. 10019

Media Equipment Resource Center
4 Rivington Street
New York, N.Y. 10002
(see p. 218)

Pacific Dance Theater Library
1929 Irving Street
San Francisco, Calif. 94122
(Orchestrations of ballet classics and original music for purchase or rental)

Sound Associates
432 West 45 Street
New York, N.Y. 10036

Stage Engineering and Supply Co.
(see p. 207)

Theatresound, Inc.
585 Gerard Avenue
Bronx, N.Y. 10451

Theatre Technology
(see p. 209)

Yale Audio of Florida
2311 North A Street
Tampa, Fla. 33606

Consult *Simon's* for more.

Audio.

Costumes

Anthropologists theorize that man probably dressed to dance before he dressed for any other reason, and we still attach great significance to costume for performance. Ballet began as primarily a costume show, and the first major technical advances came about only after costumes had been simplified. Marie Camargo, at the end of the eighteenth century, raised her skirts, lowered her shoe heels, and showed off her jump with a little beat, unprecedented for a woman at that time (see page 19).

The two great costume innovations of the nineteenth century are still with us, the Romantic and classical tutus. The Romantic tutu originated in the French ballets of the first half of the century, such as *Giselle* and *La Sylphide,* with their scenes of ghosts and spirits. The classical, short tutu emerged in Russia in the latter part of the century, and is associated with the ballets of Marius Petipa, such as *Sleeping Beauty* and *La Bayadere.*

In the twentieth century, dancers have been steadily trying to simplify costumes. One of Isadora Duncan's most shocking innovations was to dance bare-legged wearing a Grecian tunic. She wanted the body to be seen in action, and so did George Balanchine when he started presenting some of his ballets, such as *Agon,* in practice clothes instead of tutus. Martha Graham designed stunning costumes for her dancers, including ingenious skirts which fit the torso so as to require no separate trunks. Much of modern dance looks most at home in sports clothes, such as jogging shorts and T-shirts. Santo Loquasto made a wonderful costume statement about dancers' layers of practice clothes in his satin layered costumes for Twyla Tharp's dance, *Sue's Leg.*

This is one aspect of production about which many choreographers have definite ideas. Just remember that if those ideas include something fitted, you should enlist the help of someone with experience in dance costuming. Making a fitted bodice that won't slide in a lift, or curtail the dancer's breathing, is a special skill. The effect of any lighting scheme should also be considered, so that the glowing colors you choose for your costumes won't disappear in the lights. Above all, costumes, like lighting, should not detract from the dance by their fussiness. Their purpose is to enhance the dancers' bodies and the concept of the choreographer.

Some good books on the subject of costume design include:

Gorline, Douglas. *What People Wore. A Visual History of Dress from Ancient Times to Twentieth Century America.* New York: Viking, 1951. This is not about theatrical costuming, but is an excellent reference work on fashion of other centuries.

Laver, James. *Costume in the Theatre.* New York: Hill and Wang, 1964. History, with much attention to dance costumes, especially from the eighteenth and nineteenth centuries.

Motley. *Designing and Making Stage Costumes.* London: Studio Vista, 1964.

Prisk, Berenice and Byers, Jack A. *Costuming.* New York: Richard Rosen, 1970. Mainly for drama, but includes some basic patterns and cutting layouts.

Watson, Phyllis. *Designed for Applause.* Winter Park, Fla.: Performing Arts, 1972. For the daring, instructions and patterns for classical tutus.

Costume sketch by Corrado Cagli for The Triumph of Bacchus and Ariadne, Ballet Society, 1948.

WHERE TO BUY

A listing of dancewear and fabric outlets, as well as designers, can be found in the *Dance Magazine Annual.* In addition, many of these places rent and construct costumes. *Simon's* also has listings.

Associated Theatrical Contractors
(see p. 206)

Atlanta Costume
2089 Monroe Drive NE
Atlanta, Ga. 30324

Baum's Inc.
106-114 South 11 Street
Philadelphia, Pa. 19107

Brooks Van Horn Costume Co.
117 West 17 Street
New York, N.Y. 10011

California Costumes
15976 E. Francisquito Avenue
LaPuente, Calif. 91744

The Costume Collection
(see p. 251)

Dance Fashions
6 East Lake Street
Chicago, Ill. 60601

Dazian's, Inc.
40 East 29 Street
New York, N.Y. 10016

Eaves Costume Co.
423 West 55 Street
New York, N.Y. 10019

Hollywood Dancewear
6512 Van Nuys Boulevard
Van Nuys, Calif. 91401

Leo's Advance Theatrical Co.
2451 N. Sacramento Boulevard
Chicago, Ill. 60647

Northwestern Costume House
(see p. 206)

Pacific Dance Supplies
P.O. Box 16038
San Francisco, Calif. 94116

Stagecraft Studios
(see p. 207)

Teener's Theatrical Department Store
(see p. 207)

Universal Costume Co.
1540 Broadway
New York, N.Y. 10036

Makeup.

Makeup

Stage makeup completes the illusion, and varies in proportion to the dancer's distance from the audience and the tradition of the dance form. In sunlight or for a small loft or studio performance, slightly accented street makeup and a good base to give color are all that are needed. As the lighting becomes more intense and the theater larger, one enters the realm of greasepaint and false eyelashes.

When the ballet is a story ballet, such as *Peter and the Wolf* or *The Nutcracker,* there's plenty of opportunity for character makeup. Intricate shading, glue-on facial hair, false chins and noses—all can substantially change a dancer's appearance. Even for a "straight" makeup, much can be done with a skilled hand to minimize facial irregularities and draw attention to good features by shading and highlighting.

Makeup is great fun to play with, but be sure everyone is agreed on how much they are going to use. It's a good idea to have full makeup at least for dress rehearsal, if not for the technical rehearsal which precedes it, so that everyone can get used to achieving the desired effect without overdoing it, or without looking like a misplaced Wili in the midst of a corps of healthy American dancers.

For small-scale makeup, good effects can be achieved with any commercial product. If you are buying for a large group, however, you can save money by using stage makeup, which is a cheaper grade than retail makeup. If you wish to use shading and greasepaint, many of the firms can send you catalogues with color ranges, and some have pre-packaged kits for a basic stage makeup.

Melvill, Harald. *Magic of Makeup for the Stage.* New York: Theatre Arts, 1969.

Terry, Ellen and Anderson, Lynne. *Makeup and Masks.* New York: Richards Rosen, 1971. Good discussion of tools and methods.

Alcone/Paramount
(see p. 206)

Associated Theatrical Contractors
(see p. 206)

Bob Kelly Cosmetics, Inc.
151 West 46 Street
New York, N.Y. 10036
Advertises free makeup demonstrations for schools or theatres

Leichner/Stagelight Cosmetics Ltd.
Film Center Building, Suite 411
630 Ninth Avenue
New York, N.Y. 10036

Leo's Advance Theatrical Co.
(see p. 220)

Mehron
325 West 37 Street
New York, N.Y. 10018

Northwestern Costume House
(see p. 206)

Oleson
(see p. 206)

Stagecraft Industries
(see p. 207)

Stagecraft Studios
(see p. 207)

M. Stein Cosmetic Co.
430 Broome Street
New York, N.Y. 10013

Teener's Theatrical Department Store
(see p. 207)

Theater Production Service
(see p. 207)

Wolff-Fording Co.
119 Braintree Street
Allston, Mass. 01234

Zauder Brothers
902 Broadway
New York, N.Y. 10010

Running The Show

The stage manager is the person in charge of coordinating the myriad details of the production. He comes to the theater prepared to mop the floor, arrange the dressing rooms, set up the sound system, make sure the lighting is all hooked up correctly and not about to blow a fuse, check that scenery has been hung well and can be moved efficiently and quietly. He must also take care of props, setting aside a table for them in the wings, and remember to time the works and prepare curtain call procedures. The more frequently the stage manager has seen the works, the easier it will be for him to relay light and sound cues to the stagehands.

There is a great deal of good advice for aspiring stage managers in the dance production books mentioned earlier. *The Stage Manager's Handbook* by Bert Gruver, revised by Frank Hamilton, is primarily about staging drama, but is still very helpful. Drama Book Specialists/Publishers, New York. 1972 The *Dance Magazine Annual* has a listing of stage managers across the country.

Pages 222-23: Stage Makeup. George Balanchine (left) as Don Quixote in Don Quixote *and Shaun O'Brien (right) as Herr Drosselmeyer in* The Nutcracker, *New York City Ballet. Pages 224-25: Anna Pavlova in classical tutu,* The Dying Swan *(Michel Fokine), 1905.*

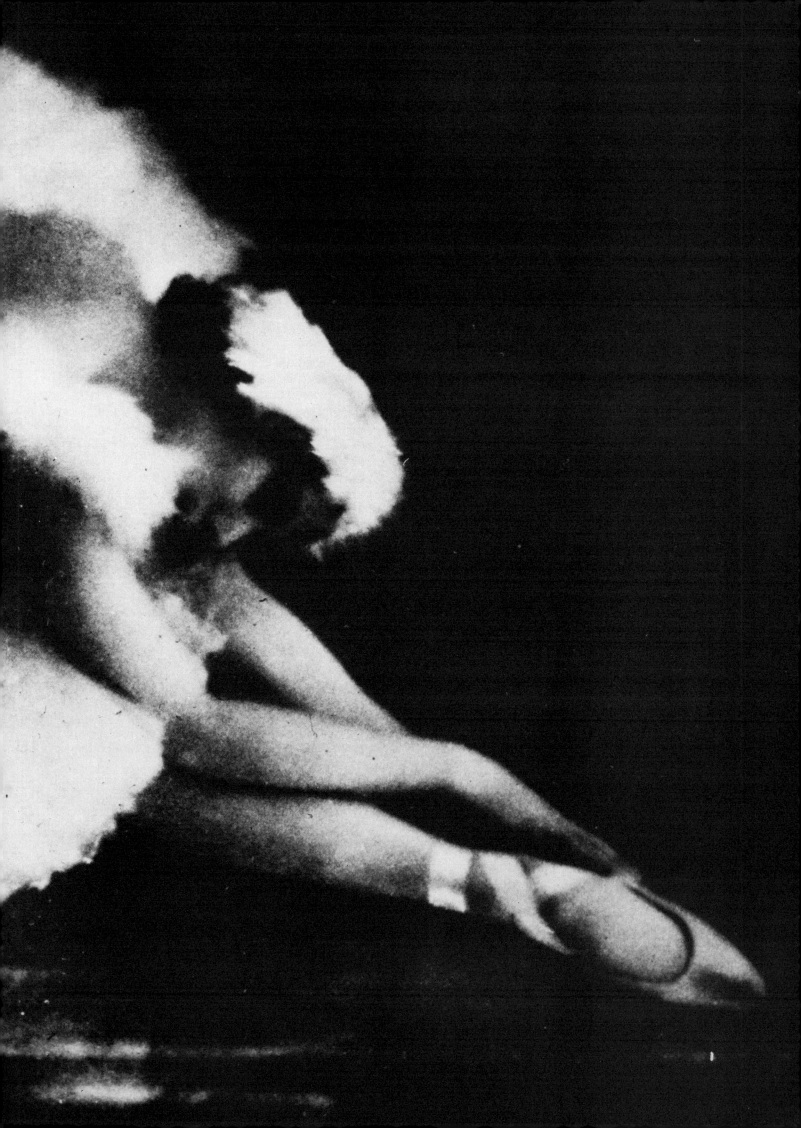

DANCE ADMINISTRATION, PRODUCING, PUBLICITY

By Ellen Jacobs

Dance Administration

The title "dance administrator" is perhaps the most elastic of all titles in dance, for it is used to describe every kind of non-artistic but dance-related work. What most dance administrators have in common is an organizational mind (most positions require an ability to deal with the multitude of details necessary for a smooth-running program), a sensitivity to the unique needs of dancers, a general knowledge of the art form, and a love of the art that will spiritually compensate for all the overtime work that often carries no financial compensation.

Since dance administration covers so many different kinds of positions, what follows are examples of the kinds of jobs that fall into this category. The descriptions of what these people do in their jobs and how they have learned how to do it should offer some idea of the range of possibilities and the kinds of experience that are helpful to anyone interested in working behind the scenes as a dance administrator:

Lisa Booth, who is now Administrative Director of the American Dance Festival at Duke University, began her career in dance the summer that she graduated from Connecticut College, where she had been a sociology major. That summer she ran the box office for the American Dance Festival, which was then located at Connecticut College. Charles Reinhart, director of the Festival, then offered her a job in his office in New York City. "That first year I did nothing but answer mail, type letters, and answer the telephone," she has said. That was in 1971. By 1972, she had begun to assume greater responsibility and that summer she became an assistant to Mr. Reinhart. As the Festival grew in scope, so did Booth's job. "I learned as I went along." Her present position is highly complex and demanding, for she is responsible for the entire financial, physical, and administrative operation of the Festival, a task which includes analyzing the Festival's financial needs, overseeing the spending of its $800,000 budget, creating and writing grant proposals, overseeing all bookkeeping and accounting procedures, defining staff positions, hiring Festival administrative personnel, and coordinating the spatial requests of the Festival's faculty and performers with Duke University. Her job also requires that she serve as liaison (and often diplomat) between the Duke University administration and the Festival's teaching faculty, administrative staff, students, and visiting dance companies.

Sandra Dilley has a long title: Project Coordinator for the National Endowment for the Arts' Artists-in-Schools/ Dance Component. The Artists-in-Schools program brings professional dancers, dance companies, and movement specialists into elementary and high schools across the United States for in-depth residencies. Dilley describes her job as being a "trouble-shooter," which means that she acts as liaison between artists, educators, the National Endowment, and state arts agencies. Her job is to make sure that contracts (between the visiting artist and the school) are fulfilled and the residency runs smoothly. The job is not quite as simple as it sounds, for it requires that Dilley spend a great deal of time ironing out the difficulties that inevitably arise when artists go into a community that may not be adequately prepared for them. She must keep track of what dance company or movement specialist is supposed to be in what school on what date, and help the schools to plan the residency so that they use the artists most effectively and to their mutual benefit. A great deal of Dilley's work depends on intangible skills that are developed through experience, such as the ability to second-guess the kinds of problems that artists may encounter in certain communities. Dilley is also responsible for planning an intensive week-long summer workshop, which is attended by all the school personnel, movement specialists, state arts agency heads, and dance companies that will be participating in the AIS program during the following year (generally about 400 people). Before assuming her present position, Dilley had been in charge of publications for the American Council for the Arts and had worked at the American Film Institute Theater in Washington, D.C. In college she had majored in journalism.

Mary Kelley Leer has been Dance Touring Program Coordinator for New York State for the past year and a half. Her job entails working with presenting organizations that are planning a residency by a dance company as well as with the dance company that is scheduled for the residency. Her work involves assisting the sponsoring organization in its selection of a dance company that is appropriate to its theater and community, helping with contract negotiations, and suggesting ways in which the sponsor can organize the residency most effectively. She also provides advice on audience development and public relations. Her job requires her to be familiar with the artistic and managerial structure of the dance companies that she is assisting, sensitive to the difficulties of touring, and have an overall understanding of the special technical requirements of dance companies. "I must also know what it means to present dance so that I know what questions to ask both the sponsor and the dance company in order to minimize problems on both sides," she has said. Before coming to New York City, Leer worked in Minneapolis where she produced the City Arts Fair, served as assistant to the director of the Urban Arts Program, and worked for the Minneapolis Arts Commission as a liaison between city government and arts organizatons. In college she majored in art history.

Robert Applegarth plays a dual role in his job as Associate Director of Dance Theater Workshop (see p. 249). On the one hand he is head of services at Dance Theater Workshop, which means that he is responsible for the advertising service that DTW offers dance companies (getting the ad copy, checking it, and placing it in the newspapers), for assisting dance companies in their use of the DTW computerized audience and sponsor mailing list, coordinating DTW's graphics department, and offering publicity and promotional help to dance companies. He also puts together the DTW Membership Kit which explains how to use the many services that DTW offers its member companies. Applegarth's other major responsibility is working with DTW Director David White on all aspects of DTW productions. During Applegarth's previous career as a stage manager, he worked with Peter Brook in Europe for three years. "After a while I realized that I had had all the experience I wanted in stage management and decided that I was interested in arts administration." Last year he worked for the Technical Assistance Group as an arts management intern on a National Endowment for the Arts grant.

Producing

Producers: short, fat men with cigars wedged between their teeth who nervously count the box office returns at the end of a day. That's the stereotyped image. Producers: men concerned about money. Like all stereotypes, the image holds a certain amount of truth, but doesn't give the complete picture.

While the producer takes the financial responsibility for a production, either by putting up his own money, convincing wealthy friends, acquaintances and colleagues to chip in theirs, or getting government or foundation support to pay for the production, he also makes, next to the choreographer or artistic director, the greatest artistic contribution to a performance—for he is the one who decides which companies will perform.

At one time, the name of a producer alone could draw a crowd. An advertisement headlined "S. Hurok Presents..." immediately attracted attention. Everyone knew the name of this legendary producer, and knew that whatever he was offering was bound to be spectacular. Hurok was noted for taking great risks and for doing everything with enormous style and flourish. Hurok's feats included bringing the American public dance attractions such as Anna Pavlova, Isadora Duncan, Mary Wigman, The Ballet Russe de Monte Carlo, Loie Fuller, and countless dance companies from the Soviet Union. He was responsible for the Sadler's Wells Ballet telecasts of *The Sleeping Beauty* in 1955 and *Cinderella* in 1957; the former was seen by a then-record-breaking viewing audience of nearly 30,000,000.

As a result of many changes in American cultural and economic life, Hurok's type of personal, flamboyant venture is now rarely found in dance. Most dance productions are backed by some kind of government or corporate funding. Though the producing of dance has become a different kind of business, the role of the producer remains basically unchanged.

The producer is top dog, overseeing and holding responsibility for all aspects of a production—from choosing the companies that will perform in his theater to making sure that the theater is cleaned up at the end of the performance. He oversees an administrative staff: the publicity, fund-raising, fiscal and audience development, box office, and house management personnel and an artistic staff: the lighting and set designers, stage managers, and technical crew.

He oversees everyone connected with the theater, which means he must also have an overall understanding of all aspects of production. He must be able to delegate responsibility, make important and far-reaching decisions, foresee potential problems, take risks, handle emergencies, and exercise imagination. He must also have a knowledge of what will be attractive to the kind of audience he has or the kind of audience he must find in order to fill the house. Ultimately, all the blame for a season's failure (the company bombs, the lead dancer gets sick and forces a change in program) and all the applause for its success (the company is a smash hit) are given to the producer.

There are many ways in which a producer can function. He can be elected by a board of directors to head an organization that presents dance in its own theater, as Harvey Lichtenstein was at the Brooklyn Academy of Music. Lichtenstein runs a different dance series in each of BAM's three theaters throughout the year. Which company performs in which theater is dependent on the spatial needs of the company and the size of the audience Lichtenstein anticipates the company will draw. The dance companies that Lichtenstein decides to present perform in the theater that he directs. A high school, university, or community theater can act as a dance producer in much the same way that Lichtenstein does, presenting a dance event or a festival of dance.

Other dance producers work independently of a specific theater. Their goal is to produce a festival or dance season or perhaps an engagement by a single company. The producer is free to arrange for the performance in the kind of space appropriate to the company, an art gallery, school gymnasium, the city streets, or inside a theater (see p. 210).

Sometimes producers are a group of schools or community centers that have joined forces to produce a season. They can also be a formally structured cooperative of people such as the Technical Assistance Group (TAG), which has been producing the Dance Umbrella in New York City since 1975 (see p. 250).

The Dance Umbrella was created to showcase modern

dance companies of artistic significance that could not afford to produce themselves for a week of performances or would suffer extreme financial difficulty if they were to do so. While TAG itself does not select the dance companies (it has an outside panel that does the choosing), it is responsible for raising the money to cover the costs of the company's fee, the rental of the theater, the salaries for all front-of-house personnel (box office, house manager, ticket takers, etc.), and backstage help (stage managers, tech crew, etc.), as well as publicity and advertising expenses.

While dance producers must be concerned about money, chances are there is little personal gain in the field for them. Their concern is having enough money to make something happen. Because of the complex and sometimes harrowing nature of their jobs, their work is inspired more by devotion to the art of dance and their desire to bring it to an audience than by any thought of earning a great deal for themselves.

Publicity

The dancers are taking their places on stage. The orchestra is warming up. Now imagine the curtain rising—to an empty house.

There are many possible reasons for such a sad story. One is that the publicist has not done his job. It is also equally possible that the publicist has done his job, but there was little public interest in the event.

A publicist can work twenty-five hours a day and succeed only in confirming what Mike Todd once said: "The genius for publicity is in the public." In other words, the public ultimately makes up its own mind whether or not it will attend an event. But the public must be notified that the performance is taking place in order to have the option of buying a ticket. Focusing attention on a coming performance is the chief responsibility of the publicist.

Publicists are responsible for all media coverage, before and during the event, which means they must secure feature stories, send out press releases and invitations to critics, and make arrangements for their review tickets. The publicist is also responsible for setting up radio, television, and newspaper interviews for the dancers and choreographers. Advertising is different; advertising necessitates buying space in magazines and newspapers or time on television and radio in which to make announcements. Publicity is free.

While it is imperative that a publicist be enthusiastic about whatever he is publicizing (he has to inspire the interest of others), the enthusiasm must be informed with knowledge. Saying that Merce Cunningham is an important choreographer becomes much more credible when the publicist is able to explain what Cunningham's importance is. Newspaper and broadcast reporters and editors rely on publicists for facts, so the publicist must know all that he can about the company, the dances the

company will present, and the performers themselves.

Publicists must also have an acute sense of timing. Productions are riddled with disaster-potential. Natural disasters are plentiful enough—a broken Xerox machine, the late arrival of program material, a change of casting—to create great backstage drama. Publicists must be aware of deadlines (every publication has a different one) since missing one can mean the loss of a story, which is ultimately the loss of a free ad.

If he works for a small producing organization, the publicist may also find himself responsible for community relations and audience development. These areas generally require giving talks, presenting slide shows, arranging for photo exhibits, and setting up lecture-demonstrations with local civic and community groups—the PTA, Rotary Club, religious groups—all of which is intended to develop interest and inspire enthusiasm in the coming performances.

There are several different structures in which a publicist may work: for a producing organization, which entails publicizing the various companies that will be performing in the organization's theater; for a specific dance company, such as American Ballet Theatre, San Francisco Ballet, or the Martha Graham Dance Company; or for a public relations firm which represents many different dance companies. Although the specific demands may differ according to the situation, in each case the publicist must be informed and enthusiastic about the company he is promoting, have a knowledge of the media with which he is working, and be able to work under deadline pressure.

Publicity is a job that has a beginning (the moment there is enough information available to send out the first press release), but no end (the possibilities for further work never stop).

WHAT TO READ

Books listed without a publisher may be purchased through Footnotes, F. Randolph Associates, 1300 Arch Street, Philadelphia, Pa. 19107.

Ashford, Gerald. *Everyday Publicity: A Practical Guide.* New York: Law-Arts, 1970. How the media works, how to get it to work for you.

Hurok, S. *Impresario.* New York: Random House, 1946.

Kaderlan, Norman. *The Role of the Arts Administrator.* (May be purchased through *Footnotes.*) The responsibilities, skill, education and attitude needed for arts administration.

Langley, Stephen. *Theatre Management in America: Principle and Practice.* New York: Drama Books Specialists, 1974. Producing for the commercial, stock, resident, college and community theater.

Prieve, E. A. and Allen, I. W. *Administration in the Arts: An Annotated Bibliography of Selected References.* (May be purchased through *Footnotes.*)

Reiss, Alvin. *The Arts Management Handbook*. New York: Law-Arts, 1974. The responsibilities of an arts administrator, including money, programming, public relations, fund raising and government.

Schneiter, Paul. *The Art of Asking: A Handbook for Successful Fund Raising*. New York: Walker and Company. An explanation of building an organization, strategy planning, cultivating and approaching donors, techniques for requesting money and follow-up procedures.

A Survey of Arts Administration Training in the United States and Canada. (May be purchased through *Footnotes*). The program content, enrollment, fees and contacts.

The following periodicals will be of interest to those involved in arts administration:

American Council for the Arts Reports (ACA)
570 Seventh Avenue
New York, N.Y. 10018
(212) 354-6655

Arts Management
408 West 57 Street
New York, N.Y. 10019
(212) 245-3850

Arts Reporting Service
2016 Coleridge Drive, #101
Silver Spring, Md. 20902
(301) 585-8560

Performing Arts Forum
Suite 605
515 John Muir Drive
San Francisco, Calif. 94132
(415) 584-6333

Performing Arts Review
Law-Arts Publishers, Inc.
453 Greenwich Street
New York, N.Y. 10013
(212) 925-4978

Washington International Arts Letter
P.O. Box 9005
Washington, D.C. 20003
(202) 488-0800

Advertising photo session.

DANCE HISTORY, CRITICISM, LIBRARIES AND ARCHIVES
By Jill Silverman

Dance History

Dance history and research are slowly becoming autonomous disciplines. For years the domain of balletomanes and amateurs, dance history is emerging today from its old position as the odd stepsister of the dance. The current popularity of dance has brought with it a renewed curiosity about historical forms, old styles, choreographic roots, and forgotten dancers. The last decade has witnessed a burgeoning of dance history courses in colleges and universities across the country. New books and journals supply the latest discoveries in biography, cultural history, and choreographic reconstruction to both the professional and lay audience.

Like all art forms, dance has a picturesque history. Unlike the other arts, however, preserving its past is a precarious task—after all, the "stuff" of dance evaporates with the moment of performance. This presents both a challenge and a threat to the researcher/historian. Unusual tools must be used to ferret out clues to lost material. Often, the only available information concerning an old work or a dancer resides in letters, diaries, technical manuals, oral history, or reviews. Research in dance often demands that the synthesis of related evidence stand in lieu of the performance itself— evidence as diverse as posters, playbills, programs, scores, scenarios, choreographer's notes, gravestones, and ships' passenger lists. Students of recent work have the advantage of film and video resources as well as the live performance itself.

After collecting vast quantities of sometimes unrelated data, the historian then begins the process of reconstruction. This can be fraught with problems. Terminology changes with time, and the meaning of a word can vary from century to century. Some things never become clear—for example, the early American dancer John Durang mentioned a step called "jockey crotch"; what the step was remains a mystery to modern historians. Moreover, the technical ability of performers changes as the years pass, and this undoubtedly affects the way movements are reassembled from old notes and manuals. Absolute authenticity and accuracy—even in mounting twentieth-century works—is nearly impossible. It is often not even desirable because of the problem of audience interest. What may once have been exciting theatrical fare may lose much of its power and charm when transported to another era. Tastes, dances, technical equipment, costumes, and conventional deportment change with time. Modern audiences are often bored by Renaissance and Baroque dance performances. The movement to us seems ornate and even stultified. When old dances are reconstructed and performed today, they are sometimes "embellished" in the interests of greater theatricality. The quantity and style of such "improvements" are, of course, the subject of lively scholarly debate.

Dance history has many uses. Aspects of historical movement, deportment, and dancing styles are invaluable to theater practitioners as well as to art, music, and theater historians. Many directors employ a movement specialist or an historical consultant to provide period dances for a Shakespearean or Restoration play. Dance history provides useful insights for social scientists and cultural historians. Anthropologists and sociologists often find the study of dance forms useful in their explorations of the social structure of a culture. They discover that dance reflects the society at large in its form and content. Those working in the area of women's studies face unbounded horizons in their historical and more contemporary analyses of women and dance.

WHERE TO STUDY

In the past, dance historians were largely self-taught creatures; today they are trained in specific courses in colleges and universities throughout the country. Though graduate programs are few and far between in dance history and criticism, related departments often permit dissertations on dance topics. The music departments at Harvard and UCLA, the American studies department at the University of Texas, Austin, and the art history department at Ohio State have recently accepted dance dissertations. The theater departments at Indiana University, New York University, Tufts, and CUNY Graduate Center also accept work in dance. The two most comprehensive guides to college dance offerings remain:

Directory of Dance in Colleges and Universities
Dance Magazine
10 Columbus Circle
New York, N.Y. 10019

Dance Directory: Programs of Professional Preparation in American Colleges and Universities
AAHPER
1201 16 Street, NW
Washington, D.C. 20036

In 1976, York University in Toronto began a unique M.F.A. degree in dance history and criticism. The faculty includes Selma L. Odom, Chairman, Dianne L. Woodruff, and Sandra Caverly. Inquiries may be sent to:

Graduate Admissions Officer
Faculty of Graduate Studies
York University
4700 Keele Street
Downsview, Ontario M3J 1P3 Canada

Opposite: Isadora Duncan. Pen sketch by Antoine Bourdelle.

For those interested in keeping abreast of current research, dissertation activities, and new departmental course offerings in dance history, Dance Perspectives Foundation and Dance Horizons co-sponsor *The Dance Scholars' Newsletter*. Address inquiries to:

Barbara Naomi Cohen, Editor
300 Riverside Drive
New York, N.Y. 10025

The following are a few listings of courses offered in dance history at colleges and universities:

Goucher College, Towson, Maryland. Major in dance history and criticism, directed by Chrystelle Bond. Courses: 1) Expository prose: magazine writing; 2) Journalism workshop; 3) New writing in the press; 4) Aesthetics; 5) Twentieth-century modern dance and its relation to other modern arts; 6) Great choreographers and dancers; 7) American dance heritage.

Indiana University, School of Music, Bloomington, Indiana. Courses taught by Frank Ries. Graduate seminars in dance history: 1) The Ballets Russes; 2) American dance; 3) Romantic ballet and Russian ballet to the present; 4) Dance theory and criticism: important theoretical material and critical writing from the eighteenth century to the present.

Sarah Lawrence College, Bronxville, New York. The Age of Diaghilev, lecture-seminar taught by Dale Harris (English department). Diaghilev within both the European and Russian cultural context of his time.

Colleges and universities offering advanced degrees in dance history or a related area:

Florida State University
Tallahassee, Fla. 32306
Dr. N. Smith, Dance Department
M.F.A. in history

George Washington University
Washington, D.C. 20052
Nancy Diers Johnson, Graduate Coordinator
Dance Program
M.A. with research emphasis

Illinois State University
Normal, Ill. 61761
Ms. G. Smith, Director of Dance
HPER Department
M.A. with history/research emphasis

Mills College
Oakland, Calif. 94613
Ms. E. Lauer, Dance Department
M.A. with history emphasis, also research and theory

Top: Poster announcing tour of the George Balanchine—Lincoln Kirstein American Ballet Caravan in South America, 1941. Bottom: Flora and Zephyr, 1796. Lithograph (1828.)

New York University School of the Arts
New York, N.Y. 10003
Mr. Theodore Hoffman, Graduate Department of Dance
Room 300 South Building , 51 West Fourth Street
Ph.D. in history

New York University School of Education
New York, N.Y. 10003
Dr. Patricia Rowe, Dance Department
675 D Education Building
Ph.D. in research and history

Ohio University
Athens, Ohio 45701
Dr. Wortman, Comparative Arts Department
Ph.D. in comparative arts, history, and aesthetics

San Diego State University
San Diego, Calif. 92182
Ms. E. Lockman, Department of Physical Education
M.A. with research emphasis

University of Colorado
Boulder, Colo. 80302
Ms. C. Irey, Dance Division
M.A. with research emphasis

University of Southern California
Los Angeles, Calif. 90007
Ms. C. Montez, Dance Department
M.A. and Ph.D. in history, research, and theory

University of Wisconsin
Madison, Wis. 53706
Dr. Mary Alice Brennan, Dance Department
Ph.D. in history, research

WHERE TO PUBLISH

Ballet Review *(quarterly)*
Box 229 Ansonia Station
New York, N.Y. 10023
Editor: Robert Cornfield

Dance Chronicle *(quarterly)*
Box 31 Village Station
New York, N.Y. 10014
Editors: George Dorris and Jack Anderson

Dance Magazine *(monthly)*
10 Columbus Circle
New York, N.Y. 10019
Editor-in-Chief: William Como

Dance Research Journal *(biannual)*
Congress on Research in Dance
Dance Department, New York University
675 D Education Building
35 West Fourth Street
New York, N.Y. 10003
Editor: Dianne Woodruff

Dance Scope *(quarterly)*
American Dance Guild
152 West 42 Street
New York, N.Y. 10036
Editor: Richard Lorber

The Dancing Times *(monthly)*
18 Hand Court
High Holborn
London WCIV 6JF England
Editor: Mary Clarke

Articles dealing with contemporary performance, twentieth-century material, the avant garde, or topics specifically related to dance and theater might be addressed to:

Educational Theatre Journal
American Theatre Association
1317 F Street, NW
Washington, D.C. 20004
Editor: Anthony Graham-White

Journal of Popular Culture
Center for the Study of Popular Culture
Bowling Green University
Bowling Green, Ky. 42101

Performing Arts Journal
Box 858 Peter Stuyvesant Station
New York, N.Y. 10009
Editors: Bonnie Marranca, Gautan Dasgupta

Restoration and 18th Century Studies
Loyola University of Chicago
820 North Michigan Avenue
Chicago, Ill. 60611
Editor: John Shea

The Drama Review
New York University
51 West Fourth Street
New York, N.Y. 10003

Theatre
Box 2046 Yale Station
New Haven, Conn. 06520

For articles dealing with aesthetic problems:

The Journal of Aesthetics and Art Criticism
American Society for Aesthetics
Temple University
Philadelphia, Pa. 19122

Research Associations

Congress on Research in Dance (CORD)
Dance Department, New York University
675 D Education Building
35 West Fourth Street
New York, N.Y. 10003

American Society for Theater Research (ASTR)
Department of English, Queens College
Flushing, N.Y. 11367

WHAT TO READ

Clarke, Mary, and Crisp, Clement. *Ballet: An Illustrated History.* 1973. Paperback, New York: Universe, 1978.

Cohen, Selma Jeanne. *Dance as a Theatre Art.* Paperback, New York: Dodd, Mead, 1974.

Dance Index (1942-48) and *Dance Perspectives* (1959-76) Two early periodicals devoted to dance-history research.

Guest, Ivor. *The Ballet of the Second Empire.* 1953–55. Repr., Middletown, Conn.: Wesleyan University Press, 1974.

———. *The Romantic Ballet in England.* 1954. Repr., Middletown, Conn.: Wesleyan University Press, 1972.

Kirstein, Lincoln. *Dance: A Short History of Classic Theatrical Dancing.* 1935. Paperback, New York: Dance Horizons,. 1962.

———. *Movement and Metaphor. Four Centuries of Ballet.* New York: Praeger, 1970.

McDonagh, Don. *The Complete Guide to Modern Dance.* 1976. Paperback, New York: Popular Library, 1977.

———. *The Rise and Fall and Rise of Modern Dance.* 1970. Paperback, New York: New American Library, Mentor, 1977.

Roslavleva, Natalia. *Era of the Russian Ballet.* London: Victor Gollancz, 1966.

Swift, Mary Grace. *The Art of Dance in the USSR.* Notre Dame, Ind.: Notre Dame Press, 1968.

Dance Criticism

Dance critics have special problems. Unlike writers reporting on the sister arts, the dance critic must catch the essence of a performance as he sees it. There are no scores, texts, or records to study beforehand. Dancing exists in a continuous span of time, and its form, qualities, and meanings must be recorded on the spot by firsthand observation. Nothing concrete remains of a dance after the performance. In recent years, film archives have provided a resource for critics who wish to study the style or early works of a specific choreographer or company (see page 202); unfortunately such tools are not available for choreography of the past or the vast majority of the current repertory.

The actual subject of a dance critic's attention appears only once, and his observation of that performance is unique. Unlike the critic of a film, a painting, or a novel, the dance critic cannot have the same experience again. The film can be seen again and the content will not change; a painting likewise remains the same. But a dance varies from one performance to the next.

Dance criticism suffers perhaps more than other kinds of criticism in that it has no clear canon of critical literature, no structure of familiar points of view, and no true historical tradition. Compared to, say, the discipline of literary criticism, which has been a full-fledged profession for almost as long as the existence of literature, dance criticism as an independent profession has been slow to develop. Dance as a form of social amusement, theatrical activity, or mass spectacle has not been treated over the centuries as something worthy of critical comment or serious study generally.

As late as the mid-nineteenth-century, dance criticism was still an avocation of writers from other disciplines. Nineteenth- and early twentieth-century critics from Europe and Russia were all art historians, art critics, and men of letters. When not writing literary criticism and poetry, Théophile Gautier (1811–72) became the foremost critic of the Romantic ballet in Paris. His pieces for *La Presse* in the 1830s and 1840s captured the revery and exoticism of sylphs and Wilis, which flourished in Romantic choreography (see pages 22-23). In Russia and Paris during the first three decades of the twentieth century, Andre Levinson's (1887–1933) criticism traced the struggles between the classical and modernist ideas in ballet. When not writing criticism, Levinson was a professor of languages and literature.

The first notable American dance critics wrote both for *The New York Times* and were professional journalists. Carl Van Vechten (1880–1964) was a music critic who later became the first influential American dance critic to record the performances of the Diaghilev troupe in this country, as well as the American appearances of Nijinsky, Duncan, and Pavlova. John Martin (1893–) was the first dance critic for *The New York Times*. His criticism was published for thirty-five years (1927–62) and both supported and championed the emerging art form called the modern dance during the thirties. While some of the work of these critics has been published in book form (see bibliography), much of it remains in scrapbooks and clipping files in libraries throughout the world. Countless other early critics have been lost as newspapers were tossed into wastebaskets, and with them, the descriptions of performances past.

A question arises: why has there been so little written criticism about dance over the years? Leaving aside the issue of dance's ephemeral nature and the lack of scores or choreographic records, the problem remains of translating the non-verbal medium of dance into words. No doubt this has inhibited many critics from writing seriously on the dance. Dance writing has yet to develop a critical vocabulary; concepts, recurring forms, and choreographic structures have not been given labels as they have in literary criticism and in art, music, and theater history. The problem of transposing dance into a workable language is still at hand. We can define the sonata allegro, the numbers of instruments used in a quartet, quintet, or octet, and the various harmonic structures when discussing the sound of a symphony, yet in this basic sense we have not discovered a set of terms to

establish form, style, choreographic patterns, or even something as elemental as the number of dancers in a given dance. The closest we come is the use of a term like "pas de deux" in ballet.

All of these questions have retarded the development of dance criticism as a respectable and self-supporting profession. The number of newspapers and magazines that employ full-time dance critics is relatively small, considering that dance is the fastest growing spectator sport in the United States. Today there are more dance critics publishing than ever before, and still newspapers often send a music or theater critic to review dance.

For those thinking about a career in dance criticism, a background in writing and dance is advisable, although many journalists with little knowledge of the art have, through critics conferences and seminars, been brought into closer contact with it. There are no professional training programs in dance criticism, *per se*. There are journalism schools on the graduate level and programs in dance history. On the whole, interested writers should be aware that the market remains fairly limited, though its growth potential still seems great. Most professional critics who publish regularly must seek full-time employment elsewhere.

Dance Critics Association

For those who write about dance or would like to, there is the recently formed (1974) Dance Critics Association, which provides a meeting ground for critics from all over the country. It organizes conferences and seminars, lobbies for the rights of dance critics, and publishes a newsletter. DCA also provides a central clearinghouse for information about critics' grants, forthcoming publications, and ethical and legal issues of concern to those who write about dance. Address inquiries to:

DCA
P.O. Box 47
Planetarium Station, N.Y., N.Y. 10024

WHERE TO STUDY

Since 1969, The National Endowment on the Arts and the American Dance Festival have sponsored a critics conference, concurrent with the American Dance Festival (formerly at New London, Conn., now at Durham, N.C., during the summers). The conference was founded by Selma Jeanne Cohen, editor of *Dance Perspectives,* and is now directed by Deborah Jowitt, currently dance critic for the *Village Voice.* The three-week seminar is aimed at professional writers—especially journalists covering

Top: Marie Taglioni in La Gitana, *1838. Stipple engraving. Center: "Tillers of the Soil" Egyptian section of* The Greek Pageant, *1916. Ted Shawn and Ruth St. Denis. Bottom:* Ballet-Comique de la Royne Louise, *1581. Chariot of Minerva. Engraving.*

dance—who are interested in broadening their understanding of dance and developing new skills in writing about it. The program explores some of the crucial elements of dance criticism—observing, analyzing, and describing movement. The daily schedule includes movement sessions, lectures on dance history and styles, writing assignments, and group critiques. The critics conference is a fellowship program. Those selected receive a grant covering transportation, tuition, room, and board. Inquiries and applications should be sent to: Deborah Jowitt, 78 Christopher Street, New York, N.Y. 10014. Applicants are requested to submit a resume, several samples of published writing (particularly dance criticism), two references, and a letter stating their reasons for wishing to attend the conference.

The Texas Institute for Dance Criticism holds a ten-day session primarily for critics in Texas. However, the entrance requirements are more flexible as far as professional level is concerned: participants are not required to be working journalists. Address inquiries to:

Texas Institute for Dance Criticism
P.O. Box 7173, Austin, Texas 78712

Many universities with advanced degree programs in dance offer courses in criticism and in critical writing (see pages 232-233).

Critics and Where to Read Them

There are many critics writing around the country; for a complete list of their names and affiliations, consult the DCA or the *Dance Magazine Annual*. A list of current writers and their outlets that might be of interest to the general reader includes:

Arlene Croce *The New Yorker*
Anna Kisselgoff *The New York Times*
Marcia Siegel *New York Magazine*
Deborah Jowitt *The Village Voice*
Walter Terry *The Saturday Review*
Nancy Goldner *The Nation*
Alan Kriegsman *The Washington Post*

Periodicals

Journals and magazines that publish dance criticism are not indexed in one place. The following list is not complete and does not attempt to cover the field; there are, of course, regional magazines and alternative newspapers in all parts of the country that publish criticism. These are a few publications:
Dance Magazine, Dance News, Ballet Review, Dance Chronicle, Dance Scope, The Soho Weekly News, The Village Voice, Horizon Magazine, The Drama Review, The Performing Arts Journal, Dancing Times, Dance and Dancers.

Top: Fanny Cerrito in La Sylphide, ca. 1841. Bottom: Mme. Augusta in La Bayadère, ca. 1839.

WHAT TO READ

Croce, Arlene. *Afterimages.* New York: Knopf, 1977.

Denby, Edwin. *Looking at the Dance.* 1949. Paperback, New York: Curtis, 1968. New York: Horizon, 1976.

———.*Dancers, Buildings and People in the Streets.* 1965. Paperback, New York: Curtis, 1965.

Gautier, Théophile. *The Romantic Ballet 1837–48.* Trans. C. W. Beaumont. 1932. Paperback, New York: Dance Horizons, 1974.

Haskell, Arnold. *Balletomania: Then and Now.* New York: Knopf, 1977.

Johnston, Jill. *Marmalade Me.* Paperback, New York: Dutton, 1971.

Jowitt, Deborah. *Dance Beat: Selected Views and Reviews, 1967–1976.* New York: Dekker, 1977.

Levinson, Andre. "Andre Levinson on Isadora Duncan." *Ballet Review* 6, No. 4 (1978).

Macdonald, Nesta. *Diaghilev Observed.* New York: Dance Horizons, 1975.

Reynolds, Nancy. *Repertory in Review: Forty Years of the New York City Ballet.* New York: Dial, 1977.

Siegel, Marcia B. *At the Vanishing Point.* 1972. Paperback, New York: Saturday Review, 1973.

———.*Watching the Dance Go By.* Boston: Houghton Mifflin, 1977.

Terry, Walter. *I Was There: Selected Dance Reviews, 1936–1976.* Comp. and ed. Andrew Wentink. New York: Dekker, 1978.

Van Vechten, Carl. *The Dance Writings of Carl van Vechten.* Ed. P. Padgette. New York: Dance Horizons, 1974.

Libraries and Archives

What makes some observers feel dance the most exciting of all performing arts is exactly what makes it impossible to store in a library or museum—its ephemerality. It leaves nothing behind and is rarely recorded as it is created. There are only costumes, scenery, and score to collect after the moment of performance. Memoirs and letters often contain thoughts and inspirations of dancers and choreographers alike, but little of the dancing itself ever actually survives. This makes the notion of a dance library or archive an exciting and dubious proposition. The unusual nature of the art makes unusual demands on traditional shapes, sizes, and services of libraries.

What does fill a dance archive? Who uses it? Although sometimes hard to find, there is material enough in many collections to provide the scholar, researcher, and critic with historical and critical information, to provide dancers with information or pictures or even films of works they need, to provide choreographers with films or video tapes of other people's works, to provide students with a wide background of dance memorabilia to page through.

The dance library is often really a multi-media research facility that houses various kinds of materials. There is written material: books, periodicals, clippings; there is visual material: photographs, prints and drawings of dancers and ballets, engravings, etchings, set and costume designs. There is manuscript material: letters, choreographers' notebooks, composers' notes for ballet scores, letters and diaries. There is audio material: taped interviews with dancers and choreographers, set designers, composers and theater managers. For contemporary dancers, scholars, and interested amateurs, the new area of film archives allows on-the-spot viewing of old repertory, historic performances, and dancers of the recent past. Video tape has revolutionized the process of putting dances on film (see pages 199-203).

For many years, dance literature and archival material was catalogued in regular libraries under such headings as social activities, recreation, court etiquette, deportment, or theater. Though common in Europe for decades, the concept of a specialized dance library or archive collection is still relatively new in America.

The collections that follow differ in size and holdings; the most extensive is undoubtedly the New York Public Library Dance Collection, which houses the Jerome Robbins film archive; the Harvard Theatre Collection would place second. There are probably fast-growing collections in cities and towns around the country that are not listed here. Local historical societies and libraries are treasure troves of material—playbills, posters, programs, clippings, and reviews. University libraries also collect widely in specific areas such as Renaissance studies, eighteenth-century social attitudes, and so forth. Dance may be found in any of these areas. Much American dance material is still sitting in dusty basements and attics, so never overlook rummage sales, auctions, and country book fairs. Valuable old periodicals and books turn up in strange places.

Libraries and Archives

Alabama

Birmingham Public and Jefferson County Free Library
Collins Collection of the Dance
2020 Seventh Ave. N.
Birmingham, Ala. 35203
(205) 254-2555
Mrs. J. L. Greene, Jr., Head Librarian
1825 books; 39 bound periodical volumes

California

Los Angeles Public Library
630 West 15 Street
Los Angeles, Calif. 90015
(213) 626-7461
Dance holdings.

Leslie Getz
239 El Camino Real
Menlo Park, Calif. 94025

Les serpentins.   Le corbeille.   L'Espagnole.

Au repos.   L'hélice.   Au repos.

Les serpentins.

LA DANSE SERPENTINE — Mlle Loïe Fuller et ses transformations

Private dance library with a collection of 1,100 books, 2,500 periodicals, and 250 programs. The collection, emphasizing the history of ballet, consists primarily of twentieth-century sources, but also includes older sources written in French, Russian, German, and Scandinavian languages. Open by appointment only.

San Francisco Dance Archive
and Archives for the Performing Arts
3150 Sacramento Street
San Francisco, Calif. 94115
Russell Hartley, Director
The performing arts in California, especially the Bay Area. Costumes, posters, clippings

Connecticut
Wadsworth Atheneum
600 Main Street
Hartford, Conn. 06103
(203) 278-2670
Betsy Hoke, Librarian
Books and programs from the American tours of the Ballet Russe. Serge Lifar Collection of set and costume designs.

Sterling Memorial Library
Crawford Collection on the Modern Drama
Yale University
New Haven, Conn. 06510
The holdings date from 1920, the year Prof. J.R. Crawford gave his theatrical collection to Yale. Programs, engravings, and photographs. No published books. Covers both musical and dramatic theater. Several thousand engravings: portraits of actors in theater, music hall, and variety: about 5,000 dance engravings.

District of Columbia, Washington
Library of Congress
Washington, D.C. 20540
The library has collected more than 200,000 plays from all periods and countries by gift, purchase, or exchange, and since 1870 has received by law almost 110,000 published plays and 130,000 mimeographed manuscripts. The more than 100,000 titles concern not only the theater but the dance, pantomime, processions and festivals, masques, royal fetes, marionettes, and works on morality and the theater.
Also the Paper Print Collection in the film section has original Edison footage of many kinds of dancers at the turn of the century.

Illinois
Chicago Public Library
Fine Arts Division—Art Section
78 East Washington Street
Chicago, Ill. 60602

*Opposite: **Loie Fuller in her Serpentine Dance, 1890,** showing her manipulation of yards of silk.*

(312) 269-2858
Marjorie Adkins, Chief
Dance collection with special card index; folk dance collection with twenty-six looseleaf volumes

Maryland
Peabody Institute of the Johns Hopkins University
Peabody Conservatory Library
21 East Mt. Vernon Place
Baltimore, Md. 21202
(301) 837-0600
Geraldine Ostroue, Librarian
Dance material; a small collection of 175 titles

University of Maryland, College Park
Fine Arts Room
McKeldin Library
College Park, Md. 20742
(301) 454-3036
Frederick A. Heutte, Fine Arts Librarian
Small dance collection

Massachusetts
Boston Conservatory of Music
Albert Alphin Music Library
8 The Fenway
Boston, Mass. 02215
(617) 536-6340
Nancy M. Forte, Librarian
Jan Veen-Katrine Amory Hooper Memorial Dance and Art Collection 10,871 books; 399 tapes; 5,021 photographs

Smith College
Werner Josten Library of the Performing Arts
Mendenhall Center
Northhampton, Mass. 01060
(413) 584-2700
Mary M. Anjudowich, Librarian
Dance holdings

Boston Public Library
Boylston Street.
Boston, Mass. 02116
(617) 536-5400
The Allen A. Brown Collection is composed of 5,000 volumes of biography, history, and criticism and polemics, scrapbooks, programs, press clippings, and engravings as well as a splendid musical collection dealing with opera and ballet.

Harvard Theatre Collection
Houghton Library
Cambridge, Mass. 02138
(617) 495-2445
Jeanne T. Newlin, Curator
Archives in the performing arts—theater, magic, minstrelsy, circus, dance with eighteenth and nineteenth century specialization; George Chaffee Ballet Collection.

New York
New York Public Library
Library and Museum of the Performing Arts
111 Amsterdam Avenue
New York, N.Y. 10023
Dance Collection (212) 799-2200
Genevieve Oswald, Curator
Varied material on all forms of dance
Special collections: Jerome Robbins Archive of Dance Film; Cia Fornaroli Toscanini rare ballet history, 15,000 items; Denishawn (dance Americana, 50,000 items); Humphrey-Weidman (modern dance, 5,000 items); Hanya Holm (modern dance in Europe and America, 1,200 items); Fania Marinoff (5,000 photos by Carl Van Vechten); Roger Pryor Dodge (Nijinsky photographs); George Platt Lynes (American ballet, 3,000 negatives); Robert W. Dowling (Albert E. Kahn photographs and negatives); Lincoln Kirstein (rare dance history); Irving Deakin (American ballet); Irma Duncan (Isadora Duncan memorabilia); Astruc-Diaghilev Ballet Russes, (13,000 documents); Craig-Duncan collection (400 Isadora Duncan manuscripts); Doris Humphrey Manuscript Collection (7,000 items on modern dance); American Ballet Theatre Archive; Jose Limon, Ruth Page collections.

Theater Collection,
(212) 799-2200
Paul Myers, Curator
Playbills, programs, memorabilia of variety shows, musical comedy, and other productions involving dance

Dance Films Association, Inc.
250 West 57 Street
New York, N.Y. 10019
(212) 586-2142
Susan Braun, President
Slides and films on dance; special collection: first film of Martha Graham; only film of Alicia Markova

Composers and Choreographers Theatre, Inc.
Master Tape Library
25 West Nineteenth Street
New York, N.Y. 10011
(212) 989-2230
John Watts, President
Modern dance, music and dance education, music and dance criticism 2,750 audio/video tapes (catalogue); 1,000 hours from concerts

North Carolina
University of North Carolina
Dance Collection
Walter Clinton Jackson Library
Greensboro, N.C. 27412
(919) 379-5246
Emmy Mills, Librarian
History of the dance, modern dance, dance notation

Special collection: Early dance books sixteenth-eighteenth century (100 vols.) Holdings: 3,000 volumes; fourteen journals and other serials
Approx. 100 titles on dancing and dance music from early eighteenth century to early twentieth in special collections
Approx. 1,500 titles in general collection
Approx. thirty periodical titles in general collection
Archives of division of dance in School of Health, Physical Education and Recreation

Ohio
University of Cincinnati
College Conservatory of Music
Gorno Memorial Music Library
101 Emery Hall
Cincinnati, Ohio 45221
(513) 475-4471
Robert O. Johnson, Librarian
Anatole Chujoy Memorial Dance Collection including books, periodicals, programs, posters, and memorabilia

Cleveland Public Library
325 Superior Avenue N.E.
Cleveland, Ohio 44114
(216) 623-2800
Dance collection of more than 1,200 volumes; ballet library in the process of rapid growth

Pennsylvania
Free Library of Philadelphia
Music Department
Logan Square
Philadelphia, Pa. 19103
(215) 686-5322
Frederick James Kent, Director
Dance annuals, biographies, costume and set designs, histories, instruction, magazines, manuals, notation, photographs, clippings; programs of local and touring companies performing in Philadelphia; material on Catherine Littlefield

Texas
Hoblitzelle Theatre Arts Library
University of Texas
Austin, Tex. 78712
(512) 471-3811
Five collections of dance and dance-related material largely comprised of playbills, programs, letters, souvenir programs, clippings, correspondence

Canada
Académie des Grands Ballet Canadiens
Bibliothèque
5010 Coolbrook
Montreal, PQ H3X 2K9
Canada
(514) 489-4959

Ludmilla Chiraieff, Director
500 books and 400 bound periodical volumes

University of British Columbia
Fine Arts Division
University Library
2075 Westbrook Place
Vancouver, BC V6T 1W5
Canada
(604) 228-2720
Melva J. Dwyer, Division Head
Dance holdings

Metropolitan Toronto Library Board
789 Yonge Street
Toronto, Ontario M4W 2G8
Canada
(416) 928-5150
Jane Suenderman, Theatre Librarian
Particular strength in Canadian dance; collection includes books, periodicals, programs, posters, clippings, photographs, and the personal papers of Boris Volkoff

---

WHAT TO READ

Beaumont, C. W. *A Bibliography of Dancing.* 1929. Reprint, New York: Rolland Press, Benjamin Blom, 1963.

Bibliothèques et musées des arts du spectacle dans le monde: Performing Arts Collections, An International Guide. Ed. André Veinstein. Paris: Centre National de la Recherche Scientifique, 1960.

Brinson, Peter. *Backgrounds to European Ballet.* Leyden: A. W. Sijthoff, 1966. Complete list of European dance archives and addresses.

Dictionary Catalog of the Dance Collection. New York: New York Public Library, and Boston: G.K. Hall, 1974. 10 volumes plus annual supplements. The holdings of the Dance Collection, Library and Museum of the Performing Arts (Lincoln Center, New York), organized under relevant headings with the aid of computers. Subscribed to by many libraries. 8,000 topical subject headings, over 45,000 titles. A major advance in cataloguing.

Enciclopedia dello Spettacolo. Rome: Maschere, 1954-66. 9 vols. plus supplements.

Forrester, F. S. *Ballet in England: A Bibliography and Survey, c. 1700-June 1966.* London: Library Association, 1968.

Young, Margaret L.; Young, Harold; and Kruzas, Anthony T., (comps.). *1974 Directory of Special Libraries and Information Centers.* Detroit: Gale, 1974. Contains a complete list of American and Canadian libraries and museums with dance materials.

Witch Dance II, *1926. Mary Wigman.*

V. Funding: Government & Private Support for Dance

V. FUNDING: GOVERNMENT AND PRIVATE SUPPORT FOR DANCE

By Ellen Jacobs

Federal Support: Past and Present

In 1926 when Martha Graham decided to give her first dance concert in New York City, she put down a deposit of $11.50 on the theater, (according to a story). She still owed another $800. There was no public money available to assist the young Graham, who would be responsible for creating a new dance heritage for her nation, and eventually became one of the greatest contributors to making America the dance capital of the world.

With the exception of the short-lived Works Progress Administration (WPA) in the 1930s, which did not have a category for dance, it took another forty years to create a federal or state program designed to assist artists financially. In Europe the tradition of government as arts patron is centuries-old.

Support for the arts in the United States had been assumed initially by the financial barons of the nineteenth century, who established museums, symphony orchestras, and opera houses. There are other reasons for the United States government's Johnny-Come-Lateness in the assistance of artists and arts organizations. For one thing, there was America's single-minded ambition for technical progress and power; the arts were considered a frill. The slow start can also be traced to the American conviction that the arts are elitist, and as such they should not be the responsibility of a democratic government.

The first major and consistent governmental commitment to providing an arts subsidy began in New York State in 1960 with the establishment of the New York State Council on the Arts. The Council had long been regarded as "Rockefeller's baby," for its existence was due in large measure to the late Governor Nelson Rockefeller's personal appreciation and devotion to the arts. The New York State Council on the Arts was to serve as the blueprint not only for the structure of other state arts agencies, but for the National Endowment on the Arts as well.

Although there had been a growing amount of talk in Washington since the end of the Second World War about the need for the Federal government to lend a hand to artists and arts groups (in 1955 President Eisenhower proposed the establishment of a Federal Advisory Commission on the Arts, and in 1961 the Kennedy administration proposed the creation of a Federal Advisory Council on the Arts), those in support of such assistance were greatly outnumbered by the skeptics.

Aside from vote-conscious politicians who did not feel their constituencies would benefit from such spending, many artists were afraid the government's hand might become too manipulative and inspire mediocrity and censorship. Artist Larry Rivers tersely summed up the fears of the arts community when he said: "The government taking a role in art is like a gorilla threading a needle." Although there was a certain amount of prophetic truth to Rivers' bleak simile, the obvious benefits that government funding has subsequently had for both artists and public have shown his warning to be overly ominous.

The National Endowment for the Arts, now the largest single source of support for American art, was created in 1965 under pressure from the Johnson administration, which believed that the arts were crucial to the Great Society it promised the American people. The sixties was a period of affluence in the United States and, by this time, too, America had firmly established a position of technological and industrial superiority. Middle-class America would finally take time out for culture.

On September 20, 1965, President Johnson signed the bill that established The National Foundation for the Arts and Humanities, of which the Arts Endowment is a part. The bill read, in part, that "a high civilization must not limit its efforts to science and technology alone, but must give full value and support to the other great branches of man's scholarly and cultural activity."

In addition to making the arts more accessible to millions of Americans, the purposes of the Endowment were stated to be: preservation of cultural heritage, strengthening of cultural institutions, and assistance to the development of talented artists.

The arts were defined as music, dance, drama, folk art, creative writing, architecture and allied fields, painting, sculpture, photography, graphic and craft arts, industrial design, costume and fashion design, motion pictures, television, radio, and tape and sound recording.

That the arts were to remain free from governmental or political influence was written into the enabling legislation which plainly stated: "No department, agency, officer or employee of the United States shall exercise any direction, supervision or control over the policy determination, personnel or curriculum or the administration or operation of any school or non-Federal agency institution, organization or association."

Unlike the WPA, which was destroyed in part by accusations of Communist affiliation and censorship on the part of some powerful legislators, the Endowment was carefully structured to prevent any governmental interference in its decision-making. Overseeing all Endowment activities is the National Council on the Arts, a Presidentially appointed group of twenty-six distinguished private citizens "who are widely recognized for their broad knowledge, or expertise in, or their profound interest in, the arts." The Council advises the Endowment

on policies, procedures, and programs, and makes recommendations on grant applications.

Each of the Endowment's twelve programs, of which dance is one, has its own panel of volunteer outside experts in the program's area who make recommendations on grant applications to the National Council on the Arts. The Dance Panel, for instance, is composed of dance critics, historians, producers, choreographers, performers, and administrators from across the United States, who represent all forms of dance. All Endowment grants are made with the approval of the Endowment's chairman, who is appointed by the President every four years.

The fact that government finally acknowledged the arts to be as important to the American people as science, technology, and education, gave the arts an official seal of approval which played no small role in legitimizing the arts in the mind of the public. This has had a visible effect in encouraging greater corporate and private support. A dramatic example is the Ford Foundation's $3.2 million grant to the New York City Ballet in 1974.

Although the United States government came to the arts scene late, it has certainly made up for lost time. In 1966, the total Congressional appropriation for the Endowment was $7 million. By 1976, the figure had jumped to $26 million. In 1978, the Endowment received $149 million from Congress. The amount of money allocated for dance in 1967 was $177,325; by 1977 it was $6,950,000—almost the total Endowment appropriation of $7.9 million in 1967.

The rapid growth of the congressional appropriation to the Endowment can be considered as both a response to the growing popularity of the arts and an inspiring stimulus to the growth of the arts, including dance. Which

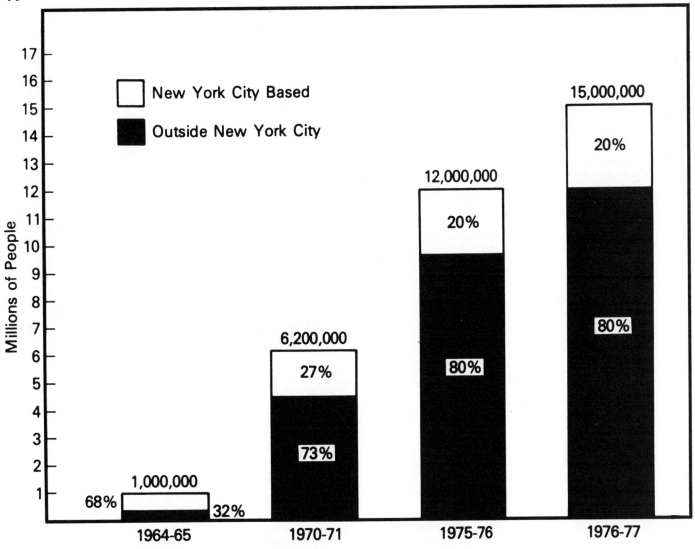

The Growth of the Audience for Dance in America since 1964. In 1975, 16% of the adult American population (16 years of age and older) saw dance in live performance, an increase of 8% over 1973 (according to The National Research Center of the Arts, Inc.).

is the cause, and which the effect, is a question for speculation. The extraordinary growth of the appreciation of dance in this country since 1965 is a vivid example: dance audiences, according to a study by the Association of American Dance Companies, have grown from 1.5 million to 15 million, or 1500% in ten years. In 1978, audiences are expected to number 25 million. Is this remarkable jump in attendance because more money was made available for touring and performing, thus making the art more available to potential audiences? Or had the cultural and psychological climate of the United States changed during the decade so as to allow the average person to begin to appreciate dance? These are questions that cultural commentators and interpreters can debate far into the night.

After the Endowment, the next most significant source of government support to dance comes from the New York State Council on the Arts, which presently gives $2.9 million to dance companies and dance organizations.

Together, the Endowment and the New York State Council on the Arts presently give almost $10 million to dance. If this seems like a great deal of money, one only has to look at how much remains unfunded in order to appreciate what small percentage of the costs government funds actually cover. The total operating budget for the New York City Ballet is $7,750,000, of which only $713,732 comes from the New York State Council on the Arts and the National Endowment for the Arts. The rest must be raised from private and corporate donations and box office receipts. Obviously the government has not taken over financial responsibility for the New York City Ballet.

Fears that the government would become caretaker of the arts and reduce corporate and private interest have proved unfounded. If anything, corporate support has increased. When the Corporate Fund for Dance began its first campaign in 1973/74 (see p. 250), it was able to raise $68,000 from fourteen corporations. In 1977, it raised $168,000 from seventy-five different corporations. As of August 1978, it had raised $222,000 from over one-hundred corporations, with four months to go until the end of the year.

Despite the growing amount of money available for dance, some financial gloom remains. In 1974, the Endowment received 294 applications for assistance in dance and funded 118, or 40%, of these. In 1977, it received a total of 964 applications and could fund 242, or only 25%. These figures imply a good deal about Federal support. For one thing, there is far greater need than the Endowment can meet. And with the growing amount of dance in America, competition for Endowment funding is becoming stiffer than it has ever been. The money is not easy to come by.

Applications for financial assistance are evaluated not only in terms of the artistic merit of the applicant, but also in terms of the company or organization's fiscal responsibility and administrative track record. The potential benefit of the proposed project to the community is also taken into consideration.

Applicants must be prepared to wait between six and eight months for an answer to their funding request. During this period the Endowment's program and fiscal staffs prepare the application for review by the appropriate Advisory Panel. The panel's job is to review applications and then recommend acceptance or rejection to the National Council. After deliberation, the Council makes its own recommendations to the Endowment chairman, who has the final word in the decision-making process. Following his decision on the application, a letter of acceptance or rejection is sent out to the anxious applicant.

"Oh, nonsense—hundreds of people have exhausted their grants and gone on to live happy, productive lives."

When the Endowment began to give its first grants in 1966, the dance program offered two forms of assistance: support for touring by dance companies and fellowships for choreographers. Great changes have taken place in response to the mushrooming of activity. The variety of needs expressed in the applications that the dance program receives is enormous: choreographers want to create new work and need rehearsal time and the money to pay their dancers during that period; a dance company wants to start a subscription drive and needs financial help to pay for knowledgeable personnel; a dance

company wants to commission a new work from a choreographer; a dance company wants to resurrect an old dance, but needs money to pay the salaries of the dancers who can teach it; a choreographer wants to film his work. Theaters want to sponsor a dance festival and to import companies from other states. Box office receipts cannot cover the gap between ticket prices and the cost of the companies' performing fees. These are just some of the more conventional needs.

To accommodate the extraordinary diversity of requests it receives, the Endowment's dance program has greatly expanded the kinds of assistance it offers. There are now at least eight different categories in which an applicant can request funds, including one for applications that do not fit into the other seven.

National Endowment for the Arts Dance Grants

Dance Touring Program

One of the most visible signs of the dance explosion can be read in the staggering growth of this residency program. Created in 1967 to develop audiences for dance and to help dance companies receive greater public exposure, DTP began with a budget of $25,000 to underwrite 50% of the fees for four dance companies to tour two states for a total of eight weeks. In 1978/79, the Endowment allocated $2 million to cover the costs of a total of 389 weeks of touring by 183 companies. At present the Endowment only underwrites 30% of a company's touring fee. DTP residencies must be for at least two-and-one-half days. Participating companies are selected by the Endowment's Dance Panel.

A recent offshoot of DTP, the Long-Term Residencies Program was created to give the visiting dance company more time (two or more weeks) to develop and strengthen its relationship with its host community and to exercise greater creativity within the community.

Choreography Fellowships and Production Grants

Ranging from $2,500 to $100,000, depending on the scope of the project, these fellowships and grants are offered to choreographers to create new works and to dance companies to commission new works from choreographers, to restage older works, or to help allay the prohibitive cost of mounting new dances.

Challenge Grants

These grants are intended to "challenge" dance companies and dance presenters to seek new, non-government sources of funding. Recipients must match every dollar received from the Endowment with three dollars from another funding source. Grants may be used to meet increased operating costs (the rising cost of rent), to eliminate accumulated debts (when box office receipts didn't meet the cost of the production), or to provide capital improvements (air-conditioning to allow for summer performances).

Resident Professional Dance Companies Program

Offering grants of up to $50,000 apiece, this program is designed to encourage high-quality professional dance activities in communities across the United States. The money is given to help create cooperative projects with other regional groups, to add new artistic personnel to the company's staff, to allow for rehearsal salaries, or for any other projects that will help to stabilize the company's performing season within a given community.

Management and Administration

With their rapidly growing audiences, dance companies have become big business. In response to their growing need for more sophisticated business management, NEA has begun to offer grants of up to $25,000 to dance companies that require more professional management or need to improve of their present one.

Services to the Field

Rather than to choreographers or dance companies themselves, these grants are given to organizations that are involved in projects that provide services to dance companies. "Services" means technical assistance (stage management, lighting, etc.), production help, management assistance, internship programs, dance criticism workshops (see pages 249-251).

Dance Film/Video

The death of choreographer James Waring in 1976 and the fear of the loss of his valuable work—none of which had been documented—inspired an impassioned plea from the dance world to make money available to preserve works by American choreographers. The Endowment responded by making money available to help underwrite projects concerned with the preservation, recording, and archival and historic documentation of dance; these funds are also offered to artists wanting to explore and improve ways of capturing dance on film and video (see pages 199-202).

General Programs

The creative nature of art makes it naturally resistant to categorization—even to the flexible categories of the Endowment. Project ideas that do not fit into any of the other areas are given consideration here. Projects must be "of professional activity, exceptional merit and outstanding quality and respond to a demonstrated need."

Non-Dance Endowment Program Categories under Which Dance Projects are Considered

In addition to grants given to dance companies by NEA's Dance Program, the Endowment offers dance companies funding from their interdisciplinary program. For instance, the Visual Arts program offers money to professional performing groups to hire artists to design costumes, sets, and posters for productions. The Endowment's Composers/Librettists program provides money to companies and choreographers who want to collaborate with a specific composer. NEA's Expansion Arts, Education (Artists-In-Schools), Media Arts, and Work Experience Internship Programs also provide various forms of assistance.

Information on these programs is available by writing to the Endowment's Program Information Office, Mail Stop 550, NEA, 2041 E Street, N.W., Washington, D.C. 20506. *The Cultural Post*, published bi-monthly, reports on the activities of NEA (same address).

NATIONAL ENDOWMENT FOR THE HUMANITIES
806 15 Street N.W.
Washington, D.C. 20506
(201) 382-5721

While NEH, twin sister of the Arts Endowment, does not fund creative or original work in the arts or performance, or training in the arts, it does support historical, theoretical, and critical studies in the arts or projects which clearly relate art appreciation to other fields in the humanities. For example, NEH has supported dance history projects and also provided the Brooklyn Academy of Music with a grant to help support teaching residencies by the Royal Shakespeare Company in several universities in the area.

Federal Jobs for Artists: CETA

When National Endowment for the Arts Chairman Livingston Biddle addressed an orientation meeting of the artists hired to work as part of the CETA program in New York City in 1978, he told them that the employment of CETA artists across the nation represented about $100 million in CETA funding, or about $37.5 million less than the Endowment's total budget in 1977. Forty-one of the 300 artists hired in New York City under CETA in 1978 were choreographers and dancers.

What is the CETA program? In Washingtonese, it is the Comprehensive Employment and Training Act, Title VI, established by the Federal government in 1973 to provide grants to state and local governments to create public service jobs for the unemployed. Similar to the WPA program during the Depression, CETA has meant a chance for artists to get paid for their work.

In New York City, for instance, participating CETA artists earn $10,000 a year for giving workshops to the elderly, lecture-demonstrations to school children, and master classes at community centers. In New York City, CETA choreographers presented a free, outdoor festival of dance on Tuesday evenings during August and September of 1978 in the garden of the Cooper-Hewitt Museum.

Since the U.S. Department of Labor does not have a category for artists in their computer, the total number of artists employed across the country through the CETA program is an educated guess resulting from an informal survey taken by the Arts Endowment. The figure for 1978 is 10,000.

Although the largest number of CETA-employed artists hail from New York City, it was among the last cities to make the program available to artists. The first CETA-sponsored artists' project developed on the West Coast in 1974, in Seattle and San Francisco. There are now approximately 465 "prime sponsors," or CETA-sponsored projects on a state or local level, that hire artists.

State Support of the Arts

In 1960, New York was the only state with a program to assist arts organizations. By 1966, there were twenty-two states with legislative appropriations assigned to the arts. By 1975, each of the fifty states had its own arts agency.

Some of the stimulus to this rapid materialization of state arts councils came from the Endowment's promise of a block grant to any state which submitted a plan describing how it would use the money awarded to it.

The first block grants of $50,000 apiece were awarded in 1967. By 1976, these grants had reached $205,000 apiece. Interestingly, even as late as 1975 only eight states had appropriated as much as $1 million for the arts. The next highest range, $500,000 to $999,000, was reached by only five states. The remaining thirty-seven states' average appropriation was only $151,000, or $49,000 less than the block grant from NEA. If all the legislative appropriations from all forty-nine states (aside from New York) were totalled together, they still would not match the $34.1 million budget of the New York State Council on the Arts in 1974.

Since the states all have different ways of allocating their funds, it is difficult to compare them in terms of how much money they each give to dance. For instance, some states fund dance residencies through community programs, while others fund them through education, others through touring. A black dance company may receive support under the category of special programs. The most definitive thing that can be said is that each state arts council works differently, and none comes close to the $2.9 million dance budget of the New York State Council on the Arts.

One thing should be noted: with the Endowment's recent trend toward decentralization, the states are beginning to assume greater responsibility for determining arts programming within their state. For example, NEA has given the states coordinating responsibility for the Dance Touring Program (see page 247) and the Artist-in-Schools Program, though the Endowment Panels still remain responsible for selecting the participating dance companies and movement specialists.

If Not Money, What Then?

While direct government funding to individual artists and dance companies has greatly increased in the United States, such support cannot begin to meet the needs of the dance community. But there are many ways in which government funds can be taken advantage of—indirectly—through the numerous service organizations that receive Federal, state and municipal support to help artists, art organizations, and the arts community.

Service organizations are a varied lot. Some offer production know-how, free space, fund-raising assistance; others provide help with promotion, publicity, booking, and management. The following are examples of such organizations. All are non-profit.

AMERICAN COUNCIL FOR THE ARTS (ACA)
570 Seventh Avenue
New York, N.Y. 10018
(212) 354-6655

Working under the assumption that in unity there is strength, the American Council for the Arts attempts to link all the state and local arts councils in the United States together to bring national attention to the arts and give them higher priority in American life. Advocates for the Arts, a sub-organization of ACA, functions primarily as a lobbying organization for the arts by seeking increased public funding (on all governmental levels), and seeking improved legislation to meet the special needs of artists.

In addition to working to improve the skills of arts councils, ACA publishes a great deal of material including *The Cultural Directory: A Guide to Federal Funds and Services for Cultural Activities*, which lists 250 federal programs offering assistance to individuals and cultural organizations; *ACA Arts Yellow Pages*, which lists more than 1,200 arts organizations throughout the United States; *Word from Washington*, a monthly newsletter containing information on federal legislation and government involvement with the arts; and *ACA Reports*, a bi-monthly news packet containing arts news on national, state, and community levels, as well as grant and funding information.

ASSOCIATION OF AMERICAN DANCE COMPANIES
162 West 56 Street
New York, N.Y. 10019
(212) 265-7824

In addition to facilitating communication among dance groups via newsletters, conferences, and seminars, AADC's lobbying efforts provide a united political voice for the dance community in America. AADC's 350 members are offered managerial assistance and information on technical and procedural questions, discounts in hotels and travel, payroll (unemployment), and medical insurance. Two recent and visible AADC projects include

the engineering of the country's first National Dance Week in May, 1978 (celebrated in part by issuance of four dance postage stamps), and the publication of *The Poor Dancers' Almanac*, a crucial book (mostly limited to services in New York City) for dancers trying to survive the physical, financial, and spiritual perils of their careers.

BUSINESS COMMITTEE FOR THE ARTS (BCA)
1700 Broadway
New York, N.Y. 10019
(212) 765-5980

The Business Committee for the Arts serves as a liaison between the arts and business communities. On one hand, it offers advice to banks, insurance companies, airlines, and other corporations interested in contributing funds to the arts; on the other, it offers arts organizations such as dance companies and individual dance artists free counseling on ways to enlist corporate involvement in their projects. Arts organizations can also receive help with accounting and administrative problems. Two BCA publications of particular value to dance companies are: *Arts and Business*, a monthly newsletter that includes examples of arts groups that have successfully solicited funding from business, and *Approaching Business for Support of the Arts*, which provides guidelines for arts organizations seeking business support.

DANCE THEATER WORKSHOP (DTW)
219 West 19 Street
New York, N.Y. 10011
(212) 691-6500

Established in 1965 as a small artists cooperative, DTW has grown to include 210 dance companies. DTW's move in 1975 to the American Theater Laboratory, New York City, provided it with a larger performing space and facilities that in turn allowed it to increase the production and administrative services it could offer dance companies enormously. Members are eligible for participation in a wide variety of production programs including: DTW Presents (DTW assumes all production costs, including promotion, technical expenses, and artists' fees); Choreographers Showcase (programs of individual works by different choreographers); ATL Presentations (artists may rent DTW's performing space and utilize DTW promotion and technical services for a nominal fee); Tangents and Workshops (DTW will help sponsor special projects such as seminars and lecture-demonstrations).

Some of DTW's other invaluable services include rehearsal studio rental; use of a computerized mailing list of over 7,000 names; discounts on advertising in New York City newspapers; a National Dance Sponsor List that includes the names of over 3,500 art centers and colleges throughout the United States; Dance Video Access, a program which allows choreographers to document their work on video. Although most DTW members are residents of New York City, membership is open to companies and individual artists throughout the United States.

THE FOUNDATION CENTER
888 Seventh Avenue
New York, N.Y. 10019
(212) 975-1120

1001 Connecticut Avenue NW
Washington, D.C. 20036
(202) 331-1400

Locating appropriate corporate or private funding sources—there are over 15,000 foundations and trusts in the United States and countless corporations—can take almost as much imagination and craft as the creation of a dance. In the past several years, fundraising has become its own business for many organizations, particularly the major dance companies, some of whom hire full-time, trained personnel to do the job. But often, particularly for smaller dance companies unable to afford a professional fundraiser, the problem of where to go and how to apply can become overwhelming. The Foundation Center is a good place to start.

With libraries in New York City and Washington, D.C., and cooperating collections in forty-five states, the Foundation Center gathers, analyzes, and disseminates factual information on philanthropic foundations. The Center's libraries offer free information on funding, including complete sets of information returns, filed with the Internal Revenue Service by all United States foundations, as well as reference works, books, reports, news clippings, and press releases dealing with philanthropy and foundations, foundation annual reports, and a history of foundation funding in each field.

The Regional Collections receive all the Center's reference works, recent books and reports on foundations, foundation annual reports on microfiches, and Internal Revenue Service information about foundations in their states. Computerized data on grants arranged in topics of broad interest are also available.

For individuals and organizations requiring frequent access to information, the Foundation Center has an Associates Program. Membership is $200 a year and offers, among other things, access to toll-free telephone reference as well as custom searches of computerized data and print-outs of specific subjects.

Of the many publications issued by the Center, *About Foundations* is particularly valuable, as is *Foundation News*, which is published bi-monthly by the Center and contains extensive current grant announcements.

The Foundation Directory. New York: Columbia University, 1977. Biennial. 7th ed. ready late 1979.
Hillmann, Howard. *The Art of Winning Foundation Grants.* New York: Vanguard Press, 1977.

THE NATIONAL CORPORATE FUND FOR DANCE
150 West 56 Street
New York, N.Y. 10019
(212) 582-0130

Founded in 1972 by Anthony Bliss and a group of dance-loving businessmen, the Corporate Fund for Dance has consolidated the fundraising efforts of nine major American dance companies: American Ballet Theatre, The Joffrey Ballet, Alvin Ailey American Dance Theater, Nikolais Dance Theater, Murray Louis Dance Company, Merce Cunningham and Dance Company, Eliot Feld Ballet, The Paul Taylor Dance Company, and San Francisco Ballet. Some of the Fund's corporate campaigning has taken the form of bringing executives to rehearsals and performances and providing dance demonstrations for the corporation's employees.

While the Fund's administrative costs are assumed by non-corporate and government sources, all money received as a result of the Fund's corporate campaigning is distributed according to the operating budgets and deficits of the participating dance companies. The larger companies receive as much as 30% of the total distribution and the smaller ones no less than 5%.

OPPORTUNITY RESOURCES FOR THE ARTS (ORA)
1501 Broadway
New York, N.Y. 10036
(212) 575-1688

Opportunity Resources for the Arts was created to help arts organizations in their search for qualified administrative staff. Its low-cost services include personnel information, counseling, and placement services. All potential employees are carefully screened via resumes and letters of reference, and if geographically possible, by personal interview. Because ORA receives financial assistance from private and government agencies its fees are low in comparison to commercial agencies.

TECHNICAL ASSISTANCE GROUP (TAG)
463 West Street
New York, N.Y. 10014
(212) 691-3500

Well-known for its production of the Dance Umbrella and the Delacorte Dance Series in New York City, TAG also provides a wide range of technical and managment assistance to dance and theater companies and producing groups across the United States. Serving as a central clearing house, TAG's staff of expert lighting designers, stage managers, tour coordinators, and administrators work individually or collectively with dance companies needing assistance in these areas. Its information services include providing sources for the low-cost rental or purchase of equipment, technical specification sheets for performing spaces, and a personnel referral service.

THEATRE DEVELOPMENT FUND (TDF)
1501 Broadway
New York, N.Y. 10036
(212) 221-0013

Originally created to make theater tickets available at reduced prices, TDF has greatly expanded its services. It now offers a dance voucher to assist small dance companies with ticket sales. Vouchers are sold for $5.00 in sets of five and then redeemed by the dance company for $2.50 apiece. TDF's other services to dance include The Times Square Theatre Centre and the Lower Manhattan Theatre Centre, which offer tickets for dance events at half price on the day of performance.

Dance companies may also take advantage of TDF's Costume Collection, which houses some 48,000 costumes that are available for rental at a nominal fee. The costumes have been donated by The Metropolitan Opera and Columbia University. The services of the Costume Collection are available to dance companies throughout the United States. The Collection also offers a work-study program for costume design students.

VOLUNTEER LAWYERS FOR THE ARTS (VLA)
36 West 44 Street
New York, N.Y. 10036
(212) 575-1150

Along with all the artistic and financial considerations of starting a dance company, there are also a series of mind-boggling legal considerations: securing tax exemptions, incorporating as a not-for-profit group, negotiating and drafting contracts, copyrighting, taxes, labor and immigration. To add to those problems, legal advice and assistance is expensive. Happily, there is an organization to help. Volunteer Lawyers for the Arts offers free legal aid from practicing attorneys in New York State. In this case, poverty helps. For individuals, VLA assistance is offered only to those earning less than $6,000 a year. Even if you don't require legal help at this point, VLA publications are of great value. They include: *Exempt Organizations and the Arts; Fear of Filing: A Beginner's Handbook on Recordkeeping and Federal Taxes for Dancers, Other Performers, Writers and Visual Artists; Housing for Artists: The New York Experience; The Individual Artist: Recordkeeping, Methods of Accounting, Income and Itemized Deductions for Federal Income Tax Purposes; Not for Profit Corporations/Unincorporated Associations: A Guide for Arts Groups.* VLA also issues a quarterly, *Art and the Law.*

Money for the Individual Artist

It seems to be a great deal easier for a choreographer to receive money to help pay the operating expenses for his dance company than for the choreographer to get funds to make the dances that his company will perform. This irony is dramatically underlined in the fact that the New York State Council on the Arts had not until recently been allowed to give money to individual artists.

Aside from Endowment fellowships and the sprinkling of state arts agencies with commissioning programs, the following three programs represent major opportunities for funding to individual dancers and choreographers who want to perform or create new works (see also the NEA Choreography Fellowship program, p. 247). While none in itself is a government agency, all except for the Guggenheim Foundation receive part of their funding from local and federal sources. None is profit-making.

AFFILIATE ARTISTS
155 West 68 Street
New York, N.Y. 10023
(212) 580-2000

Affiliate Artists brings dancers, in addition to singers, mimes, instrumentalists, and actors into communities throughout the United States. During the artist's fifty-six day residency in a selected community, the performer is expected to act as a "performer at large" by offering informal performances in such off-beat places as factories, shopping centers, churches, schools, libraries, firehouses, and Rotary clubs. Thus, Affiliate Artists helps to close the gap between the artist and his audience.

CREATIVE ARTISTS PUBLIC SERVICE PROGRAM
250 West 57 Street
New York, N.Y. 10019
(212) 247-6303

Since the New York State Council on the Arts had originally not been permitted to give money to private citizens, the Council created the Creative Artists Public Service Program as a funding conduit to individual artists. CAPS provides fellowships to artists in twelve fields, including dance. Each year approximately ten CAPS fellowships are offered to choreographers to create a new work and to perform community services—lecture-demonstrations, master classes, workshops. Grants range from $4,000 to $10,000 a year. Fellows are selected by an outside panel. Applicants must be residents of New York State. CAPS Fellows have included Lucinda Childs, Louis Falco, Rosalind Newman, Dan Wagoner, and Jacques d'Amboise.

JOHN SIMON GUGGENHEIM MEMORIAL FOUNDATION
90 Park Avenue
New York, N.Y. 10016
(212) 687-4470

The highly selective and highly prized fellowships offered by the Guggenheim Foundation are available to choreographers to create new works and to dance critics and historians for research and projects. Of the 300 Guggenheim fellowships given out annually to artists and scholars, about four are offered to those working in dance.

INDEX